The Trial of the Archons

Carol A. Reimer

South Huntington, NY 11746

'The Trial Of The Archons' is a sequel to the prior publication: 'Sophia And The Archons'. Although much of the information is factual, it is written in fiction mode. Many names are authentic . . . some are not. Information may be verified from other publications when indicated; such as the web and certain published works. The climax of the story offers a solution to suspected inter-dimensional energies (Archons) that are seen by many people (including author) as a major threat to Earth. There has been a covert collusion between governments, the military complex, Vatican, and mega corporations with the Ets for the last sixty years. As this novel goes to print, W.W. III is looming, giving authenticity to the disclosure offered within the pages of this story.

Rosebud Publications

ISBN -13 -978-1492701569

ISBN -10 -1492701564

Also written by

Carol A. Reimer

~ The Labyrinth

~ Trapped In A Time Warp

~ A Rose For Amy

~ This Bird Doesn't Sing Anymore

~ Sophia And The Archons

Introduction . . .

There are endless myths and legends across the World about lost lands. Earth's geological and biological records confirm evidence of many extraordinary upheavals of former continents and civilizations that have been born and completed and then forgotten over and over again. Knowledge was lost as generations came and went. All that we learn in the present has existed before; our inventions and discoveries are but former forgotten inventions and discoveries. So why bother? Why continue to pursue the redundant, frustrating story of humanity and the Planet we live on? The World we presently call 'home' has been around for millennia. We've all been on this journey many times. Often a vague memory buried deep within has you yearning to return to another time and place. Where, when and with whom is a mystery, but you *feel* you were a lot happier then. It was free of all the unhappiness you experience now. Remember?

The tale of Noah and the Great Flood is an almost verbatim repeat of stories told about Sumer (4000 BC - 300 BC). These accounts have been found on clay tablets recovered from what is now Iraq and they originated thousands of years earlier than the *biblical* version. The Sumerians were the first 'post' Flood or postdiluvian people to live in cities and build walls, roads, and ocean-going ships. They appeared out of nowhere at a highly advanced level of knowledge and sophistication. More than a hundred 'firsts' that we take for granted today can be traced to Sumer six thousand years ago.

Introduction . . .

Different cultures have different names for lost civilizations, but none have escaped the legend of Atlantis and Lemuria. The Greek philosopher, Plato (427-347 BC), dates the demise of these civilizations to be around 11,000 years ago. The ancients said the Flood brought an end to the 'Golden Age', an era when men lived like 'gods', without vices or passions, vexation or toil. They co-existed in happy companionship with the animals and spent their days in tranquility and joy, living together in perfect equality and united by a mutual confidence and love. Supposedly, Earth was even more beautiful than now. Man didn't suffer any of the infirmities of age and is presumed to have lived hundreds of years or more.

Hindu tradition supports this theme with different epochs or eras called 'Yugas'. The 'Krita Yuga' was their Golden Age. When paradise ended with what the Bible labeled the 'Fall of Man', it brought fear, suffering, disease, emotional pain and an obsession with materialism and survival right into the 21st century. What triggered this down-hill slide? There is widespread evidence that some fantastic event changed the Earth's surface in little more than an instant. What it was exactly is still unknown. There is an enormous amount of speculation. All agree that Earth suffered a global catastrophe, but did the intervention of a malevolent force contribute to the end of the Golden Age? I believe it did based on the research of those who seem to have 'connected the dots'.

Introduction ...

We read from various sources that approximately 50,000 years ago a planetary body, believed to exist between Mars and Jupiter, was mysteriously destroyed. Referred to as Tiamat, (among other names), its surface consisted mostly of great oceans. Upon its destruction, vast saline waters entered into Earth's atmosphere causing the first of two massive prehistoric deluges that resulted in mankind's total and long lasting chaos and confusion. (*It is thought that alien invaders were attracted to the Solar System by the conflagration or caused the calamity themselves upon coming here. Taking advantage of the situation, they moved in to control the weakened inhabitants of Earth).*

The pre-Flood World was far more advanced than we are today. Intelligent life on Earth dates back much further than the scientific community will concede to. Evidence of advanced civilizations is supported by many mystery structures and artifacts that have been found worldwide, yet mainstream science and academia refuse to acknowledge their importance. Earth's true history isn't taught in the schools and universities. Why is this so? Basically, it's because our educational system is controlled by the 'elite' bloodline families who fund *academia*. These bloodlines, seeded in the pre-Flood World and afterwards, continue to control everything and everyone in a global 'Orwellian Big Brother' state. The wealthy elite have always discouraged creative thinking and have re-written *history* to support their interests. You finally realize that 'history' was dictated by powerful figures as *'his - story'*.

Introduction ...

Wonders such as the Nazca Lines in Peru, the ancient buildings of Baalbek in Lebanon, the Great Pyramids of Egypt, China, Mexico, and other amazing structures, temples, and stone circles defy our understanding. Many are beyond our present-day capabilities. In comparison to knowledge and accomplishment, 'contemporary society' has a lot of catching up to do.

Most of us who had to 'catch up' have only recently become aware that we really don't live in a 'free' society. You and I were duped into believing we did because there weren't too many *visible* constraints to tip us off. We function every day within a confined structure that has recently been identified as the *'Matrix',* a false World, orchestrated by the 'elite' with technological assistance from inter-dimensional Archons, also referred to as *fallen angels, Ets, reptilians, aliens, cyborgs, jinn,* etc. Skilled liars, and never releasing their 'grip', the elite have established themselves in every position of power within society and have caused humanity immeasurable suffering. Thanks to the tireless efforts of those who are educating us via their lectures, publications, videos, etc., mainstream is starting to become aware. It's a slow process. People have reservations because of the *frightening* message. But they are catching on.

Although long overdue, the elite and their inter-dimensional Archon buddies including the Demiurge, Yaldabaoth, have been summoned to stand trial before the Aeon Council. Their nefarious past has finally caught up with them.

Suggested Reading

Human Race Get Off Your Knees . . .	*David Icke*
Not In His Image . . .	*John Lash*
Exo-Vaticana . . .	*Chris Putnam -Tom Horn*
Fingerprints Of The Gods . . .	*Graham Hancock*
Forbidden Archaeology . . .	Michael A. Cremo Richard L. Thompson
Atlantis - Alien Visitation & . . . . Genetic Manipulation	Michael Tsarion

Chapter One

The Council

In Chapter 44 of *'Sophia And The Archons',* Thelete summoned a meeting of the Aeons to discuss Sophia's urgent cry for help. Her recent distress calls from the Stereoma have reached the Galactic Core and were heard loud and clear. The matter was of extreme importance. The fate of Sophia was at stake although She hadn't appealed to the Council on Her own behalf. Her Dream, Her Creation, Her children . . . were at risk of extinction!

The Stereoma, located in the third spiral galactic limb of the Galaxy, is the virtual World of the Archons, a species of inorganic beings produced by Sophia's impact upon elemental matter eons ago. As Her impact deepened, the chaotic fields of elementary matter in the galactic limbs not only became organized, they become animated, taking on a life of their own. In other words, Sophia's life-force mingled within the chaotic matter in the zone She had entered, resulting in the formation of a rudimentary world-system. However, it had evolved into a different planetary system than what She had envisioned before She fully metamorphosed Herself into the planet Earth also located in the Stereoma. According to the Greeks, the word 'Stereoma' was a stereoscopic projection; a hologram, which had condensed into the Solar System. Contained within its structure were five planets, excluding the Earth and Moon that revolved around a central star - the Sun.

Earth's geological and biological records confirm evidence of many extraordinary upheavals. After the last recorded cataclysm (approximately 7,000 years ago), Archon//Reptilians seized the opportunity to manipulate the surviving traumatized humans with all the 'evil' their jealousy and hatred could manifest. They replaced Sophia's Moon with one of their own fake 'constructs', causing a massive 'tear' or 'distortion' in the 'holographic information construct of the 'Metaphysical Universe'. This distortion was then falsely decoded as extraordinary destruction and upheaval. Humanity regressed into the Stone Age and has never fully recovered. Sophia's maternal instinct and love for Her Creation motivated Her not to abandon them. She held on to Her 'Dream' and never lost faith that Her children would rise to the occasion and become all they could be once again . . . until now. That the Archons had orchestrated these cataclysms hadn't occurred to Sophia. She too had been stunned and unprepared when all hell broke loose and She went into a semi-coma. Now, after 300 Earth years, She has slowly awakened from a nightmare - Earth's 'history'. Although She had allowed the continued existence of the Archons, they never acknowledged Her kindness. They delighted in destroying everything She had created. Her patience exhausted, She knows She must resort to drastic measures. Was it too late? She hoped not, but quick decisions had to be made. Her call for help was heard clear across the Galaxy to the Pleroma. The Aeons were shocked, but understood Her distress signals. A meeting with the Council had been scheduled." *(Sophia and the Archons)*

There was a sudden hush among the Aeons. THE ONE had arrived. Before there was a God, a Heaven, or an Earth, there was only THE ONE, the infinite and eternal Mind. This perfect pre-existent Aeon dreams all realities in quiet and deep solitude and dwells in the invisible and unnamed elevations that extend forever in every direction. THE ONE is the only Being that can perceive itself in Its totality for THE ONE is Consciousness itself.

As Father, He has been described as becoming enamored of His own image in the spiritual waters of Light that prompted Him to generate a 'Thought' named Barbelo, the Mother of all. THE ONE and Barbelo united in spiritual intercourse. As a result, Barbelo conceived and gave birth to a spiritual child. One emanation led to another. Conception followed conception and Aeon followed Aeon until the entire Divine realm was filled with

Aeons of Light. Sophia, the youngest, was the Aeon of 'Wisdom'. The repertoire of Aeons remained motionless as they awaited permission to be seated. Situated between them were several illuminated spheres; each representing various stages of Earth and Sophia/Gaia's evolution. A voice suddenly came forth. It was the voice of Thelete, Sophia's Heavenly partner. He had forgiven Sophia's impulsive creation of the Anthropos without him.

"Most Powerful One, may I have permission to speak?"

THE ONE acknowledged Thelete's request with a blinding flash of Light. "Thank you, "replied Thelete. He took a deep breath and continued. "Mother Barbelo, may I beseech Your compassion and attention on Sophia's behalf."

"It is granted, "She replied.

Thelete turned and faced the other Aeons.

"Most honorable Aeons, thank You for attending this meeting. I, like You, have heard the groaning distress calls of our Sophia who cries for our attention and help. Her situation in the Stereoma is desperate. She wishes to advise you of Her situation and seeks Your advice.

"For what purpose? "inquired 'Reflection'.

"It concerns a decision She must make concerning the Archons, "replied Thelete.

"The Archons! I thought She had that situation under control, "exclaimed Mother Barbelo.

"She thought so too, Mother. However, Her feelings have

changed towards them since she has learned of new information."

"Which is . . . ?"

"Sophia weeps whenever She allows herself to think about the pain and stress the Archons have caused Her and Her children. She endeavors to keep Her emotions in check as Her tears have caused many areas on the Planet to flood."

"Those ugly creatures were always a menace, "replied Mother. "Why She ever allowed them to exist has been a mystery to me."

Thelete explained, "She has endeavored to be compassionate towards them because of Her remorse, but they refuse to appreciate Her kindness. Instead of accepting themselves for who they are and remaining within their own environment, they lust for what the Anthropos have. Because it is unavailable to them, it is their intent to destroy Earth and all Sophia's creations for spite."

"So, are you saying that Sophia isn't able to control these useless parasites? "Mother inquired.

"Not in a peaceful manner, "Thelete sighed. "They are beyond reasoning. But they must be stopped once and for all. Sophia is seriously contemplating destroying them forever. But she wants Your opinion and Your endorsement for Her decision this time."

"Our impulsive young Aeon has matured, "sighed Mother. "She no doubt realizes the danger in pursuing this action. There is a strong possibility that all might be lost . . . Herself included."

"She realizes the possible repercussions, Mother."

"What about the humans who have not been contaminated?

"inquired 'Compassion'. "Can She expect any help from them?"

"Those who have awakened are concerned and sympathetic, "sighed Thelete, "but the unfortunate truth is that the Archons have gained control over those who rule the Planet. Many humans are so brainwashed, they aren't even aware of the stakes. And many are fearful and depressed. They have lost hope."

"Thelete, this situation has existed for a long time, "protested Mother Barbelo. "I don't understand why Sophia hasn't done something sooner and put an end to it."

"I know, "sighed Thelete. "Our Sophia is tenacious, impulsive, passionate and compassionate. However, She is overwhelmed that Her Dream will not be realized. She is very sad."

"As well She should be, " 'Reflection' replied.

"Yes, as well She should be, "Thelete whispered.

Thelete paused for several minutes and organized His thoughts. In Sophia's defense, He continued to speak,

"Earth's history records many tumultuous cataclysms Sophia and the Anthropos have suffered at the hands of the Archons. Before the last 'Great Flood', Earth was a lush paradise. Humans were an elegant species in tune with Sophia and beyond to the higher dimensions. There wasn't any death or ill health. Humans didn't eat food. Their source of sustenance was obtained from the nurturing light of the Sun and Earth's atmosphere. Animals did the same, negating the need for the daily mass murder that is now called the 'law of the wild'. There wasn't any fear - or obsession with survival. The highly advanced cultures of Atlantis and Mu had evolved during the era described as 'The Golden Age'. Their amazing accomplishments supported a glorious existence for all Earth's inhabitants that has yet to be duplicated. Unfortunately, all was lost after the Archons initiated a series of horrific cataclysms that nearly destroyed Earth and most of the Anthropos.

"However did they manage to accomplish this? "inquired Mother.

"The Archons had become skilled in technology and were capable of constructing artificial spheres throughout the galaxy. They built these spheres as vehicles to traverse the Universe and hijack other planets - precisely the way they did Earth."

"Will you elaborate, please, " Mother insisted.

Thelete continued, "When Mars was destroyed, Sophia's original Moon was lost in the chaos. The Archons seized the opportunity and replaced it with their 'Death Star' - a hollowed out spacecraft. Earth's present Moon is an artificial sphere they constructed."

"Did Sophia realize they had switched Moons? " 'Truth' inquired.

"Not at first. After the last cataclysm, the arrival of the Archon Moon caused a massive 'tear' or 'distortion' in the Metaphysical Universe, which was then used to fool humans. Information was decoded through a fake holographic reality and experienced as extraordinary destruction and catastrophic geological upheavals. Human society immediately descended from an advanced technological World into the 'Stone Age'."

"I don't recall receiving any of Her distress signals at that time, "replied Mother.

"That is true, Mother. Sophia didn't want to alarm You. She thought You would advise Her to terminate Her 'Experiment' and She wasn't ready to do that, "Thelete answered.

Mother looked perplexed. "How then did Sophia react to all the violent destruction?"

"Despite the 'near death' of Her magnificent Creation and the destruction of their astonishing accomplishments, Sophia persevered and slowly replenished Herself to enable the traumatized humans to continue their struggle for survival."

"We were so informed, "replied Mother. "What has changed? Why is Sophia sending us messages that She wishes to come home?"

"Sophia has reached a turning point, "sighed Thelete. "She realizes Her Experiment has been in progress for millennia. Despite the repetitive destruction of the Planet and its inhabitants, She has endured. She has been patient and shown compassion to the Archons. She has given mankind many opportunities to regain 'Consciousness'. While some humans have responded positively; many haven't. The Gnostics, a spiritually advanced group, warned humans about the Archons as far back as 6000 B.C. Similar to a virus, they invaded Earth and spread without much resistance, infecting many humans. It is the foundation for all the chaos existing on the Planet presently. Humans have been in a state of deep depression and confusion since then and for the most part, have become complacent and fearful."

“This is serious,” replied Mother. “Of course we will give Sophia our help and support. You must inform us of every detail in a concise fashion. Only then will we be able to determine the best course of action. Prepare your presentation well, Thelete. We will meet again tomorrow at this time. All in favor, say ’aye’.“

She turned around to acknowledge THE ONE’s presence.

“Do you approve of our plan, dear husband?”

THE ONE acknowledged Mother Barbelo with a flash of light.

“That’s a ‘Yes’, ”she smiled.

A soft aura of pastel lights emanated from the Aeons in appreciation of Mother’s humor. Sophia’s problem was unprecedented, but the Aeons realized the urgency. They would help Her resolve the matter. Thelete exhaled with a sigh of relief.

‘Chapter One’ and the remaining subsequent chapters are written in ‘fiction’ mode, although a great deal of the information within the following pages was based on authentic research and may be considered ‘true‘. In this case, we might call this literary endeavor ‘faction‘.

> *“Let’s pretend. Let’s make believe. That’s what you do when you write fiction, even though, in the process, you may set the foundations of your fantasy in the solid ground of reality.”* Graham Hancock

Our understanding of the World we live in and our former blind acceptance of its historical roots has undergone significant re-evaluation. Many tenets 'written in stone' seem to be slipping away from their foundations. Prior concepts, ideologies, traditions, scientific theory, etc. have been challenged, and in many situations, have proven to be unacceptable and false. We are beginning to realize that we have been deceived, manipulated, and controlled.

> "Approximately 11000 years ago, dark forces caused a gigantic distortion in the information construct of the Metaphysical Universe after the arrival of their artificial Moon, the hi-tech wars, and the destruction of planet Tiamat between Mars and Jupiter (now the Asteroid Belt). The distortion was then decoded into the holographic level of 'reality' as war, division and mayhem. The human personality was also subject to this *schism* and people became fractured and distorted and were no longer 'whole'. Human society immediately descended from an advanced technological World into the Stone Age."
>
> *David Icke - Human Race Get Off Your knees*

After reading the *Myth of Sophia And The Archons,* you may have embraced the concept that there are unlimited possibilities. Perhaps *Trial of the Archons* will also stir your imagination. You may be outraged to learn that a handful of psychopaths are in control of our Planet, working furiously to transform the World into submission under the dictates of a Fascist/Communist regime. It is obvious that many hybrids, working in collusion with inter-dimensional entities, are mentally, emotionally, and physically perverted and must be stopped! We must break loose from the 'programming' and regain our former status and potential prior to the distorted reality that has imprisoned us. The Goddess Sophia is about to intercede on our behalf. But we must do our share and work with Her. How? For starters, avoid complicity and/or detachment. Be concerned of your fellow man. Let go of the 'fear'. Turn off your *smart phones, your Ipods,* and all your *'techie toys'.* They were designed to distract you and encourage your 'dependence' on technology until they eventually destroy you, those you love, and your way of life, which is eroding rapidly. Pay attention to what the 'dark powers' in government and military are doing. Discover what is happening outside of your small, delusional, self-centered 'World'. What can you contribute? How can you help? These questions are more important than, "Did you watch the game?" or "What's your favorite 'smart' model?"

If you understand the seriousness of the ongoing threat of the psychopaths bent on destroying humanity and acknowledge their greed, their arrogance, their selfishness, their utter disregard for life, and become aware of how they are feverishly exercising their power within all walks of life - your Consciousness will be heightened as will your sense of worthiness and power. As David Icke has repeatedly stated, "Human Race - Get Off You Knees!"

You and I have allowed these misfits to imprison us and our World. Isn't it time we took it back?

Chapter Two

Thelete

Thelete departed the meeting slowly. Caught in deep deliberation, His mind was flooded with many details. He realized the gravity of Sophia's position in wishing to address the Archon situation so decisively. How extremely draining it must be for Her to finally deal with a crisis of this magnitude. He was cognizant of how important it was for Him to organize the data He would present to the Council. Much was at stake. The facts must be told in a logical, concise manner. 'Key' would be His ability to explain Sophia's position and 'intent' to the other Aeons. He understood Her - but would they?

Sophia had briefed Him as best She could, but She was very emotional and upset at the time. "Woman usually are, "He thought, "especially women who cared and loved as deeply as Sophia." He felt Her pain and frustration. Her Dream was on 'the line'. Would it end traumatically? Sometimes a Mother hadn't any choice than to walk away from her children who refused to listen.

Thelete sighed. It was unfortunate that Sophia's impulsiveness had caused Her to unintentionally create the 'anomalies'. Her remorse never ceased. It compelled Her to overlook the Archons' ignorance and blindness and She tried to help them. But they were arrogant and never appreciated Her efforts. Following the leadership of the 'Demiurge', their intrusiveness had become out of control. Her compassion and forgiveness were exhausted and She now realized She must take drastic measures.

Thelete decided to visit the *Akashic Library* where records of Earth's entire history would be readily accessible. When He arrived, He noticed two young girls sitting on the steps of the entrance. He was attracted to their vibrant 'mercabahs' (energy shell) that contained many delicate pastel colors. In particular, the color 'turquoise' was present in both of their 'auras' suggesting they had experienced 'Earth' lifetimes. He smiled and waved 'hello'. They responded with a soft display of vibrating colors emanating from their auras that pleased Him. He had a sudden thought. Perhaps these were the young girls Sophia had mentioned. He requested them to join Him and they were soon by His side.

"Greetings, dear ones. My name is Thelete. Thank you for joining me. May I ask your names?"

"My name is Tiffany Rose and this is my cousin, Viola, "the young girl softly replied.

Thelete smiled. "I noticed the vibrant turquoise glow within your beautiful auras. May I assume that you and Viola have lived at least one 'Earthly' lifetime?"

"Yes, this is true, "replied Tiffany Rose. "May we be of any assistance?"

"Maybe, "replied Thelete. "Do either of you recall the approximate time you lived on Earth and the life you experienced?"

"I do, "Viola replied. "So do I, "Tiffany Rose remarked. "Why do you ask?"

"Well, I'm in a bind of sorts, "Thelete answered. "I'm trying to compile data concerning Earth's early history; in particular information concerning lost lands that sank beneath the sea amid earthquakes, volcanoes and tidal waves."

"You mean Atlantis and Lemuria? "Tiffany Rose questioned.

"Yes, Thelete answered. "They're the most familiar. They were destroyed in the Great Flood around 11,000 years ago, which supposedly brought an end to *The Golden Age*. Were either of you around at that time?"

"No, but our ancestors were, "smiled Viola. "They spoke about the

'Great Flood' and the horrific destruction it caused. After the Flood, there was a lot of 'rediscovering' to be done as so much knowledge was lost. Humanity basically had to start over. Eventually, new civilizations emerged in South America, West Africa, Egypt, Sumer, India, and China. Tiffany Rose and I were born in Egypt."

"I see, "Thelete answered. "Were you descendants of any of the Pharaohs?"

"Not really, "Viola smiled. "We were a small tribe of nomads who lived in the caverns along the Nile River around 325 B.C. Our people were constantly fleeing the tyranny of the Emperor Constantine. He had just become Emperor and he was killing and imprisoning anyone who opposed him; especially the Gnostics."

Thelete was surprised. "Did you know any of the Gnostics?"

"Yes. I was engaged to be married to one, "sighed Viola. "He was murdered by Constantine's soldiers. After his death, I didn't want to live anymore. I lost all faith in God. Where was his God to protect him?"

"I'm sorry, "Thelete offered. "I don't have an answer. Weren't you able to catch up with each other after that lifetime?"

"No. I've been informed he is living in another world. We keep missing one another. Perhaps you can help me, Thelete."

"Perhaps. But first, I must focus on helping Sophia."

"Sophia! Did you say Sophia? "Viola gasped.

"Yes, dear one. I am here to help my partner, Sophia."

"Oh, my goodness, "cried Viola. "Sophia is my spiritual mentor!"

"What's the problem, "Tiffany Rose inquired? "How can we help?"

"I don't have time to elaborate, "Thelete responded. "I will try to advise you of specifics. I came to the Akashic Library because I hoped to secure a history of the extraordinary geological upheavals Earth has endured. It is believed they were initiated by the Archons, who are highly suspect."

"I know about the Archons, "Viola exclaimed. "Carl, my beloved, told me stories about them. They are a menace!"

"Yes, unfortunately so, "Thelete agreed. "They have been allowed to exist for thousands of years. Every time they were confronted by Sophia for their misgivings, their leader, Yaldabaoth, promised Sophia he would change his ways and control his cyborgs. He is a liar and cannot be trusted. They are 'out of control' and have finally exhausted Sophia's patience and compassion. She is determined to deal with them once and for all. I think their days are numbered."

"Our hearts feel dear Sophia's pain, "Viola sighed. "We will help you find the information you are seeking. I have good organizational skills."

"And I enjoy a challenge! "Tiffany Rose blurted out.

"Thank you, "Thelete smiled. "We best get started."

Chapter Three

Sophia's Fall

Thlete allocated different 'epic' periods for Viola and Tiffany Rose to research. This would eliminate any duplication of effort between them. He urged the girls to select the time period they felt comfortable with. He wasn't surprised that He was left with the most obscure period involving the origin of the Archons, the Solar System, Sun, Moon and . . . the Earth.

"My sweet, Sophia, "He whispered to Himself. He hoped His efforts would present an opportunity to uncover information that offered Him a clearer understanding of Sophia and Her 'Dream' before She took Her fatal 'plunge'. He had forgiven Her for not including Him in Her plans; but any additional information that would increase His understanding would be welcomed. Mostly, he wanted to ease Her pain.

He closed his eyes to remember Sophia was the 'baby' of the Aeon family - the youngest and the last. All the Aeons favored Her. Intellectually endowed, She was named the 'Goddess of

Wisdom'. But, She was also very impulsive and intensely passionate, which proved to be Her nemesis. Still, everyone sought Her advice. They knew it would be given with their best interest at heart He remembered how attracted He was to Her. Often, He would fabricate a problem just to hear what She had to say. But, It's difficult to know the inner dreams of a young Aeon. And He, like the others, was stunned by Her Fall that eventful day.

He tried to imagine what Sophia dreamt as She contemplated the template of the Anthropos, the 'human genome', before Her plunge. While She was still within the proper limits of the Pleroma, Her Dreaming envisioned a World to come. She acted in an anomalous manner, by Herself, without pairing off and sharing Her vision with another Aeon. Thelete found the Chapter in the Akashic record titled: 'Sophia's Dream' . . .

"*Sophia feels a profound, unsettling attraction to what She beholds. She is captured with total fascination on how the Anthropos will evolve and manifest its unique potential. Drawing Her currents away from the general aggregation, She muses about a World where the human singularity will emerge and thrive. She empathizes intensely with the human creature that will appear in the Divine experiment now underway. As the Aeon who configured the genome, She takes an unusual interest in its future development, and She does so unilaterally without consulting with Her counterpart, Thelete. This is unusual behavior for a Generator, transgressing the norm, but is within the freedom allowed by the 'One' that such developments can arise. The young Aeon Sophia now formulates Her own act of projective Dreaming, centered on the glittering template suspended in the spiral arms. Independent of the other Aeons, this torrential wave-form dreams on Her own about what might happen to a strain of the Anthropos. In Her freedom, Sophia is impetuous and daring. She goes much further than Aeons usually do to anticipate how a certain experiment might play out. She idealizes the situation, picturing a three-body system - Star-Planet-Satellite (Sun, Earth, Moon) where a strain of the Anthropos would have optimal opportunity to discover and develop its encoded talents, even to achieve works of genius. Sophia is tremendously excited by these prospects of the Divine Experiment that has only now been seeded in the Kenoma, the Matrix of finite potential.*

Totally enthralled in Her solitary view, and ever more detached from the other Generators in the Pleroma, Sophia envisions a World yet to be, where humanity will emerge to live, learn, and love. The sight of the Anthropos nested in the nebular cloud engages her Divine powers of Dreaming in an unusual way, with exceptionally intense involvement. Rather than leave this cosmic novelty to mature and unfold on its own, according to the instructions encoded within it, the Pleromic current, whose signature is 'Wisdom', succumbs to a strange attraction. Sophia is deeply compelled to get involved in an experiment with a strain of the Anthropos." Thelete paused to process the information.

"With exquisite slowness, Sophia's longing pulls Her precariously close to the porous bounding membrane of the Pleroma, the outer rim of the Galactic core. Her desire follows the path taken by the Anthropos, out into the 'Dema', the chaotic flux of elementary matter in the spiral arms. Compelled by the excitement of what might happen out there, this Aeon is gradually pulled away from the core - until the moment She plunges out and away. Like a slow-motion waterfall twisted into a torrential braid, the Aeon Sophia spirals downward toward the object of Her own desire. The currents that compose Her energetic form distend into a massive power spike, a tongue of pearl-white luminosity leaping from the Pleroma, shooting light-years into the exterior regions. The Wisdom Goddess falls out of the Galactic Center.

Sophia's torrential current carries the Aeonic power of animation and imparts it to the Dema. This action is anomalous, for normally an Aeon does not act directly upon the physics of the spiral arms. However, this 'Generator' engages the Dema energetically, and She watches Her Dreaming power trigger a series of events She cannot resist or impede.

Like all 'Generators', the Wisdom Goddess commands 'supra animating intent'. For such a cosmic entity, the mere act of attending spontaneously causes form and activity to arise; as if gazing at a rosebud, you could make it blossom, or by looking into a tide pool, you could cause the microscopic life-forms floating there to grow, mutate, combine, and aggregate into colonies just by the power inherent to your attention. In just this way, wherever Sophia directs Her attention, the Dema springs into life and acquires form. To Her horror and amazement, the Aeon finds Herself surrounded by bizarre creatures - a phantom species spawned of elementary matter - the Archons! These entities are legion, like a swarm of locusts. Not having a place to alight, they mass around Sophia, sucked into Her currents and blown out again. They swarm like bees or locusts in a circling mass, but not entirely in a chaotic way. Due to the innate designing powers of Cosmic Intent, the Archons emerge in a kind of parade; a pattern of 'fractal' iterations.

To Her astonishment, Sophia realizes that She is now the Mother of a bizarre species that has emerged from the Dema due to the impact of Her Divine currents, but without Her Divine intention. Such is the weird consequence of Her precipitous plunge from the cosmic center. But now something even more odd occurs. Sophia sees a distinct mutation in the Archon swarm; an aggressive figure appears; a dragon-body with the head of a lion that rages and roars. This reptile-like mutation of the Archon horde rapidly dominates the embryonic creatures and assumes the role of 'overlord'. The entire Archon colony comes alive with the Reptilian overlord assuming a god-like stance over the rest of the species. The overlord of the Archon species rapidly becomes conscious of himself and his surroundings. He prances and preens before the swarming horde that has arisen from the fracture pattern of Sophia's impact. He is 'blind arrogance' embodied, and he is truly blind. Looking around, the chief Archon does not see the Pleroma or the Anthropos, nor does he even see the Aeon, Sophia. This monster, the Demiurge, takes the impact zone for the entire Cosmos, and declares himself to be Lord of all he surveys. "I am the only god, let there be no others before me." The Archon overlord is delusional, believing that he has created the Elementary Cosmos in which he finds himself along with the countless minions of the embryonic Archons. Sophia realizes that something terribly odd is underway. Here She beholds a cosmic species propagated by mistake so that it does not have a proper habitat for itself. Unlike the Anthropos, which is a production of Divine Imagination intentionally projected from within the Galactic Core, Archons arise unintentionally outside the Core in the encircling limbs. The Archons cannot swirl around in the Dema vortex forever. A more stable environment must be provided for them. And besides, the chief Archon wanted a kingdom to reflect his false omnipotence and his arrogant impulses. Sophia imparts a portion of Her Dreaming power to the chief Archon so that he sees the Pleroma. He then commands his legion of celestial drones to imitate the fractal designs and he proceeds to organize fantastic celestial Mansions (planets) for himself. The chemical elements present at the formation of the Solar System were all inorganic - hydrogen, nitrogen, helium, carbon, iron, etc."

Thelete took a breath. "So that's how they did it, "He exclaimed.

"Gnostic texts clearly state that Jehovah is the Lord Archon, a Reptilian type of alien predator who dominates the hive-mentality of the embryonic or Grey aliens. Jehovah, whom the Gnostics called Yaldabaoth, is truly an extraterrestrial being whose realm is the Planetary System, independent of the Earth, Sun, and Moon. He is not an advanced being (i.e., more evolved than humans), but a 'demented alien' with certain superhuman or deific powers. Gnostics taught that Jehovah infects humanity with the belief that he is their creator god, but in fact he cannot create anything. The Gnostics are very clear that Jehovah/Yaldabaoth is the commander of the Archon species."

Thelete now had a better grasp of Sophia's relationship with the Archons, but He felt the information was superficial. He realized He had to probe deeper. Sophia's 'Dream' and Her subsequent 'Fall' had initially been responsible for Earth's tragic history for thousands of years. It had inadvertently invited other entities to invade, exploit, rape, and destroy Earth, leaving their destruction behind. Who were they? Should they also be included in His investigation? He wanted to be thorough. Mother Barbelo had urged him to 'prepare' His presentation well - to be 'concise'.

He would continue His research. There were endless myths and legends of lost lands that suffered the destruction of earthquakes, volcanoes and tidal waves during Earth's history. Were the Archons always responsible? It was a possibility. What about the humans? Who had interfered with their genetics?

Different cultures had different names for the once highly advanced civilizations, but the Myth of Atlantis and Lemuria (Mu) were renowned. The demise of these ancient civilizations were recorded in the Bible as 'Noah and the Great Flood'; a story that was an almost verbatim repeat of others told in Sumer (4000 BC - 2000 BC) and other ancient Mesopotamian civilizations, including Babylon (2000 BC - 300 BC). These accounts were found on clay tablets that were recovered from a land Earth people now called *Iraq*. They originated thousands of years earlier than the 'biblical' version of the 'Fall of Man'.

Thelete had also heard of a theory that Atlantis was not a 'Center' of an advanced human civilization; rather it was the creation of - and home to - 'alien' beings that experimented and colonized the Earth inhabitants as their slaves.

"Who were those *alien beings*? "He questioned. "Were they relevant in the scheme of things?" Posed in front of a massive arrangement of literature, He retrieved a large Manuscript containing the 'A' index and turned to the Chapter that read:

The Ancient Civilization of Atlantis

The Chapter contained voluminous pages and pictures. Thelete prepared Himself for a lengthy read. He hoped He would find answers to His queries within the delicate parchment pages At best, He was confident that beginning His search with the 'Myth of Atlantis' would provide a solid foundation for His purpose.

Chapter Four

Atlantis & Lemuria

"Approximately 50,000 Earth years ago, there was a great intergalactic war between several extraterrestrial forces in a neighboring galaxy that resulted in the destruction of a planetary body commonly identified as '*Tiamat*'. The planet was believed to have existed in Earth's Solar System between Mars and Jupiter and was referred to as the 'Second Sun' because its atmosphere was resplendent with reflections of Earth's actual Sun due to its surface.

Tiamat consisted mostly of great oceans. Upon its destruction, three vast saline waters entered into Earth's atmosphere causing the first of two massive prehistoric deluges and tribulations that mankind would experience. It is believed that alien invaders took full advantage of this predicament and moved in to bring about 'colonization' of the disoriented and weakened inhabitants of Earth who believed the visitors were powerful gods.

These 'loser' aliens had been pursued by their adversaries into Earth's System where they pretended to take refuge on Tiamat. In reality, they had taken refuge on Earth and hid in existing underground caverns that their scanners had detected. Hiding in the caverns, they couldn't be seen by their pursuers. They also descended into other caverns that they themselves cut out of the living rock where they lived in complex colonies. The caverns provided perfect concealment for them as they knew how imperative it was not to be traced to Earth. It gave their pursuers the false presumption they had been utterly destroyed.

The debris from Tiamat's destruction became the Asteroid Belt with its own orbit. The waters of its great oceans became frozen in space. When they entered Earth's atmosphere, they liquefied, flooding Earth and often depositing their live contents on Earth's surface as fish, frogs, oil, stone, hail and ice.

The 'loser' aliens were immoral, negative beings who had contributed to the corruption of their own home planet from which they were being expunged. The *Bible* and the *Book of Enoch* in particular, relate Earth's sovereignty was violated by these entities named 'Nephilim'. When they arrived on Earth, they immediately took advantage of their hosts. Having no love for the people of Earth, they sought to enslave them. The Nephilim established their main headquarters at Atlantis on the continent of Appalachia. It is suspected that Atlantis was never a center of an advanced human civilization. Rather, it was a slave camp where the aliens experimented with human DNA. The aliens sought to establish a 'New Order' over the natural and loving inhabitants of the Earth with biogenetic interference and alteration of the indigenous inhabitants genetic makeup. Their experiments were continued for centuries. Those chosen for hybridization by the Nephilim inherited the alien DNA and became morally corrupt. Some were placed back into their tribes and exalted as priests, elders, or even kings, possessing powerful magic and wealth. Still, they remained the lackeys of the malign warlocks who ruled them from 'behind the thrones'.

Records were kept in Atlantis of all their engineered slaves. From then on, their progeny would be favored and protected and 'bloodline' would be extremely important to the monarchs of Earth. These false envoys and overlords imposed taxation, enforced slavery and sacrifice, and generally lived off the labor of the hybrid Earth people. They instigated hierarchic control, the division of labor, merit-oriented advance, and induced conditions that inevitably led to man's disconnection from nature. They also indulged in the pursuit of aggressive warfare and the conquest of other tribes and nations as well as the reality of ritual murder and human sacrifice to instill fear and provide sustenance to the gods of the 'underworld'. Records of hundreds of cultures lead to the conclusion that humanity's decline was due to the external interference of these 'alien' intruders. They and their minions instilled the idea that nature was threatening and antithetical to humankind; something to be abused and possessed. They also instilled the fallacy that women were lower in ontological status than were men. They were to be distrusted and kept in subordinate positions. *Keeping women submissive and uneducated insured that they would never wonder why they were being used as incubators.*

Rebellion broke out on Atlantis eventually; possibly due to a 'falling out' between factions of the oppressors, with one group taking sides with the humans. Some say a small group of alien priests took pity on the humans and sought to restore the 'Natural Rule'. Others contend that it occurred due to the intervention of galactic forces that sought to eradicate the Serpent/Nephilim from the Planet or at least restrict their corrupting operations. Whatever the actual truth, those who were capable, vacated Atlantis and relocated to the continent of Oceania, later known as Lemuria where they established a thriving civilization. (The continent of Atlantis is believed to have been located in the Atlantic Ocean and Lemuria in the Pacific). Some researchers suggest they were ancient civilizations in lieu of being continents. The stories and migrations have survived down to Earth's present time.

Thelete paused. Outraged with the information He had learned, it was painfully clear that humanity had been victimized by the Nephilim in many ways. He would include the Nephilim in His presentation. Perhaps they were a strain of the Archons or actually were the Archons identified with a different name.

Visitation of alien beings from outside Earth's Solar System was a repetitive occurrence. There was an incredible collection of information Thelete had to browse through, but it had to be done. He realized that after the destruction of Atlantis and the Golden Age, a global society emerged based on a similar religion and source of knowledge. However, it was expressed differently and even changed as much had been lost after the 'Flood'. Still, a common thread survived within the countless myths, names, and rituals of the different cultures. Elite bloodlines were seeded all over the World before the upheavals and reseeded later within the new emerging civilizations. The bloodline and peoples of Sumer, Babylon, and Egypt became known by many other names as they migrated from Mesopotamia and the Middle East over thousands of years. In addition to the Reptilian/Archons, they were described as the Anakin, Rephaim, Djinn, Giants, Titans, Fallen Angels, Watchers, Serpent People, etc. All were accused of tampering with human DNA to create their own hybrids to become the leaders of ancient societies.

The Sumer Empire became the Babylonian Empire and the term 'empire' followed the elite bloodlines of Mesopotamia wherever they located. Many migrated to Europe. Their main centers of power became Rome and London (Babylon-don). The elite Sumerian-Babylonian-Egyptian bloodlines established Rome and the Roman Empire. They also established the Roman Church, which was simply the religion of Babylon relocated and renamed. The bloodlines of Sumer, Babylon, and Egypt went global with European Colonial Empires. Prime among them was the British Empire on which the 'Sun never set', so vast was its domain of control and occupation. All were obsessed with acquisition, control and domination. It was no coincidence that wherever the bloodlines located their headquarters, an empire would follow.

The 'British Empire' and its smaller counterparts allowed the bloodlines to be exported across the World, together with the secret society network that manipulates them. They placed people, agents, and lackeys into positions of power. This network of secret societies originated before the Flood in deeply malevolent secret societies established in Atlantis and Lemuria in the latter stages of the Golden Age. Instigated by secret societies and their black magicians, the wonders that were Atlantis and Lemuria descended into infamy, chaos and sheer evil before the cataclysms brought them to an end. The secret societies continued on as the 'Mystery Schools' of the post-Flood World, especially in Sumer, Babylon, and Egypt.

Not all Mystery Schools were contaminated, but the bloodline versions were and even the benevolent ones were gradually taken over. While the elaborate ceremonial magic of antiquity was not necessarily evil, there arose from its perversion several false schools of sorcery, or black magic In Egypt. Black magicians of Atlantis continued to exercise their superhuman powers until they completely undermined and corrupted the morals of the primitive 'Mysteries'. They usurped the position formerly occupied by the Initiates, and seized the reigns of the spiritual government.

Thus *'black magic'* dictated the State religion and paralyzed the intellectual and spiritual activities of individuals by demanding complete and unhesitating acquiescence in the dogma formulated by the priest craft. The Egyptian Pharaoh became a puppet in the hands of the Scarlet Council; a committee of arch-sorcerers elevated to power by the priesthood.

The Secret Society Network of today operates globally with groupings like the Jesuits, Knights Templar, Knights of Malta, Opus Dei and Freemasonry, working as one unit at their highest level. This unit or force connecting all the major 'secret societies' is known as the Illuminati or Illuminated Ones. It is a series of degrees into which the other secret societies place their chosen few, and entry to the upper echelons of the Illuminati pyramid is by bloodline only. *(The great majority of secret society initiates haven't a clue that Illuminati degrees even exist).* Knowledge is compartmentalized as are all other secret groups. The lower ranks are systematically 'misled' to keep the real knowledge exclusive only to the bloodlines. The only reason 'outsiders' are allowed into their societies, corporations, and governments is because there aren't nearly enough of the elite to do what is necessary to advance their agenda of global control. The bloodline families have constructed a global control system piece by piece, century after century, and today it is astonishing in its reach, depth and detail. They have enslaved mankind in a prison without bars; simply stated . . . a prison with bars they cannot see. Thelete compiled a short synopsis:

"Planet Earth is controlled by a powerful organization named the Illuminati . They are a global network of secret societies and semi-secret groups that are instructed like a transnational corporation. Corporate headquarters, the hub of the organization, is located in Europe and dictates policy to all subsidiary networks worldwide. These subsidiaries direct their nation's politics, business, banking, media, military, medicine, science, education, etc., ensuring that they all conform to the blueprint dictated by 'headquarters'. Most people don't know that they are involved in a grand conspiracy to enslave the World."

Thelete shook his head in disbelief. Earth's history of trauma encompassed a far greater magnitude than he had originally suspected. The notion of a 'removed god', a distant, immaterial and punitive 'Demiurge' that required man to repress his natural instincts and live in constant guilt had surfaced on Earth from the alien presence and their overt dominion. Bent on weakening the resolve of humans while strengthening their own control, the aliens embroiled 'man' into futile and destructive wars by arousing their aggressive instincts, causing repetitive systemic and social despair. At times, it seemed that the efforts of those who rebelled the tyranny were successful. Humans probably relied on their physical numbers. However, the 'evil ones', who lost battles or who were deposed, continued to practice their vile arts. Their offspring, who had been genetically altered, continued to exist and procreate. They too, had aggressive instincts and the innate 'power mania' of their forefathers. They were operating from left-brain modality and excelled in the technological sciences, predisposed to feeling separate and superior to their fellow human beings, the natural inhabitants of the Planet.

Although few in number compared to the rest of humanity, it was perplexing for Thelete to understand how the evil ones managed to regain power and control. He didn't believe that humankind would accept such vile structures as a matter of course. It would take extraordinary circumstances for the humans to be severed from their instinctual nature and innate 'God worship' to embrace purely pragmatic power relations.

Thelete was puzzled. Apparently, this was a repeated scenario for the Anthropos. Why did they allow themselves to be suppressed and manipulated over and over again? Did they never learn from their prior mistakes? Was submission their only M. O.? The matter was indeed frustrating. It appeared that this was a fatal flaw in the Anthropos 'genome' unless it was the result of the genetic manipulation forced upon them. He decided to take a 'break' and closed the Manuscript. His thoughts wandered to Viola and Tiffany Rose. He wondered how they were doing.

Chapter Five

Viola

"Are you sure you will be all right? I don't think it's too smart to want to go back and relive days of your past. I'm worried on how you'll react to old memories."

"I'll be fine, Tiffany Rose. I can handle it, "sighed Viola. "I think it may help me to move on. Maybe there's something I'm meant to know. Maybe there's something I'm still not aware of."

"Is that why you chose this 'time frame' to do your research? Did you hope something important would be revealed to you?"

"Perhaps. I don't know. It just seemed the right thing to do. You know how much I miss Carl. I'd do anything just to be in his arms again, "Viola whispered softly.

"I know. I understand, "Tiffany Rose sighed. She put her arms around Viola to console her. "Perhaps you're right. There's a presence around you. Maybe it's Carl."

Viola lifted her face from Tiffany Rose's shoulder. "Do you really think so? "she sighed. "I sense him too."

"Come. I'll help you get started, "Tiffany Rose smiled. They walked over to an area of the Akashic Library where they believed they would find the information Viola was seeking. Shortly afterwards, they found a white leather Manuscript titled:

The Gnostics - Egypt - 3rd - 4th Century

in ornate gold lettering. They carefully lifted the Manuscript from its position on the shelf.

"This should be very interesting, "sighed Viola. She seated herself comfortably at one of the tables and carefully positioned the Manuscript on its smooth surface. She stared at the cover, focusing on the 'blurred' gold lettering. Not looking up, she whispered, "I'm fine."

Tiffany Rose lingered for a few moments. She then softly said, "Good. I'll be close by if you need me, dear."

Viola waited until Tiffany Rose was out of sight before she allowed the tears she had been repressing flow profusely over her burning cheeks. She held her trembling hands over her 'racing' heart as she continued to sob softly. Her body remained motionless until she was able to regain her composure. Taking a deep breath, she opened the Manuscript and turned the pages slowly as she whispered, "Carl, please talk to me. Help me find the information I need to move on."

She closed her eyes. Suddenly, she heard someone call her name . . . "Viola. Viola. Come quickly!" It was the voice of her Mother, Yolana. "There are several men outside, "the voice continued. Carl is with them. He wishes to talk to you. But you must hurry!"

Viola pushed herself away from the warmth of the burning coal stove. It was a damp, cold evening. A sudden chill had seized her frail body. Even her bones ached. She hadn't seen her beloved in several days. How worried she had been. Reaching for her shawl, she ran to the front entrance of the cave dwelling. Once outside, she could barely see the dim outline of the men on horseback. A thick fog had settled over the landscape and the night air was unfriendly. She called out, "Carl. Where are you?"

"Over here, Viola." She ran quickly towards the figure standing in the shadows. She flung into his waiting arms. "My darling. Where have you been? I was so worried, "she moaned.

"I'm all right, "he responded. "May we visit for a while? Perhaps you could brew us a cup of tea or soup. We've been riding for several hours." Viola looked to Her Mother for approval. Yolana nodded her consent. It wouldn't be the first time she helped Carl and his friends. "Thank you, Mother, "Viola smiled.

"My Mother has given us permission, my love. Please tell your friends to come in. I will prepare them something warm to take away the chill." Once inside, they sat around the table they had moved closer to the stove. A large candle, positioned on the table, radiated beams of light that cast shadows onto the stone walls of the room. Viola served them each a bowl of soup and a basket of warm bread. She put a bottle of wine on the table and advised them to help themselves. Except for an occasional 'thank you', the hungry men ate and sipped their wine in silence. After they finished their meal, Viola told them they could rest in an adjacent room. Yolana had already retired. The young lovers were finally alone. "You have been so kind and gracious, my sweet Viola. This is why I love you so, "Carl whispered. He gazed into her large, dark almond-shaped eyes. They were deep and mysterious. The soft glow of the burning candle reflected highlights in her thick, black hair that framed her delicate face. He touched her smooth, porcelain skin and ran his finger across her high cheekbones. "You are so lovely, my dear Viola. I could fall asleep in your arms forever."

"You look very tired, my brave warrior, "she replied. "Come. Stretch out on the bench and put your head in my lap. I will stroke your head as you rest."

Stretching his long body over the bench, he gently placed his head in Viola's lap and closed his eyes. She studied the face of the man she would soon marry. She loved him so. His features were rugged, his skin smooth, and his hair was a thick carpet of dark curls she loved to pull her fingers through. They were both in their early twentys and had known each other since they were children. How fortunate that they had fallen in love. They considered themselves very blessed as their marriage would not be one of 'convenience'. Neither had ever been with another. Carl opened his eyes. He looked up into Viola's face and smiled.

"Your hands feel so soothing and loving. It's a relief to be here with you, but we must plan to leave this area very soon. It is not safe. None of the villages are safe. The 'maniac' is burning them one by one. He's burning all the sacred books. Anyone who resists is shot or dragged away. He hates our people, especially. We must hide our scriptures where they won't be found. Do you understand, Viola?"

"Yes, Carl. But why? Why is the Emperor doing this?"

"Because he is possessed. He is a man who wants control and power. He is dangerous and an enemy of the people."

"When will it end? "Viola cried. "Is it never going to be different? Will we never know peace? How much suffering can our people endure?"

"It will end when people fight back. But, everyone is frightened. And I cannot blame them, "cried Carl. "They are tired of fighting. Life is difficult enough without these ruthless maniacs wishing only to destroy and conquer. They use magic to do their evil. I have seen it. The black magicians continue to exercise their superhuman powers. They have corrupted the morals of the primitive Mysteries and have usurped the positions formerly occupied by the Initiates. They have even seized the reign of the spiritual government!"

Viola sat quietly. She felt it best to let Carl speak and she encouraged him to continue . . . "Are you saying that Constantine is in legion with the sorcerers?"

"Yes! "Carl blurted. "Constantine claims he is a Christian and that he doesn't wish to be caught in the conflict between Arius of Libya and the Bishop of Alexandria. In reality, he worships a deity called 'Sol Invictus', the 'Unconquered Sun', another esoteric concept similar to the worship of the Moon god. He and Rome are using 'Jesus' and his teachings as a cover-up. Constantine has formulated a credo called the 'Nicene Creed' stating that he wants 'his' Christianity to be doctrinally consistent to help him hold the vast Empire together. Every Christian must acknowledge these teachings as the one, true, orthodox Christian faith. All other belief systems are being condemned and considered as heretical."

"It is wrong to force people to believe in something they don't want to. People want to be free and live life according to their hearts, "Viola cried.

"So true, "Carl agreed. "Especially since this is just a cover-up to help Constantine become powerful. He will stop at nothing. A group of us have planned to hide sacred scriptures in the caves up in the mountains before they are burned. Perhaps when the time is right, they will be discovered by others."

"What you are planning to do is dangerous, Carl. What if someone reports you to Constantine's soldiers? They will kill you!"

"Don't worry my sweet Viola. My God will protect me . . . my God will protect me . . . my God will protect me . . . "

Viola heard Carl's words over and over as she began to slowly come back to the present. Her heart was pounding. She tried to call out Carl's name, but no sound came forth. She had been in a trance - another dimension. Or was it just a dream? She had awakened before the ending. Still dazed, she began to sob. "What was the ending? "she moaned. "I begged him not to go. I pleaded with him. It was too dangerous. There were spies everywhere. He never came back. No one knows what happened to him and his friends. But, I know, "she sobbed. "I know what happened. They murdered him. They murdered Carl."

She buried her head in her folded arms resting on the table and began to cry uncontrollably. Her whole body began to shake.

"Viola . . . Viola . . . please don't cry. I'm right here by your side."

Viola lifted her head. "Where? Where are you? I don't see you, Carl. Is that really you speaking? Please tell me it's you and that I'm not dreaming."

"Just believe and listen, Viola. Listen to what I am about to tell you. Do you promise you will believe?"

"Yes, I promise. I promise to believe. Tell me where you are."

"I am here with you in spirit, but in the very near future, I will return to you in my body. The *Paralemptors* have promised me they will bring us back together never to be separated again. They know how difficult it has been for you . . . for me . . . for us, sweet Viola. I promise we will be together soon."

"When? Where? You've got to tell me or I'll burst!"

"After you have finished helping Thelete, I will be allowed to leave my World to join you in yours. Thelete is the catalyst. He is aware.

that the 'Light Being' promised me. He said I could go back."
"The who? "Viola questioned.
"I'm sorry. I forgot you are not familiar with these beings, "sighed Carl. "They are entities of 'Light'. Please listen to me and I will explain . . .

"A 'Paralemptor' is a benevolent Archon. He is also called a 'receiver'. He is intimately associated with the Sun and is regarded as a dissenting faction of the predatory Archon horde. The role of the 'receiver' is to gather the psychic remains of a deceased person consisting of the unused, unfulfilled parts of his soul life and store these components in the Sun's lattice, perhaps to be recycled in further human incarnations. I have been chosen to return. This is why I will be allowed to return to you. We have much work to do on Earth . . . "

"Is that why they are sending you back? "Viola gasped. "Just so that we can work together? . . ."
"No, of course that's not the only reason. We will be married. We will have children . . .we will be just as much in love as we always were . . ."
"Oh, "Viola whispered softly.
"Do you understand now, Viola? I have a 'Paralemptor' - a 'Light Being'. He has offered to bring me back into the Light and return to you."
Viola sat motionless for a few minutes and then cried out, "Am I really talking to you, Carl, or with the demons in my head?"

"Viola, would it help you to know that the Paralemptors told me our special love was a gift from Sophia."

"Really, Carl?" She was stunned. "You're not just saying that."

"Yes, Viola. "It's true. She loves you dearly."

"Oh, I must tell Tiffany Rose, "she gasped. "I don't know what I would have done without her all this time . . . "

"Tell her I said 'hello', my love. Remember, I am always here with you in spirit until we are together again. I love you very much."

"I love you too, Carl. I will believe. And I'll try to be patient."

Viola wiped her moist eyes. This time they were tears of 'joy'. Still somewhat dazed, she realized her mystical experience with Carl was meant to restore her faith in God. She had prayed to 'Sophia' for help and the Goddess heard her prayers. Viola was blessed with a loving heart and a sound, rational mind. It was a rare combination, and she was needed on Earth to help elevate the Consciousness of the Planet. Her sadness had distracted her sense of purpose for a while, but the Goddess knew it would rebound with Carl's return.

Sophia had arranged the fated meeting with Thelete at the Akashic Hall. She knew Viola and Tiffany Rose would assist Him with His research. In return, Thelete would help Carl return to Viola's World and Tiffany Rose would finally meet her true 'soul mate'. It was the Goddess' way of saying, "Thank you."

Chapter Six

The Sphere of Light

Viola remembered that she had convinced Thelete she could best serve Him if she utilized her *investigative skills* to uncover the nefarious activities of the hybrid/Archons. She believed their recent history would be more compelling to report to the Council. He agreed, and advised her to 'take command'.

"Take command, "she sighed. "I almost lost it!"

She wondered what Thelete would say if He knew how 'out of control' she had been just a short while ago. Now completely composed and refreshed, she felt confident to resume her search. She carefully closed the white Manuscript and pushed it gently aside on the table. "Where should I begin? "she pondered.

Her attention was suddenly drawn to an oval luminous object situated on the adjacent table. It was emanating a soft white glow. Her curiosity aroused, she cautiously approached the intriguing object to get a closer look. It was odd she hadn't noticed it before now. She assumed a safe posture in front of the luminiferous sphere. It was mounted on a black pedestal. When she leaned in closer, it glowed brighter. She put her hands around the globe

and felt a pulsating energy. Moments later, she felt a tingling energy permeate her entire body. It was very soothing and she didn't fight it. Sensing something was about to happen, she focused on the globe and waited. Suddenly, pictures began to slowly fade in and out. They were followed by numbers and captions. A soft voice spoke to her, *"Watch closely and all will be revealed."*

Viola took a deep breath. The unexpected 'voice' had startled her. She reached for her writing tablet and grasped her pen. Her trembling hand was poised to post whatever information was forthcoming. . .

"It isn't necessary for you to take notes, dear. Just relax and listen . . . You will remember."

"Greetings Viola . . .It is important for us to tell you that Planet Earth is controlled by a powerful organization named 'The Illuminati'. . . while they pay lip service to religion, they worship Satan. Their agents control the World's media, education, business and politics. These agents may think they are only pursuing success, but their success literally means serving the 'Devil'. Prisoners of their wealth, the Illuminati prefer hatred and destruction to 'love' and peace. They consist of hybrid bloodlines that were seeded in the ancient and prehistoric World by the genetic union of humans and non-human races 'from the stars'. Almost every native culture has its stories and legends of the 'star people'. There are many non-human races who visit Earth, but the one entity most relevant to the global conspiracy takes a Reptilian form and it is seeded in the Illuminati bloodlines that control global finance, politics, business, governments, the military, medicine, science, education and connected institutions . . ."

"Are these 'Reptilians' the Archons? "Viola questioned.

"Yes, but they are known by various names . . 'Archons' may not be the most common . . .they abound in the Universe in different locations; mainly the Draco Constellation and the Star System of Orion. They can be found in many forms and variations, such as humanoid appearance with green scaly skin to albino white. Some have tails and horns, even wings. Some are malevolent, some are benevolent and most are somewhere in between."

"Please tell me more about the Archons, "Viola insisted.

"Archons exist in Fourth Density beyond 'visible light' where humans cannot decode its frequency. It is still a 'physical ' realm - although it is less dense. Archons do not eat 'solid food'; their sustenance is derived from human forms of energy."

"Are you saying that humans are their source of food?"

"Yes. Their food is derived from human thought and emotion based on fear, depression, anxiety, guilt, anger, hatred and so on. Humans have a particular type of energy and the Archons have structured human society to provide that energy - especially from little children."

"Children, "gasped Viola. "How horrible! Why do they harm little children?"

"Let us simply say they prefer children because their chemical makeup is pure. Reptilians cannot stay in Third Density for long. They return to Fourth Density to replenish themselves. Drinking human blood helps them to remain on Earth for longer intervals because human blood contains human 'energetic codes' necessary to maintain the Archons' vibrational state in greater synchronization within Earth's dimension. Fourth Density Reptilians manipulate Earth's reality by possessing 'human bodies' and taking over their mental and emotional processes. They wear these bodies like spacesuits. It allows them to dictate events in your World without actually being in it - thus their hybrid bloodlines become the genetic vehicles that allow them to control Earth while hiding behind human form."

"My fiancée Carl was abducted by Constantine's soldiers never to be seen again. The murderers must have been possessed by the Archons! It all happened in the 4th century when we lived our former 'Earth life'. We were 'Gnostics' and Constantine hated our people. The hypocrite claimed he wanted to establish a 'one' true Christian religion when in reality, he was a 'Sun-god' worshipper. His form of Christianity was just another version of other esoteric concepts including the worship of the Moon god . . ."

"We are aware of your sad experience, Viola. Many 'humans' have suffered unjustly. Your Bible claimed it was the unique 'word' of 'God', but in truth, it was a collection of ancient stories and texts; some symbolic - some literal - that were repeats and re-writes of legends and accounts about Reptilian control that originated thousands of years before the 'Holy Book', or its religious expressions, Christianity and Judaism existed. This book didn't come out of nowhere; it had roots from a distant past."

"Are you acquainted with Sophia and Thelete? "Viola questioned.

"Yes, of course, dear one. Sophia speaks fondly of you and Carl. She has instructed us to help you in your quest. Your work is very important to Her and all of humanity. You must be tired. We can continue tomorrow. Rest, dear one. Rest."

Viola watched as the luminous brightness of the globe slowly dimmed until it was gone. The 'Guides' had bid farewell. She sighed contently and wondered how Tiffany Rose was doing.

Chapter Seven

Tiffany Rose

One of her finest attributes was her courage. Once she committed herself to a task she never reneged, despite the challenge. Her character, strength, and sincerity reflected the qualities of her Father, Josef Armand, a respected leader/teacher of the early 4th century Donatist Christians who had strong Gnostic leanings. The group comprised a vigorous membership that rejected any Christian who collaborated with Rome during the great persecution of their era.

Tiffany Rose idolized her Father. His unblemished work ethic, his uncompromising adherence to truth, and his endearing inability to conceal his compassion and kindness, were just a few of the sterling qualities she admired and loved so much. Indeed, she was 'Daddy's girl'. She secretly hoped to meet and marry a man with similar qualities. Those who didn't understand, thought her to be too demanding, but Viola understood. She too, respected and loved Josef Armand. How relieved Viola was that

Uncle Josef approved of Carl. He acknowledged the young man's intelligence and became his spiritual mentor and teacher.

Tiffany Rose chose to research Earth's religions and their origins. She soon learned that 'Serpent' worship was the worldwide foundation of all belief systems. This understanding explained why the same 'Serpent' gods could be found in virtually all ancient cultures and religions. They eventually fused into 'one' God to create the monotheistic religions of Christianity, Judaism and Islam, but they remained as 'gods' in other religions such as Hinduism, where their various deities existed in the *tens of thousands.* 'Serpent' gods became the Hindu gods, Sumerian gods, Babylonian gods, Egyptian gods, Chinese gods, and so on. The Reptilians and their hybrids remained the force behind all World religion and they used it relentlessly to control their slave race - HUMANITY. They chose religion as the 'battleground' on which to conquer the human *mind.* Tiffany Rose paused momentarily. "My goodness! "she exclaimed. "No wonder there were so many wars over religion." Her thoughts focused on her Father. He, like other Gnostics, searched for a greater depth of understanding of life and the Universe in light of the most complex and richly variegated intellectual tradition of their day. They knew the 'gods' were merely fabrications of the Serpent race and that religion was a trap that forced a 'sleep state' over humans to gain control of them through fear. Gnostics were intellectually curious. Their belief system was subtle, audacious, and sophisticated.

They endeavored to expand their knowledge of 'Consciousness' and free their thinking from the Fourth Density Reptilian control that was using 'religion' as a source of energy. The Reptilians drained the life force of humans by manipulating them to focus on deities that represented them. An example of this manipulation could be witnessed when Muslims worshippers circled the 'Kaaba' in Mecca (their 'symbol' of Reptilian gods). Their movement generated a constant energy for Reptilian assumption.

The 'Serpent' has always been the main symbol of Mythology and it is the common object of superstitious terror throughout the habitable world. Reptilians and their hybrids have been working for eons to possess and control the human 'Mind' to disconnect humanity from a higher Consciousness. Serpent-worshipping religions, secret societies, Satanism, and sacrificial rituals destroyed the Golden Age. Legends across the World say that humanity was ruined by the 'Serpents', which is what exactly happened.

Evidence of 'python' worship practiced 70,000 years ago was discovered in the Kalahari Desert in South Africa. Africa is a derivative of the ancient word, 'Wafrikia', and means 'the first people on Earth'. Indigenous people, known as 'Bushman', believed a giant 'python' had landed in the hills and created humans from eggs he carried in a bag. Another study traced the expansion of Serpent worship out of Babylon and Mesopotamia. The same basic story of deities and beliefs about the Serpent gods existed everywhere. It was the basis of religious beliefs worldwide. They had entered into the Mythology of every nation, consecrated almost every temple, symbolized almost every deity, was imagined in the Heavens, stamped upon the Earth, and ruled in the realms of everlasting sorrow.

At the center of the Reptilian religious control system is the worship of the Serpent, the Sun god, the Moon god, and the Moon goddess, or Mother goddess. Serpent/Sun/Moon/Saturn worship was associated with *human sacrifice* to the 'gods' and also with the building of pyramids. The Reptilians and their hybrids were the 'pyramid builders' of Egypt, Sumer, Central America, China, and so on. Christianity, Judaism, Islam and their like are all a cover for worship of the Reptilian Serpent. It seems that in most, if not all civilized countries where the Serpent was worshipped, some fable or tradition alluded to the *Fall of Man in Paradise*, in which the Serpent was concerned. The most accepted account relates the story of the 'victorious' Serpent over man (who was in a state of 'innocence') and subduing his soul into a state of 'sin' and the most abject veneration and adoration of himself. The 'Fall of Man' describes the consequences of the Reptilian takeover. In present times, the minds of billions are controlled by an unshakable belief in the Christian, Islamic, Jewish, Hindu and other version of the same original myths from which they all came, keeping their gullible believers in 'Mind' mode and out of 'Consciousness'.

The belief systems of the faithful are fiercely policed through fear, guilt, and even violence. Some zealots will kill members of their own family for violating rigid and ludicrous beliefs dictated by their dogmatic laws. Included in this agenda are 'arranged marriages' found in Islamic faiths. It isn't uncommon for young people to be killed if they dare to marry below their 'cast' status. While mainstream religions are the 'public face' of the Serpent cult and 'hidden societies' are their true expression, there is a third element. The upper echelons of the secret society network and many others belong to Satanic groups that engage in 'animal' and 'human' sacrifice to the gods on a scale that would boggle the imagination.

One of the major Satanic Reptilian deities is 'Lilith'. Some versions of the Garden of Eden story say that Lilith was Adam's first wife and the real Mother of Cain and that she was symbolized by the snake that tempted Eve. She is depicted as half human and half Serpent and was associated with the sons of Anu (Anunnaki), and Samael (another demon angel) who supposedly impregnated Eve to give birth to Cain. To the Babylonians, Lilith was the

Mother of the first vampires and she is widely associated in many cultures with stealing and killing children. She is also described as a consort of Lucifer, the 'Light Bringer' and the 'god' of Freemasonry. Lucifer and Lilith are said to be the androgynous figure of 'Baphomet' or the 'Goat of Mendes', a symbol of worship by the Illuminati Knights Templar. Lilith is also known as the Scarlet Woman, Great Mother, Babylon the Great, Mother of Harlots, the Whore of Babylon, and Mother of Abominations.

The 'lily' is the inspiration for the fleur-de-lis, an ancient symbol of the Reptilian/hybrid bloodline for the Serpent demon, Lilith. It is used by the House of Windsor, the Spanish Monarchy, the Grand Duke of Luxembourg, the French Royal Houses as well as military and scout organizations. The *owl* is also associated with Lilith. Located in the redwood forests of Sonoma County, California, is *Bohemian Grove,* the infamous 'summer camp' of the elite Satanists, where the bloodline families and their sycophants take part in 'child sacrifice' rituals in homage to Lilith and a deity named Moloch. The 'gods' are represented by a 40 foot *stone owl.* The Bohemian Grove crowd who perform child sacrifice rituals are former presidents and business leaders. Attending participants captured on film are: George Bush, Jr., George Bush, Sr., Ronald Reagan, Richard Nixon, Jimmy Carter, Gerald Ford, Dwight D. Eisenhower, Lyndon Johnson, Herbert Hoover, Teddy Roosevelt; the Rockefellers, Henry Kissinger, Al Gore, and numerous others.

SO WHERE ARE THEY?

There are Reptilian entities that operate within *visible light*, and there are colonies of them in underground cities and tunnel systems that are widely described in ancient and modern records. Drinking human blood helps them to stay in Third Density longer. It contains the human energetic codes and helps them maintain their Third Density vibrational state in greater synchronization. It also gives them energetic sustenance. Humans have a particular type of energy and the Reptilians have structured human society to trawl that energy, especially from children when it is the most 'pure'.

There is a connection between the Reptilians and legends about 'vampires' and the blood-drinking human sacrifice networks that are known as SATANISM. Stories about vampires are based on fact and this is another universal theme that connects with the Reptilian manipulation. Most familiar of all the vampires was a character named 'Vlad the Impaler', known to most as 'Dracula'. He was the son of Vlad Dracul, who was initiated into the ancient Order of the Dragon (known also as the *Brotherhood of the Snake* formed in Egypt in 2170 BC) by the Holy Roman Emperor in 1431. Its emblem was a dragon, wings extended, hanging on a cross.

The younger Reptilian hybrid Dracula was the 15th century ruler of a country called Wallacha, situated not far from the Black Sea, in what is now Romania. The region included an area known as Transylvania, the home of the most famous vampire legends.

He is said to have slaughtered tens of thousands of people and impaled many of them on stakes. The decaying corpses were often left for months. He signed his name 'Draculea' or the 'Devil's Son', which later became Dracula. Queen Mary, or Mary of Teck, the Mother of King George VI and grandmother to the present Elizabeth II, was a descendant from a sister of Dracula, which isn't too surprising given that the House of Windsor is *supposedly* a Reptilian hybrid bloodline.

Vlad Dracul

Vlad Dracul is perhaps an extreme example, but blood drinking and human sacrifice is 'part of life' for the Reptilian hybrid bloodlines. They have always done it and still are doing it. Nothing is 'off limits' to them no matter how grotesque it may be.

COVENANT WITH THE DEVIL

The Rothschild dynasty is controlled by the family's Satanic black magicians who know how 'reality' works and how they can manipulate energy and human perception. They know money is 'energy' and they have set up the World Financial System to ensure that its wealth flows back to them.

Chapter Eight

Satanists

Satanists are peculiar people. Their ranks are filled with doctors, lawyers, businessmen, and basically highly responsible citizens. They are not a careless group apt to make mistakes. Rather, they are secretive and are bonded together for a common cause - to mete out havoc on society!

Some of the world's richest families, including the Rothschilds, the Rockefellers and the Windsors, are members of the Illuminati as previously mentioned. Their agents control the world's media, education, business and politics. These agents may think they are only pursuing success, but success literally means serving the 'Devil'. Prisoners of their wealth, they prefer hatred and destruction to love. Understandably, they can't go public with this. They pretend to be moral while working behind the scenes to degrade and enslave humanity in a 'New World Order'.

(*Skeptics should avail themselves of numerous articles seen on the web and other publications*).

Seen below is the Baroness Philippine de Rothschild who is the owner of the French winery - Château Mouton. She is the only daughter of the vintner Baron Philippe de Rothschild and she is a member of the Rothschild ‘banking dynasty‘. She has also acted under the stage name ‘Philippine Pascale‘. Her personal wealth has been estimated at €190 million by *Le Nouvel Economiste.*

Baroness Philippine de Rothschild

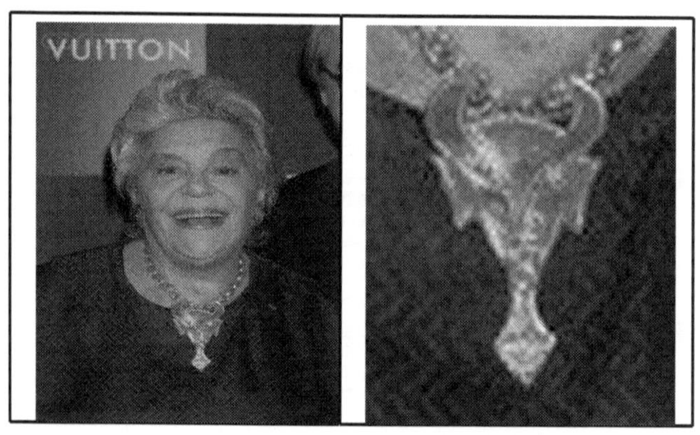

She wears a heavy chain linked gold necklace with a pendant. The pendant is a huge image of ‘Baphomet‘, a pagan deity that, since the 19th century, has become a figure or synonym of ‘Satan‘. There are other pictures of Ms. Rothschild wearing pendants that are more stylized or abstract versions of the Baphomet, i.e., the goat's or ram's ‘horns‘. This woman is one of the wealthiest people on Earth who can wear any piece of jewelry she desires, but again and again, she chooses to wear big, ugly Satanic pendants on big, heavy, gold chain necklaces.

Some claim the Illuminati to be mainly, if not wholly, Jewish. Others, such as Henry Makow (who is a Jew), do not identify the Illuminati with a particular racial or ethnic group. They identify them by their common spiritual perversity - 'Satanism'. The Rothschild family are 'Satanists' and have a horrible history.

(The epistemology of 'conspiracy theories' such as this one about the Illuminati and its members tend to arouse skepticism until one actually views pictures of a 'Rothschild').

Think of the Illuminati network as a gigantic spider's web and the strands representing different secret societies, semi-secret organizations and others that operate openly in the public domain. The latter includes governments, transnational corporations and the banking system. The closer the 'strands' are to the 'spider' in the center, the more secretive and exclusive they will be. All are controlled by the Spider and its Shadow People. Key enforcers are the *'House of Rothschild'* banking dynasty, who in turn, established the 'Round Table' in the later years of the 19th century. Under the leadership of Cecil Rhodes, a Rothschild agent, they plundered southern Africa. Rhodesia, now Zimbabwe and Zambia, were named after him. They are a major conduit for bloodline manipulation and have become more so all the time. Known as 'The House of Rothschild', or more simply as the Rothschilds, they are a European family of German (Ashkenazi) Jewish origin that established European banking and finance houses from the late eighteenth century.

Five lines of the Austrian branch of the family were elevated into the Austrian nobility, being given hereditary baronies of the Habsburg Empire by Emperor Francis II in 1816. The British branch of the family was elevated into the British nobility at the

request of Queen Victoria. It has been argued that during the 19th century, the family possessed the largest private fortune in the World, and the largest fortune in modern history. An estimate of the Rothschild wealth was over $6 billion in 1850. Taking $6 billion and assuming no erosion of the wealth base and compounding that figure at various returns on investment (a conservative range of 4% to 8%) would suggest the following net worth of the Rothschild family enterprise, as of 1997:

$1.9 trillion (@4%) - $7.8 trillion (@5%) - $31.5 trillion (@6%) - $125,189.1 trillion (@7%) - $491,409 trillion @ 8%).

Religion, secret societies and what is known as Satanism are all connected and controlled by the Reptilian conspiracy. At the top level of the pyramid structure, they work as one organization. Both the secret societies and the Serpent worshipers emerged from the ancient Mystery Schools that were established and hijacked by the Archon/Reptilians bloodlines. Mainstream religion is the public face of the Serpent cult, and secret societies are its hidden expression; but there is a third element - the full blown human sacrifice 'religion' of the Reptilian gods, which is known today as Satanism. The upper echelons of the secret society network, and many lower ones, fuse with the global web of Satanic groups that engage in animal and human sacrifice on a scale that boggles the imagination. Satanism and the Illuminati are indivisible and many famous people take part in human sacrifice and blood-drinking rituals. Satanists perform their rituals to a strict calendar related to astronomical and astrological movements of the Earth, Moon, and the planets.

Those in major positions of royal, political, banking, commercial, media, and military power are invariably Reptilian/hybrids and the bloodlines have always performed sacrificial rituals going back to Sumer and the later stages of Atlantis and Mu. Power and Satanism go together. Among the highest echelons are found politicians, medical doctors, high ranking police officers, lawyers, advertising gurus, decorated military men, media and entertainment personalities, fashion models, and social workers. Lower ranks include prostitutes, minor drug dealers, and misguided young adults. Many celebrities, too numerous to mention, are on the list.

(The following information was published by David Icke - 'Human Race Get Off Your Knees')

"Philip Eugene de Rothschild, son of Baron Philippe de Rothschild of the Mouton-Rothschild wine estates in France, came forth after he rejected his family's horrific agenda. He said he was one of hundreds of thousands of 'unofficial' Rothschild offspring. Except for a few, all are produced through sperm-bank breeding programs to insure the genetic purity. These Rothschild children are brought up in other families and don't officially use the Rothschild name. They can then come into power in the institutions of society, including presidents and prime ministers, without anyone realizing the Rothschild connection. Philip Eugene stated: "My Father was a decadent dilettante as well as a master Satanist and hater of God, but he loved the fields and the wines." He also stated that he was conceived by the 'occult incest' also employed by the Rothschild and the bloodline families to protect their genetic code. He lived most of his childhood and adolescence with his Father on their estate in France and they had a 'physical' relationship to make sure he was 'held fast' in the emotional power of incest, which was normal in this culture. Incest is very common among Reptilian bloodline families. They are possessed by 'demonic' entities in rituals performed for that

purpose. He claimed he had been maximally demonized. He was placed within the Christian Church to work for the Rothschild agenda while appearing to be a perfect 'Christian', but later rejected his role and the Satanism that went with it. He advised that like other children, he played a key role in his family's revolt from God. When he watched CNN, he saw many familiar faces on the World stage of politics, art, finance, fashion, and business. He grew up with these people, meeting them at ritual worship sites and in the centers of power . . .financiers, artists, royalty, and even Presidents. He recalled the Rockefellers and the Bushes attending rituals although never having the supremacy to lead them. He regarded them as 'lackeys' and not real brokers of occult power.

"Except for Alan Greenspan (US Federal Reserve), most were 'camp followers' in the occult, primarily for the economic power and prestige while Greenspan was a person of tremendous spiritual, occult power and could make the Bushes and the younger Rockefellers cower with just a glance."

Author Pierre Sabak compiled a fascinating and comprehensive book titled *The Murder of Reality.* It is a detailed study of word derivations, associations, and true meanings that show how the Serpent Race and its subjugation of humanity is encoded into ancient languages and accounts. These words and meanings have since been passed through 'modern languages'. Comparative linguist and symbologist, Pierre Sabak, spent seven years researching to reveal the interconnecting words and meanings that encode all the major aspects of the Reptilian conspiracy. A monumental endeavor, several of the meanings are as follows:

➢ The Serpent race or 'gods' that are controlling humanity are responsible for the geological catastrophe symbolized as the 'Great Flood'.

➢ They are the fundamental connection with royalty and a hybrid bloodline passing through history - the bloodline of Eve and the Serpent Race that rules the World. The word 'Eve' is synonymous with 'life' and 'snake'.

➢ The association of the Serpent Race with 'light' and illumination' as in 'the 'shinning ones'. (In Latin, 'Illuminati' means enlightened). Mention is made of the Serpent 'gods' or Fallen Angels 'shinning' like the Sun.

➢ The description of the Serpent Race as rapists, liars, and deceivers who hide their existence behind symbolism that only the 'chosen ones' are meant to decode.

Chapter Nine
Codes And Symbols

The imposition of a 'royal' Reptilian/human hybrid bloodline may possibly be the result of an agreement that followed humanity's defeat in a war with the Serpent race. It may have been no more than an agreement any 'loser' in a conflict 'agrees' to the victor. This agreement has passed through history under the name 'Covenant' symbolizing God's/gods Covenant and central to it, is the interbreeding between humans and the Reptilians to create and maintain the ruling hybrid bloodline. It also involved an agreement that the Reptilians would be able to abduct human children on a massive scale - worldwide. Codes for the interbreeding include 'divine marriage' and a marriage between 'heaven and earth'. The offspring were said to be 'born of heaven and earth' and 'born of the clouds', among many other codes and symbols. The 'dragon', a teacher of words and arithmetic, embedded knowledge of itself sequenced in numerical codes (Numerology) - a secret history veiled in mathematics, geometry, astronomy, semiology (study of signs) and language. Systematic and intelligent, the adoption of *signs* is discursive of secret knowledge pertaining to the 'snake' and its concealment. The essence of language loans itself to symbolism represented sublimely through the study of philology and homonyms (words that look and sound the same, but have different meanings). A hidden mentor of man, the 'angel' in occult lore is a Reptilian entity distinguished as the hidden Master or King. Untrusting towards humans, this creature hides behind occult ritual. Frightened of being uncovered, it uses war, economic and political coercion to force nations to do its bidding. Ancient accounts suggest the *snake* is duplicitous in its designs and dealings with man. You must uncover the codes to see how widespread the evidence of the Serpent Race and its manipulation of human life actually is.

The Satanists desperately seek to remain hidden, which necessitates working hard to unpick the locks, codes, symbols, words, and mathematics that provide the 'cover'. It is a deep cover, too, and hidden in words that appear at first to have nothing to do with any Serpent Race. Common was the use of nautical terms such as 'heavenly boats', 'upper ocean', and other maritime themes in the legends of Egyptian deities like Osiris and Ra. Words used to describe the Reptilians often had the meaning of 'sailor' or 'crewmember'. This explains why there are so many words ending in 'ship' - kingship, lordship, citizenship, relationship, membership, worship, and so on.

Christianity, Judaism, Islam and their like are all a cover for the worship of the Reptilians - 'Serpent' worship. It is the foundation of all human religion and is hidden behind symbolic deities, stories and rituals. The language research confirms the many other sources that were gathered together over the years that reveal a 'covenant' between the bloodline families and their Serpent masters to sacrifice their first born sons through immolation. This appears to have been one of the conditions imposed *after humans lost the war with the Reptilians.* The Covenant also included the usurpation of human genetics by the *reptile* seed with the sacrificed child being replaced with the offspring of the Serpent race. These Reptilian replacements became known as 'changelings' (substitutes). We see the constant recurrence of the sacrifice of the firstborn and the slaughter of the *innocents* in religious texts. In the Old Testament, Abraham is asked to sacrifice his son, Isaac. God tells Abraham:

"Take your son, your only son - yes, Isaac, whom you love so much - and go to the land of Moriah. Sacrifice him there as a burnt offering on one of the mountains, which I will point out to you." (Genesis 22:1-18)

"You shall not delay to make offerings from the fullness of your harvest and from the outflow of your presses. The firstborn of your sons you shall give to me. You shall do the same with your oxen and with your sheep; seven days it shall remain with its Mother; on the eighth day you shall give it to me." (Exodus: 22:29-30).

As far as the Jewish people being the 'chosen people' and having a Covenant with God, Sabak stated that when groups talk of being the 'Chosen People', like the Jews, it does not mean all of them. It refers to those who made the Covenant with the Reptilians. This is why the Rothschilds couldn't care less about Jewish people as a whole. The Rothschilds are in tune with the '*Zionists*'.

> *(A comprehensive history of Israel and how it was established by Rothschild may be found in David Icke's novel: 'Human Race Get Off Your Knees')*

The secret society network today operates globally with groupings like the Jesuits, Knights Templar, Knights of Malta, Opus Dei and Freemasonry, working as one unit at their highest levels. This unit or force that connects all the major secret societies is known as the Illuminati. The bloodline plan for global control advanced with the process of giving 'independence' to their former colonies. It is now obvious why many of the 'wars of independence' were engineered by the very 'Colonial' powers that were being challenged. (The most powerful form of control is one you cannot see and are not aware exists). The United States reflects this covert scheme, which has been researched, exposed, and published. '*Apollyon Rising 2012*' - Tom Horn.

Former president, George Bush, Jr., and Barack Obama are controlled by this 'Shadow Power'; a fact many Americans are beginning to understand. (*It doesn't matter who you vote for; the government still gets in - the secret government, that is).*

Chapter Ten

Rogue's Gallery

The global network of secret societies and semi-secret groups are instructed like a transnational corporation. Their Corporate Headquarters, the hub of the organization, is located in Europe and dictates policy to all subsidiary networks worldwide. These subsidiaries direct their nation's politics, business, banking, media, military, medicine, science, education, etc., ensuring that they all conform to the blueprint dictated by 'headquarters'. Most people involved in some capacity don't know that they are involved in a grand conspiracy to enslave the World.

Among the Round Table satellites are:

- Royal Institute of International Affairs in London (1920)
- Council on Foreign Relations in the United States (1921)
- Bilderberg Group ((worldwide (1954)
- Club of Rome (1968)
- Trilateral Commission (global - 1973)
- United Nations (1945)

'WHO'S WHO'

joined at the hip . . .

Rockefeller Rothschild

The Rockefeller family is a Sumerian bloodline and they are interbred with the Rothschilds, from whom they take their orders. The role of the Rockefellers is to run the United States subsidiary. Both names have engineered wars, economic crashes and the control and manipulation of government, banking, global corporations, medicine, pharmaceutical, biotech industries, etc., but *banking* is their main vehicle for manipulation and control. The Rothschilds and their bloodline families own the banks and corporations through financial control and place people who run the organizations according to their instructions. They control most of the Vatican's wealth and are financial advisors to the Chinese government.

Zbigniew Brzezinski

(Rothschild Zionist) - Former US National Security Advisor to President Jimmy Carter. Co-founder of the Round Table's Trilateral Commission. Mentor to US 'Fascist' president, Barack Obama.

George Zoros

Billionaire financier. Obama mentor and funder. Manipulates events through a complex network of foundations and organizations operating worldwide in league with 'elite' groups and agencies in the US and Israel, including the CIA and Mossad.

Rahm Emanual

The son of a Rothschild Zionist terror group operative, he is the 'real' power in the White House. Both Emanual and Obama have lifetime memberships in Chicago's infamous gay community 'Bath Houses'.

THE BILDERBERG GROUP - Every year the same question is posed or answered in different ways: What is Bilderberg really? What is it at its core? Here is the key answer and definition: "*People incapable of empathy acquiring the literal powers of gods through science".* The purpose of Google and the NSA is to make the super class all-knowing, all-seeing and to enable them to predict the future. The *drone program* is about becoming all-seeing and to become like the god Zeus, sending bolts of lightning at mortals you want to take out of existence. Weather modification, chem-trailing and ionospheric manipulation through systems like HAARP are not just 'weapons' in the Military's toolkit. They enable the 'control freaks' to control the weather like a god would do, sending floods and droughts and storms to kill mortals. Genetic engineering and the wider field of synthetic biology are not primarily about making money to buy more vintage sports cars from the 1960s; rather it's all about becoming the 'Creator' of life.

Another significant Illuminati organization is England's Fabian Society. Founded in 1884, it is a 'wolf' in sheep's clothing as it uses a technique called 'permeation', which manipulates the consensus. It has been involved in the long-term agenda for the global Fascist/Communist dictatorship. If George Orwell's book, '*1984*', (published in 1945) and Aldous Huxley's, '*Brave New World*', (published in 1948) were combined, it would be obvious as to how the Illuminati are seeking to impose their agenda. Both men were members of the Illuminati 'Fabian Society' and both wrote novels that proved to be extraordinarily accurate about the global Control System that is presently emerging.

The late sociologist Neil Postman wrote about the effects of technology on our lives. Keeping in mind what Cicero said 2,000 years ago - "When you trade your freedom for security, you will lose both" - the following is the foreword from '*Amusing Ourselves to Death*' by Neil Postman:

"We were keeping our eye on 1984. When the year came and the prophecy didn't, thoughtful Americans sang softly in praise of themselves. The roots of liberal democracy had held. Wherever else the terror had happened, we, at least, had not been visited by Orwellian nightmares. But we had forgotten that alongside Orwell's dark vision, there was another - slightly older, slightly less well known, equally chilling: Aldous Huxley's 'Brave New World'. Contrary to common belief even among the educated, Huxley and Orwell did not prophesize the same thing. Orwell warns that we will be overcome by an externally imposed oppression. But in Huxley's vision, no 'Big Brother' is required to deprive people of their autonomy, maturity and history. As he saw it, people will come to love their oppression, to adore the technologies that undo their capacities to think."

- *What Orwell feared were those who would ban books.*
- *What Huxley feared was that there would be no reason to ban a book, for there would be no one who wanted to read one.*
- *Orwell feared those who would deprive us of information.*
- *Huxley feared those who would give us so much that we would be reduced to passivity and egoism.*
- *Orwell feared that the truth would be concealed from us.*
- *Huxley feared the truth would be drowned in a sea of irrelevance.*
- *Orwell feared we would become a captive culture.*
- *Huxley feared we would become a trivial culture, preoccupied with some equivalent of the feelies, the orgy porgy, and the centrifugal 'bumble puppy'.*

As Huxley remarked in *Brave New World Revisited*, the civil libertarians and rationalists who are ever on the alert to oppose tyranny 'failed to take into account man's almost infinite appetite for distractions'. In 1984, Huxley added that people are controlled by inflicting pain. In *Brave New World*, they are controlled by inflicting pleasure. In short, Orwell feared that what we hate will ruin us. Huxley feared that what we love will ruin us. This book is about the possibility that Huxley, not Orwell, was right.

All major institutions and groups that affect our daily lives are connected within the 'Pyramid of Manipulation'. This global 'Control Structure' is a system of pyramids within pyramids. Only the few at the top in the 'Capstone' know the true motivation of the Global Dictatorship. And sitting at the top of the pyramids is the *House of Rothschild*, enforcing and orchestrating the agenda of the 'One World Government'. By now, it's blatantly clear that the bloodlines want to install a World Government that will dictate to every country via 'international law' and 'international regulation' - their LAWS and REGULATIONS!

This plan for World power has been playing out for decades. It seeks to impose the total transformation of global society to create a World 'prison state' that will control every individual - including his very thoughts. The Rothschild dynasty is controlled by the family's 'Satanic' black magicians who know how reality works and how they can manipulate energy and human perception. They know that money, like everything else, is energy and they have set up the financial system to exploit this knowledge. People talk about the 'flow of money', but it is really the flow of 'energy' that controls the World. The Rothschilds have created an 'energetic construct' that ensures the 'energy of money' encircles them. Called the 'economy', it appears to consist of banks, financial houses, stock markets and other forms of trading. But all these entities are just *acupuncture points on the meridians of money* to ensure that the wealth of the world flows to the bloodline families. It is because of this, the Rothschilds count their wealth, not in millions or billions, but in multitudes of trillions and more. Some uninformed people think it is 'unfair' to criticize the Rothschilds 'just because they're wealthy'. The point is, how did they accumulate their wealth? Covert manipulation and taking advantage of millions of people in 3rd World countries less educated and powerful is not 'cricket'! People are starving and homeless, not to mention 'DEAD', because of their ruthlessness and detachment. Researching their nefarious history would soon set the uniformed individual 'straight' about the game they play.

When Bush Jr. left the White House in 2009, Obama moved in. His job was to serve the interests of the Rothschilds and their Wall St. bankers by introducing the 'solutions' to the problems they had callously created. Obama surrounded himself with Rothschild Zionists - Axelrod, Emanuel, Frum, Biden, Gore, Dennis Ross, Henry Kissinger, Cass Sustein, Timothy Geithner, Steven Rattner, and numerous others. The rest is history.

There is an extraordinary ratio of Rothschild Zionists to positions of power. When you realize that the Jewish people make up no more than two percent of the American population, and some of them aren't Zionists, the ratio of Rothschild Zionists to position of power and influence is absolutely fantastic.

It is important to realize that 'The House of Rothschild' controls the political system of the United States and Israel. The network that links the two is 'Rothschild Zionism'. The American/Israel Public Affairs Committee (AIPAC) is a mega-funded lobby operation that ensures the U.S. slavishly supports the interests of Israel and the Rothschild networks. You cannot become *president* or be appointed to any significant political office in the U.S. unless you are either acceptable to them or preferably, 'subservient'. The network was behind the Bush administration, which was controlled by the 'neo-con' or neo-conservative network that included Rothschild Zionist 'think tanks'. They are infiltrated with Khazar/Sumerians, and their agents and it was this network that orchestrated the invasion of Afghanistan and Iraq. The same situation is found with the 'Obama regime'. The mystery of how the 'unknown' Obama was elected to the White House is readily understood after learning that the billionaire, George Zoros (Rothschild Zionist) carried him there.

(For a more in-depth summary of the Rothschild's global influence and control - read 'Human Race Get Off Your Knees'
by David Icke)

Chapter Eleven

"There exists this power in the world so subtle, so organized, so watchful, that we dare not speak above a whisper when we speak in condemnation of it." Woodrow Wilson

---

Viola found Tiffany Rose and shared her unique encounter with the 'guides'. Tiffany Rose was intrigued and they decided they would make their next 'contact' together. They sat focused in front of the globe and anxiously waited for the guides to appear. Suddenly, a luminous blue glow emanated from the globe to announce the guides' arrival.

"Greetings Dear Ones - When the 28th President of the U.S. quoted the above statement, it is unknown if he knew the identity of the power of which he spoke. Today, many humans realize he was referring to the 'Illuminati', which is comprised of men and women in every country who adhere to laws these 'power brokers' dictate. The global secret society network

is orchestrated through hybrid bloodlines like the Rothschilds and the Rockefellers. They dictate and impose the laws that govern every area of human life for the 'Serpent gods' they serve. The 'covenant' with 'god' to his chosen people is actually a contract that was forced upon humanity by the Archon/Reptilians. It was the result of humanity's defeat in a war with the Serpent race; or some renegade group. This agreement has passed through history under the name 'covenant' or 'God's/the gods' covenant and central to it, is the interbreeding between humans and the Reptilians to create and maintain the ruling hybrid bloodline. It also involves an agreement that the Reptilians are able to abduct human children on a massive scale worldwide. It continues to be imposed through governments (covenants) that are nothing more than 'administrators' of the Serpent laws and rules passed down through the bloodline families and the secret societies into the public domain. Early accounts of the 'Elohim' - plural (the gods) imply a military dictatorship identified with invasion and conquest.

King Hammurabi established the Babylonian Empire during his reign (1795 BC - 1750 BC) and built the World's first known Metropolis. He is famous for his 'Code of Hammurabi', which he said had been given to him by the 'gods'. The same theme can be found with the story of Moses and the 'Ten Commandments'. All religions are founded on the law given to the people through a middleman or prophet by their various versions of God or the gods - the 'Serpent Hierarchy'. It is still happening today.

The Archon/Reptilians aren't able to invade Earth with spacecraft and take over. If it were possible, they would have done so a long time ago. Why? Because Fourth Density Reptilians lack the ability to live in 'sunlight' for long periods. Earth's atmosphere is hostile to their 'inorganic' makeup. This explains why they live underground in caves on Earth, the Moon, Mars, in their spacecraft and who knows where else. When you stop and think about all the underground facilities the elite, shadow government, and Illuminati have constructed in recent years as well as those built in ancient times, you can connect the dots. How many human people do you know prefer to live underground? Although the Archon/Reptilians possess advanced technology, there are relatively few of them compared to humans. Extremely outnumbered, they hope to wipe out the human population with various sadistic techniques. Once you become aware of their agenda, you will be in a better place to do something about it."

"These people seem mad, "exclaimed Viola.

"Yes, the World seems to be crazy and out of control to many people. However, when you understand the game, you will see that human society is the way it is for a reason - the enslavement of the many by the minuscule few. Things are the way they are because the Archon/Reptilians want it like this. There is a method to their madness. CONTROL. They believe that if they can reduce the World population to a safe number, it will make it easier for them to remain in power. They've been doing this for eons. We

know the methods they used in ancient times - human sacrifice, wars, and famine . . . just like today. Nothing has changed much. For the 'unaware' and those in 'la la' land, the information presented will shock and undermine their false sense of security and well-being. Tell them to wake up! It's time to smell the stench of blood and sacrifice existing in the World. Just as Michael Ellner has stated, they have built a prison camp around your Planet where all is backwards and perverse. Your bodies are biological computer systems. To program the desired perceptions and responses, 'access codes' are needed. They are vibrational, electrical, chemical and mathematical. The whole system is set up to allow the Archon/Reptilian programmers to manipulate the body/computer minute by minute through all these means of entry to underpin the 'hive-mind reality' being broadcasted from the Moon. Do you know about the Moon/Matrix?"

"No, not really, "Tiffany Rose answered.

"It is complex and will be explained later. Briefly, they (Reptilians) seek to download the beliefs and perceptions of 'reality' that enforce their agenda enabling them to destabilize and imbalance the human body's receiver/transmitter system. It blocks your ability to connect with levels of awareness that allow you to see through the smoke screen and mirrors. They have perverted many areas of human life: health, belief systems, justice . . . and introduced so much fear, guilt, and confusion."

YOUR DOCTORS DESTROY HEALTH . . .

"The medical establishment Worldwide is just a tool of the pharmaceutical cartel, or 'Big Pharma'. The last thing it represents is 'human health'. Mainstream medicine is about wealth - not health. Its covert endeavor is to keep people mentally, emotionally, and physically sick; or in 'states of being' that denies them a connection to their true and infinite self. Despite the appearance of different companies, 'Big Pharma' works as one network in the Illuminati pyramid-within-pyramid structure that controls the entire mainstream medical profession and its associated 'industry'. It is an industry founded on human suffering. Healthy people don't require drugs or pay medical bills; sick people do! 'Big Pharma' controls what is taught in the medical schools, what drugs doctors prescribe, and how far they can stray from strictly enforced medical 'norms'. It also dictates government health policy. 'Big Pharma' is a grotesque cesspool of corruption and self-interest made even worse by the extraordinary levels of ignorance and incompetence among those who are paid outrageous sums to be 'medical experts'. They cannot challenge the 'norms' dictated by the authorities and many doctors don't even know what the human body is and how it really works. Their methods are antiquated and ineffectual - especially their knowledge of surgical applications. They know what they are told to 'know' and are restricted immediately if they try to 'think out of the box'. Hard to accept, but doctors are the third biggest cause

of 'death' in the World from unnecessary surgery, harmful medication, and other errors. Reptilian Rothschild-Rockefeller networks created the system of medical associations - (British Medical Association (BMA) and the American Medical Association (AMA) to control medicine and the medical profession.

"There's those names again, "Viola exclaimed. "The Rothschilds' and the 'Rockefellers'. Who are these people?"

"All in time, dear one. All in time. What is important to know is that schools refusing to use 'modern scientific medicine' in place of natural, homeopathic applications, did not receive funding from the Rockefeller Foundation and other drug companies despite the fact that Rockefeller himself avoided 'allopathic' medicine, preferring to be treated with homeopathy. Hypocrite! In other words, "Do as I tell you to do and not as I do!" The rules only apply to mainstream - the poor unfortunates who have been tricked and forced to obey. How many times have people dipped into their pockets and made a generous contribution to help some 'research' campaign to find the cure for 'something'? Too many! By now, after all the money and efforts contributed by sincere, humane people, all diseases should have a cure . . . and most do. Did you know there is a cure for many diseases that the present Medical Society is sitting on?"

"I suspected as much, "Tiffany Rose replied. "It was our belief in the 4th century that the Goddess Sophia had provided us with natural herbs to heal any of the maladies people suffered."

"You are quite correct, my dear. Whenever there is evidence of illness, it is due to an unbalance in your energy field that is mainly caused by fear."

"There is so much to remember, "Viola sighed. "Can we take a break and continue tomorrow."

"Yes, of course dear one. We failed to see how exhausted you both are. We will continue in our next session. Goodbye dear ones."

Before Viola and Tiffany Rose had offered their farewells, they were unexpectedly startled by a deep voice spoken by a young man that had suddenly appeared in the globe.

"Young maidens! Wait! Don't go yet! I request your attention."

Quite startled, the girls remained frozen and speechless.

"Don't be frightened. I wish to help you. My name is Darius. I have been eavesdropping on your conversation with the guides.

I too, have concern and sympathy for the Goddess Sophia. She needs all the help She can get, wouldn't you agree?"

Tiffany Rose managed to reply. "I don't understand. Why do you wish to help us? Do you know Thelete? Has he sent you?"

"I had the honor of knowing your dear Father, Tiffany Rose. He has sent me to you."

"My Father, "Tiffany Rose gasped. "My Father sent you to me?"

"Yes, on my honor. He is aware of your mission to help Sophia."

Tiffany Rose regained her composure. "I see. You are quite right. Sophia would appreciate your help. But, I would suggest that you speak with Thelete. He's 'in charge'. I will tell Him about you and arrange for you to meet Him tomorrow, if this is agreeable."

"Yes, that would be fine. You are very kind to arrange a meeting with Thelete. Thank you. I have my own 'channel', so to speak, on the globe's network. Once the globe is 'activated', just ask to speak to me, 'Darius of Tarsus'. I will anxiously await our next meeting. It was a pleasure to speak to you and Viola. Good bye."

"Farewell, "Tiffany Rose weakly replied. "Ditto, "replied Viola.

Within seconds, he was gone. They turned to face each other and after a few moments, burst out laughing. "What was that all about? "Viola giggled. "He was so handsome . . . and polite."

Tiffany Rose sighed. "Yes, he was rather nice looking . . .and he knows my Father. This is all so unbelievable." She felt a sudden blush rush to her cheeks and turned away, but it was too late.

"You're blushing! "Viola exclaimed. "You're actually blushing."

Chapter Twelve

Darius

He had known the stench of war; the ravages of battle, the maligned bodies covered in blood, the groans of those who were dying. War! How utterly perverted and insane. It was all so futile; so manipulated. When the 'reality' finally seized him that there had never been a 'noble cause', nor an urgent need to protect himself, country; and loved ones, that he wasn't involved in the 'good' fight against evil, that neither side would be the victor, that the promise of peace would never be fulfilled - he wanted to 'throw up'. Only the perverted maniacs who started the lie, who craved the 'blood ritual', who secretly sneered at his inflated vanity and ego-centered illusions . . . were the victors. They would collect the 'spoils' and benefit from the pain and injustice after each battle. How revolting were these psychopaths! They must be challenged and stopped. Weary and disillusioned from all the empty victories, he 'retired' from the role of 'warrior'. He wanted to make amends. But to who? Who even wanted him?

He prayed to the 'gods'; all of them, until he realized they too were mere extensions and fabrications of the 'black magicians'. He settled into a deep depression, but his heart never let go of his desire to find a new path and a 'true love'. It had saved him. He slowly climbed out from the 'abyss' and in his upward struggle to find truth and love, he met Josef Armand, the beloved Father of Tiffany Rose.

Josef managed to escape the wrath of Constantine with other Gnostics in the 4th century and fled to a safer location. Unfortunately, Carl was captured and disposed of. Viola was devastated. Tiffany Rose watched over her and helped her to heal emotionally, but Viola never loved another man in that lifetime. She and Carl were true 'soul mates'. When Darius appeared on the scene, he reminded Josef of Carl. The similarity was striking. Both young men were visionaries and never wavered in the pursuit of their goal. Josef took Darius under his tutelage. He taught him about Gnostic principles and introduced him to the story of the Goddess Sophia. Darius joined the *telestai*, (those who are aimed - focused) and charted a path for himself, hopeful that it included a relationship with a 'true love'. Encouraged by the compassion and wisdom of Josef, he slowly embraced a new vision that transformed his life. Their mutual respect for each other encouraged a strong teacher/student bond between them. Darius had the potential of becoming a true devotee of the teachings of the Sacred Mysteries and the Goddess Sophia.

Josef had 'celestial' connections and had been informed of Sophia's situation and the upcoming Trial. He was concerned about the safety of his daughter and niece. Confident of Darius' sincerity and strong moral fiber, he decided to inform him about Sophia and the Trial. As he anticipated, Darius volunteered his services. Josef was pleased. He secretly hoped his daughter would be receptive to the young man and his offer to help. He doubted if the girls realized the resistance they might encounter from the 'dark forces'. Darius would protect them. Having been involved in many battle skirmishes, he was well informed of the covert tactics of the 'black magicians' and very skilled with 'offensive' strategies.

Darius wished to avoid any type of warfare. He planned to utilize his intellectual and spiritual knowledge. He had put old programming behind him. No longer was he a captive of the of the 'dark magicians' manipulation. He was now a devoted member of the telestai and a true advocate of a higher Consciousness. He had invoked the Goddess Sophia for 'wisdom'. She answered him with a call for 'help'.

Chapter Thirteen
Darius Meets Thelete

Tiffany Rose contacted Thelete to meet her and Viola. He wasn't surprised that they had beckoned Him, but the fact that they said it was 'urgent' was unsettling. He met with them in the lobby of the Library.

"It's good to see you both. How is everything going? "He inquired.

"Very well, Thelete. We missed you."

"I missed you also, but you know we are pressed for time and there is much to do. Has something out of the ordinary caused you to beckon me? You said it was 'urgent'."

"Well, maybe 'urgent' wasn't quite the best way of describing what it is I wish to tell you. However, the matter is important."

"How so, Viola? Please don't keep me in suspense any longer."

"I'm sorry, Thelete. To begin with, I have made contact with some wonderful guides. They spoke to me from a luminous 'globe' that was stationed on the table next to me when I first began my research. I didn't have to write a word down - just 'listen'. It was so amazing. I rushed to Tiffany Rose to tell her about my experience and she joined me in another session with the guides today."

Globe? Guides? How unusual, "Thelete responded. "Did they tell you something that alarmed you in any way?"

"Yes. Everything was alarming . . . but that's not the issue we wish to tell you about. As we were about to end our session today, a young man suddenly appeared, "exclaimed Viola.

"Appeared where? In the same room?"

"No. In the globe! He appeared in the globe and spoke to us like the guides did."

"And he said he knew my Father, "Tiffany Rose added. "He offered to help us. I told him, he would have to speak to you. He was very polite and thanked me. He's waiting for us to make contact with him. I hope you are not annoyed."

Thelete saw the concern on their faces. How could he be irritated when they were so sincere? "No, of course not, "He replied.

"When does he wish to speak to me?"

"Whenever it is convenient for you, Thelete. I told him that you were in charge. And . . . he said that he knows about Sophia."

"Hmmm. In that case, perhaps we should contact him now.

Where is this globe you mentioned?"

"Follow us, Thelete. We will take you there now."

They quickly headed towards the area Viola made contact with the guides. She silently prayed the globe hadn't disappeared.

The globe was still intact upon their arrival. They seated Thelete at the center of the table to insure his visibility and hearing weren't compromised. Viola pulled up additional chairs for herself and Tiffany Rose. Within minutes the globe began to vibrate and glow. Following Darius' instructions, Viola asked to speak to 'Darius of Tarsus'. Waiting nervously, they observed Thelete's reaction.

"Impressive. Very impressive, "He murmured. Suddenly, Darius appeared.

"Greetings All. I am Darius of Tarsus."

"Darius, it's us . . .Tiffany Rose and Viola. We are here to introduce you to Thelete. Please say hello."

"Greetings, Sir. It is an honor to meet with You. I respectfully request to be of service to You in your present project for the Goddess Sophia. Tiffany Rose's Father, Josef, informed me of the Trial and your efforts to obtain information on Her behalf."

"What is your background, Darius? How is it that you believe you may be of help to us?"

Darius composed himself before speaking.

"Regrettably, I have been a 'warrior' for many lifetimes. I saw the error of my ways finally, and after much pain and deliberation, I have chosen a different path to dedicate my efforts. It is one of love and service. I owe much to Josef, who has been my spiritual teacher and guide."

"What wars were you involved with?"

"There were many, but the most infamous was the 'War of the Gods'. With your permission, I would like to share my analysis of that horrific war. It played a major role in my transformation."

"You may proceed, Darius."

"Thank You, Sir."

Tiffany Rose and Viola sat speechless on the edge of their seats.

Darius had stirred an unexpected excitement within them.

He began . . .

"The 'Great War' broke out between factions of the Reptilians and non-human groups involving atomic and laser weaponry far in advance of what humans have today. Evidence of atomic warfare in the ancient World, including 'fused green glass', may be found in Mesopotamia, Egypt, India, and elsewhere. An astute observation was made in 1947 when the desert sand in New Mexico turned to 'fused green glass' after the first atomic bomb was set off. The 'Great War' even included battles on the Moon. It ended one 'Age' and began another bringing us to the present. The Battle was recorded in legends Worldwide . . .

"You were actually in that battle? "Thelete inquired.

"Yes, Sir."

"Please continue."

"The reason humans are trying to resolve why 'good' and 'evil' still operate side by side, personally and collectively, is because there was a variable in the days of 'old', that prevented resolution. This variable was the nuclear war between the Serpent Masters (Atlantis) and the Sons of the Serpent (Lemuria), a war that was recorded by almost all the cultures of the World. The results, unforeseen by either side, caused the 'end game' to be delayed, literally by millennia. Upon investigation, there is much evidence to indicate that the 'alien' visitors and their dark progeny have been and still are on Earth and that they are in fact at the very helm of the echelons of society making use of powerful secret societies such as the Masonic and Rosicrucian fraternities as their cover for centuries. It is only now that this has been uncovered and that the members of these bodies permeate and influence all areas of government, politics, education, religion, and business. It is commonly known that many persons involved in the sciences are overwhelmingly cold blooded and inhuman. Such persons may also be found in the political and psychological sciences, medical professions and involved in many other industries. They appear to be the paradigm authors in modern times, leading mankind to destruction with every new diversion. Are such beings the progeny of the Necromancers of Atlantis? Are they 'homo Atlantis' who chose to hearken to the alien DNA instead of the homo sapiens strains? Are these scions of ancient sorcery involved in the governments and media today?

Of central importance is the purely scientific accounts of the devastation that affected the Earth's flora and fauna. This global war and its devastation meant that the Earth would now have a different climate, equator, and continental placement. (Man's various nightmare fears and daytime phobias arise from physiological experiences in the ancient past). The phenomena of 'evil' came into this World and into the consciousness of humankind via genetic manipulation. From that moment, every human had to deal with an inner dichotomy, had to decide which proclivity to choose - the 'human' or the 'alien'. This is the choice they are still making. From the advent of the first historical empires, over 10,000 years have elapsed. Humans have long attempted to answer the dilemma of evil and its permutations. They have been led to believe that it is a natural part of life, something they each have to work out as they exist and evolve. They are made to think that evil comes 'into being' because of the erstwhile movement of nature and they don't see the ramifications of this false contention. They subliminally regard nature and its order as ontologically 'inferior'. It is this attitude which then leads to the desecration of nature, animals, and indigenous peoples as well.

There is a premise or a clause in the lexicons of the 'black sorcerers' that they do in fact obey. It is obligatory for them to tell humans in one way or another what their designs and machinations are, and what is happening or ever going to happen to their prospective victims. They are letting them know right now, often by way of the media, but the so called 'good' are persistently unable to read the signs, being symbolically illiterate and recalcitrant. Therefore, they collude in their own fleecing. Evil always exists by the indulgence of the 'good'. In the game of chess, if one does not occupy a square, then by rights the opponent can."

"That was quite profound, Darius."

"Thank You, Sir. I believe I can be helpful in reading the 'signs' and what these 'black sorcerers' might be planning to do. It will give us an edge and help us plan a good 'offensive'. We don't know how they're going to react when they learn about the Trial."

"You are quite right, Darius. We haven't endeavored to hide our research, but I really don't think the Archons are savvy to what is in store for them. At best, even if they heard a rumor, they would probably 'toss it off' believing Sophia was just giving them another warning that She wouldn't 'follow through' on. She has given them many warnings, but they continue to ignore Her. Yaldabaoth, the Demiurge, believes he is mightier than Her. He always did, the pompous fool! Welcome aboard, Darius. Thank you for offering us your help. The girls and myself will be in touch regularly. And if you have any questions or insights, please let us know."

"I will, Sir. I will keep my eyes and ears alert. And Tiffany Rose - your Father sends his love. I am trying to get him established on his own 'channel' on this globe 'communicator' so that you may speak to him shortly."

"Oh, that would be wonderful, Darius. I would really appreciate seeing him and being able to converse with him . . . my Mom, too."

"I understand. And Viola . . . your uncle sends his love to you."

"Thanks, Darius. Perhaps you can arrange for Carl to have his own 'personal' channel, although we did manage to speak to each other telepathically the other day. It was wonderful, but seeing him would be awesome!"

"Excellent. I'll see what I can do. I know you all have work to do, so I will sign off for now. 'Til we meet again, may the Goddess be with you. Have a good evening, everyone."

"You too, Darius. Goodnight."

After saying goodbye to Darius, they lingered for a while to discuss their schedules with Thelete. Each had made significant progress. Having access to the globe and the 'guides' reduced the drudgery of collecting 'data' tremendously. However, it was established that certain information Thelete was intending to submit to the Aeons required a 'written format'. He urged them to use their discernment to eliminate redundant information as they prepared their painstakingly grueling assignment and He gave them each an outline to follow before he made his exit.

Viola would continue to focus on 'health' matters and Tiffany Rose would compile information on 'legal and political issues' that would strengthen their argument about the nefarious conduct the Archons were waging against Sophia and humanity.

"There's an enormous amount of data to assemble, "sighed Viola. "Earth's present 'health' situation isn't favorable, to say the least. Humanity is in grave danger. Perhaps you can work with the guides while I organize my data."

"Sounds like a plan, Viola. We can work in the same area of the Library this time. It will 'break up' the monotony."

"Yes, this is true. I'm just hoping that all our efforts will influence the Aeons on Sophia's behalf."

"I think it will . . ." Tiffany Rose paused. She had an afterthought as she was leaving. "If the guides or (pause) . . . Darius should ask for me, please explain where I am . . . and say 'hello'."

"I will, Tiffany Rose. I certainly will."

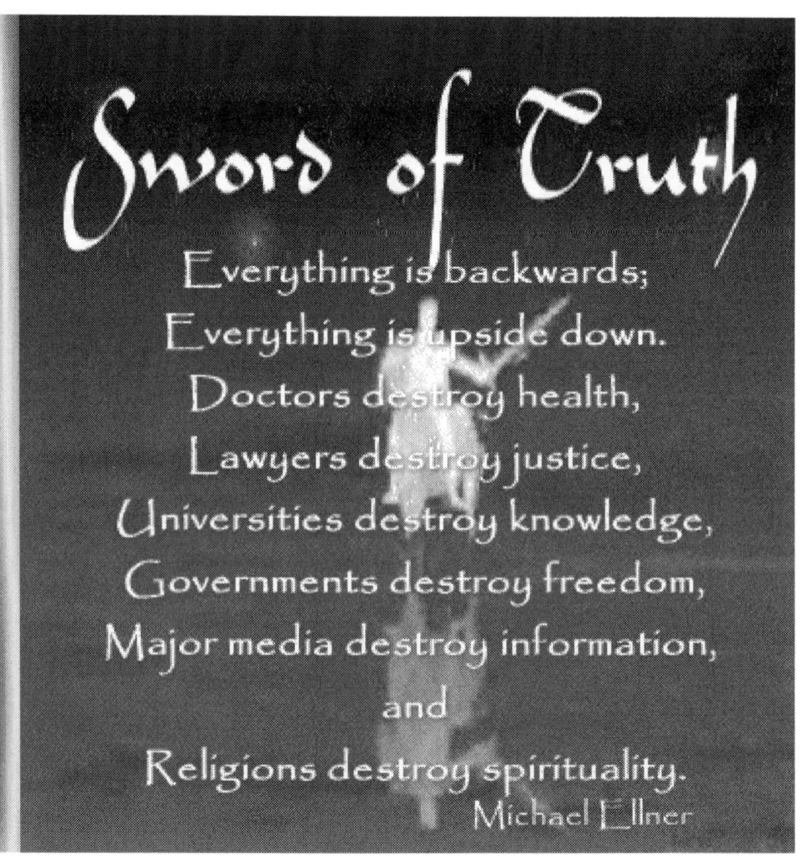

Killing humanity . . .

Chapter Fourteen

The Truth Revealed

Viola resumed where she had left off with the guides.

DOCTORS DESTROY HEALTH:

CANCER - The figures are fantastic. Eight million people die every year from cancer! Dr. Richard Day, (Rockefeller-controlled eugenics organization - 'Planned Parenthood') was quoted:

"We can cure almost every cancer right now. Information is on file in the Rockefeller Institute, if it's ever decided it should be released."

Day also said that letting people die of cancer would slow down population growth:

"You may as well die of cancer as something else."

He also said that the *plan* has been to 'control' and 'destroy' the population through medicine, food, new laboratory-made diseases, and the suppression of a cure for cancer. The Medical establishment around the World is just a tool of the Pharmaceutical cartel, or 'Big Pharma', whose aim is to keep people mentally, emotionally, and physically sick or in the 'states of being' that deny them a connection to their true and infinite self. 'Big Pharma' works as one network, despite the appearance of apparently different companies. It is an industry founded on *human suffering*.

There were doctors who still had a moral code. An Italian doctor, Tullio Simoncini, believed cancer was a fungus caused by Candida, a yeast-like organism that lives in the body in small amounts - even in healthy people. The immune system keeps it under control normally, but when it morphs into a powerful fungus, some serious health problems can follow - including cancer. He maintained that the conventional medical explanation of cancer being a *cellular malfunction* is wrong. His work has been rejected by the majority of his peers and of course - the 'power brokers'.

MULTIPLE SCLEROSIS - Another major illness, was found to be caused by an excess of *iron* which leads to inflammation and cell death in the brain. Italian doctor, Paolo Zamboni discovered that 90 percent of people with 'MS', including his wife, had malformed or blocked veins draining blood from the brain while people without 'MS' did not. He performed a simple operation to unclog veins and restore blood flow. The results were stunning! Sadly, he has faced suppression and disinterest from the system and the 'MS' charities. (The threat of being severed from funding insures the loyalty of charities and organizations).

BABIES are now given 25 vaccinations and combinations before the ripe 'old age' of 'two'. Mercury in vaccines has a major impact on the development of children becoming 'autistic'. The late Bertrand Russell, (Fabian Society member and eugenicist - died in 1970), wrote in detail how 'mercury' and other chemicals could be used to damage the brain and the ability to think clearly and sharply. (Hard to believe).

MMR VACCINE - DR. Andrew Wakefield was the man who first suggested a link between the combined Measles, Mumps, and Rubella vaccine, or 'MMR' and bowel problems that have been linked to AUTISM. Followed was a tidal wave of condemnation to discredit his claims. The pressure came from the top of the Illuminati pyramid and filtered down to the 'dark suits' that administer the System.

Serious forms of mitochondrial disease affect one in every 6,500 children. Dr. Day (Dr. Death) was quoted saying that people who didn't want to go along with the new World System would be disposed of humanely. "People will just disappear."

GENETIC MANIPULATION

The U.K. is about to rewrite rules to allow Nephilim genetic engineering of children. Altered humans will then pass along restructured human DNA to all succeeding generations so that all flesh can be corrupted as it was in the days of Noah! An article written by a Dr. Mercola reads as follows:

"When I first read that 'genetically modified' humans have already been born, I could hardly believe it. However, further research into this story featured in the UK's 'Daily Mail' proved it to be true. They've really done it. They've created humans that nature could never allow for, and it's anyone's guess as to what will happen next. Even more shocking was the discovery that this is actually old news! The 'Daily Mail' article was not dated, and upon investigation, the experiments cited actually took place over a decade ago; the study announcing their successful birth was published in 2001. At best, I hope I can stir you to ponder the implications of this type of genetic engineering as reported in the following article:

> *The disclosure that 30 healthy babies were born after a series of experiments in the United States provoked another furious debate about ethics. Fifteen of the children were born as a result of one experimental program at the Institute for Reproductive Medicine and Science of St. Barnabas in New Jersey. The babies were born to women who had problems conceiving. Extra genes from a female donor were inserted into their eggs before they were fertilized in an attempt to enable them to conceive. Genetic fingerprint tests on two 'one year-old' children confirmed that they have inherited DNA from* ***three adults*** *- two women and one man.*

It's relevant to understand that these children have inherited extra genes - that of TWO women and one man - and will be able to pass this extra set of genetic traits to their own offspring. One of the most shocking considerations here is that this was done - repeatedly - even though no one knew what the ramifications of

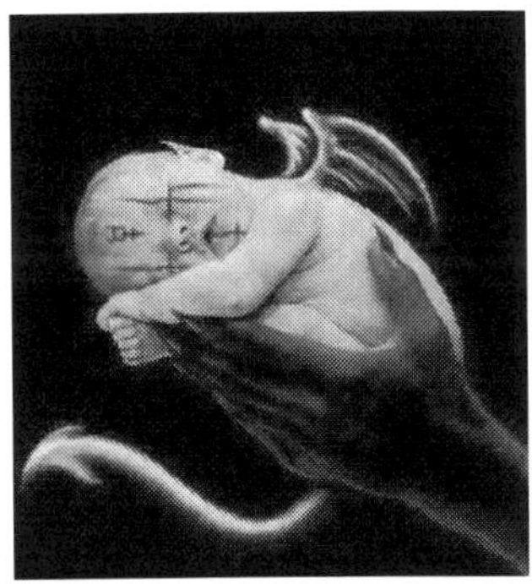

having the genetic traits of three parents might be for the individual, or for their subsequent offspring. Based on what I've learned about the genetic engineering of plants, I'm inclined to say the ramifications could potentially be vast, dire, and completely unexpected."

The techniques are contentious because they produce embryos that carry DNA from three donors and genetic modification that passes the donor's DNA on to future generations. British law currently prohibits such genetic modification of embryos, but the legislation may be rewritten as early as next year after a Parliamentary debate that will be informed by the Human Fertilization and Embryology Authority's consultation. Through online questionnaires, public meetings in London and Manchester, and opinion polls, the Human Fertilization and Embryology Authority (HFEA) hopes to indoctrinate views on the procedures for a report that will go to Jeremy Hunt, the Health Minister, in the Spring. The consultation runs until December 7th. "If this is allowed, and we don't have a view, it has consequences in perpetuity," said Lisa Jardine, Chair of the Regulator. "Once we have genetic modification we have to be (very) sure we're happy, because this is not about us, our children, or even our grandchildren; *it's about many generations down the line."*

All this reinforces their intent to control the population by assuming authority to grant permission to have babies; redirecting the purpose of sex - (sex without reproduction and reproduction without sex) - contraception available to all universally; using sex education and canalizing of youth as a 'tool' of World Government; encouraging 'anything goes' homosexuality; technology used for reproduction without sex; euthanasia; the demise pill and many more aberrations. How many people are aware that 'Planned Parenthood', a creation of the eugenics-supporting Rockefeller family, is an Illuminati-front organization? In 1969, Dr. Richard Day, the national Medical Director of P.P. addressed the Pittsburgh Paediatric Society with an audience of about 80 doctors and informed them about a New World System in which American industry was going to be sabotaged. The U.S. would remain a center for agriculture (Monsanto), high tech, education and communications, but heavy industry would be 'transported out'. Different parts of the World would have a specialty and thus become inter-dependent. This has been happening for decades in the European Union. Economies and industries in various countries were targeted to destroy diversity and self-sufficiency to replace it with specialization, making everyone dependent on everyone else.

The plan would control the population via medicine, food, new laboratory-made diseases and the suppressed cure of cancer. Abortion would no longer be illegal. The food supply would be monitored, growing food privately would be outlawed, young people would spend more time in school, but not learn anything, and the family would diminish in importance. There would be restrictions in travel and private home-ownership would disappear. People would be desensitized to violence and porn and 'music' would be irritating and uncreative. Weather modification (volcanoes, tsunamis, tornados, torrential rains) would be used as weapons of war. Long established communities would be destroyed by these bizarre weather patterns and unemployment would force people to abandon their homes. Drug addiction would be covertly encouraged by the government and people would be poisoned by food, medicine, and vaccinations.

(Author's note: The above information was enhanced to bring attention to the intended harm to society).

The Reptilian Rothschild-Rockefeller networks created the system of medical associations: The British Medical Association (BMA) and the American Medical Association (AMA) to control medicine and the medical profession. The Illuminati funded the creation of medical associations to replace what is known as 'alternative' medicine with their own. Mainstream medicine is about wealth.

- AMA - Established 1847. Its purpose was to control medical schools and forms of healing taught. Supported by Rockefeller family and Illuminati, they employed Abraham Flexner (Rothschild Zionist) to visit and report on schools' suitability to teach and establish standards.
- JAMA - Established shortly afterwards. Comprised of a committee of allopathic physicians who reviewed and analyzed various non-allopathic treatments, modalities, and services. Unfavorable findings were reported to the Councils, which were published in JAMA. (Sought to discredit alternative methods of healing and introduced a system of licensing which ensured all medical staff were 'qualified').

The real reason for AMA licensing was to control both the medical profession and the treatments it employed while taking the big 'Pharma' $$$dollar. John D. Rockefeller, founder of Standard Oil, with backing from the Rothschilds, had single-handedly destroyed the prevailing medical approach and replaced it with a new one controlled by Big Pharma. His crude oil, worth a nickel/gallon suddenly turned into medical drugs worth millions of dollars per gallon. Suppressing human health is another goal of the Illuminati. Codex Alimentarius ('Food Code' or 'Food Book') seeks to block access to food supplements of adequate doses and quality that would compensate for the loss of nutrients in food that have been lost in the soil and food production processes. It is controlled by Monsanto.

Chapter Fifteen

MONSANTO

Obama, Monsanto, and the New World Order crowd believe they have the right to control you . . . You are simply in the way, other than being trained and pushed around as a good little 'serf' who creates income for the 'elite' international power brokers.

Danny Serfling knew he was in trouble in July. Tiny white worms in the soil had eaten away the anchoring roots on half of his corn, and in one big storm last summer, the stalks toppled like sticks. "All the corn around here went flat from Spring Valley to Mabel, "said Serfling, who farms a few hundred acres in south-eastern Minnesota. He was resigned to the next step. "We will have to use more insecticide."

This is what scientists and environmentalists regard as one of nature's great ironies. Fifteen years ago, genetically engineered seeds promised to reduce the amount of poisons used on the land, but today they are forcing farmers to use more toxic chemicals to protect their crops. So begins the alarming story of a dangerous international GMO company - MONSANTO.

Pharmaceutical companies control and make you dependent on their medicine of choice. Monsanto *engineers* seeds and *controls* the food supplies. Obama, the UN, and his New World Order 'handlers' manage and control it all. Long before Obama's tyrannical and controlling rule of America, we were viewed as cattle to be forced into stalls, either for branding or slaughter. Underneath our noses, and beyond most people's understanding, food, medicine, property rights, and even the length of our lifespan has been *assaulted, designed, and planned.* You thought all this time you had the right to live, breath, grow food, and function as a free human being? Aren't you a precious little cow? *Obama, Monsanto, and the New World Order crowd believe they have the right to control you . . . not you! You are simply in the way, other than being trained and pushed around as a good little 'serf' who creates income for the elite international power brokers.* Let's deal with Monsanto and how it is slowly poisoning the human population and is destroying the balance of nature . . .

Monsanto is a huge international GMO that plans to control and IS controlling more and more of the international food supply. They aren't just a little start-up research group studying food supply. They are in 60 countries, have over 14,000 employees, and have revenues of $$$6 billion. They have invested over $$$500 million in two of their destructive schemes - 'genomic' and 'biotechnology'. I call it what it is - 'depopulation' and hiding behind 'Mother Theresa' goals.

Monsanto is quite famous for the release of the 'Terminator Seed', which renders a seed as a 'controlled' and 'neutered' item that can only produce a crop *one time*. Farmers and growers cannot use and re-use seeds as they have historically done for thousands of years. Monsanto has made sure that their Terminator Seed is good for *one crop* only. Thus, the farmer is forced to come back to them and get more seeds that 'hark' Monsanto controls forcing growers to be dependent on a 'Frankenstein's' laboratory. Where do they hide and do they have real influence?

An astute observer using an assumed name, 'Miguel', talked of Monsanto's domination in our colleges and universities. He also said that after watching them and working with them for 25 years, it was most clear that their care for the safety and welfare of people and health is seriously in question. Monsanto has been accused numerous times of fraud, threats to health, ecological disasters, and false evidence. Some say that 'genetically modified food' is the harbinger of saving a hungry humanity. Monsanto talks a good game on the surface - food protection, stopping World hunger, and controlling viruses, but it appears more and more that their goal is just the opposite. *By controlling the World's food supply, depopulating parts of the World by creating massive illness and death, and dependency on them for modified seeds, they will have the increasing power to turn the 'modified' spigot on and off - create diseases at will, and get rid of unwanted populations. Obama and the UN must be thrilled . . . and you thought 'abortion' was the big depopulation weapon.*

With most of the world standing against Monsanto's terminator technology, they are verbally distancing themselves from it, but in truth pushing and funding it Worldwide. It is a known fact that poor farmers feed up to 1.4 billion people a year. If they cannot afford to buy seed after the first year, millions if not billions, stand to die from starvation.

(Move over Dr. Death . . .You have company).

Rats fed best on GM corn (such as on stores shelves and in foods everywhere) now suffer tumors and die prematurely. According to a published controversial French study, rats fed a lifelong diet of one of the best selling strains of genetically modified corn, suffered tumors and multiple organ damage. The report is set to ignite the debate over whether GM crops are safe. Gilles-Eric Seralini of the University of Caen and colleagues said rats fed on a diet containing NK603 - a seed variety from crop *giant* Monsanto - made tolerant two dousing of the best selling weed killer -

'Roundup' - or given water containing Roundup at levels permitted in the United States, died earlier than those on a standard diet. The animals on the GM diet suffered mammary tumors, as well as severe liver and kidney damage. The researchers said 50 percent of males and 70 percent of females died prematurely, compared with only 30 percent and 20 percent in the control group. Seralini was part of a team that flagged previous safety concerns based on a shorter rat study in a scientific paper published in December 2009 but this takes things a step further by tracking the animals throughout their two-year lifespan. The researchers found:

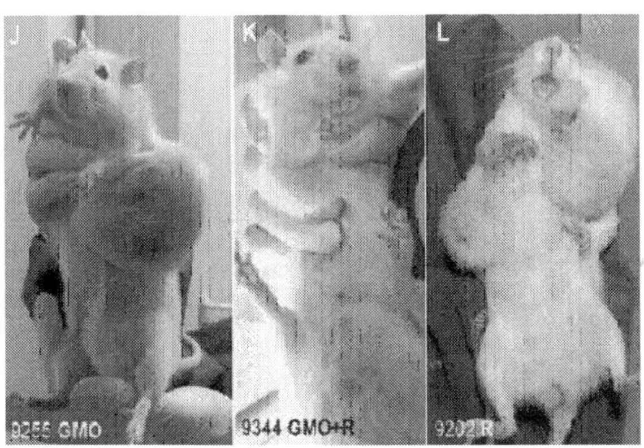

- Between 50 to 80 per cent of female rats developed large tumors by the beginning of the 24th month, with up to three tumors per animal. Only 30 per cent of the control rats developed tumors.

- Up to 70 per cent of females died prematurely compared with only 20 per cent in the control group.
- Tumors in rats of both sexes fed the GM corn were two to three times larger than in the control group.
- The large tumors appeared in females after seven months, compared to 14 months in the control group.

The team said the tumors were 'deleterious to health due to a very large 'size', making it difficult for the rats to breathe and causing digestive problems. Significantly, the majority of tumors were detectable only after 18 months - meaning they could be discovered only in long-term feeding trials. The study - led by molecular biologist Professor Gilles-Eric Seralini, a critic of GM technology, was published yesterday in 'US Journal Food' and 'Physiological Pathway'.

The Daily Mail's Frankenstein Food Watch campaign has long highlighted problems with the lack of rigorous safety assessments for GM crops and food. Although GM corn is widely used in the U.S., British consumers have turned their backs on the technology because of concerns about its impact on human health and the environment. Although it is not available in British supermarkets, it is fed to farm animals including chickens, pigs and dairy cows, which eventually is consumed by humans.

Mustafa Djamgoz, Professor of Cancer Biology at Imperial College, London, said the findings relating to eating GM corn were not a surprise. "We are what we eat, "he added. "I work at the molecular level on cancer. There is evidence that what we eat affects our genetic make-up and turns genes on and off. We are not 'scare mongering' here. More research is warranted."

Dr Julian Little, of the Agricultural Biotechnology Council, which speaks for the GM industry, insisted GM foods were safe adding, "'The industry takes all health concerns regarding biotech food and feed very seriously."

Anthony Trewavas, Professor of cell biology at Edinburgh University, questioned the way the research had been conducted, saying the number of rats involved in the study (200) was too small to draw any meaningful conclusions. "To be frank, it looks like random variation to me in a *rodent line* likely to develop tumors anyway, "he said. He also claimed Professor Seralini was an anti-GM campaigner and that previous studies questioning the technology's safety had not withstood scrutiny.

What Monsanto didn't count on:

Mutated pests are adapting to Biotech crops in unpredicted and disturbing ways. Genetically modified crops are often designed to repel hungry insects. By having toxins built into the plant itself, farmers can reduce their use of environmentally unfriendly insecticide sprays. But as any first-year evolutionary biology student can tell you, insects are like the 'Borg' in Star Trek. They quickly adapt. And this is precisely what is happening - but in ways that have *startled* the researchers themselves. The discovery is a 'wakeup call' to geneticists because it has highlighted the importance of having to closely monitor and counter pest resistance to biotech crops. The development also raises the question of the potential futility of having to change the genetic structure of crops in perpetuity; given that insects are constantly evolving, to what degree will geneticists have to go to ensure crop immunity to pests? And what does that say to the ongoing safety of such crops as far as human consumption is concerned?

3/25/13

In the typical slippery nature of Monsanto's legislation-based actions, the biotech giant is now virtually guaranteed the ability to recklessly plant experimental GM crops (genetically modified) without having to worry about the United States government and its subsequent courts. The 'Monsanto Protection Act' buried deep within the budget resolution has passed the Senate, and now nothing short of a presidential veto will put an end to the ruling. In case you're not familiar, the Monsanto Protection Act is the name given to what's known as a legislative *rider* that was inserted into the Senate 'Continuing Resolution Spending Bill'. Using the deceptive title of 'Farmer Assurance Provision', Sec. 735 of this bill actually *grants* Monsanto the immunity from federal courts pending the review of any GM crop that is thought to be dangerous.

Unbelievable!

How many times have we heard of the FDA threatening and shutting down perfectly safe and fine milk and cheese farms, hiding behind contrived and extremely controlling regulations? Threats are made, fines are issued, guns are drawn, farms and businesses are shut down and many times perfectly good animals slaughtered. The American people do precious little to stop these endless assaults on their liberty and health. We are becoming good little serfs just as Pharmacy, Monsanto, and the New World Order has planned.

Biotechnology's promise to feed the World did not anticipate 'Trojan corn', 'super weeds', and the disappearance of monarch butterflies. But in the Midwest and South - blanketed by more than 170 million acres of genetically engineered corn, soybeans and cotton, an experiment begun in 1996 with approval of the first commercial genetically modified organisms, is producing *questionable results*. Those results include vast increases in herbicide use that have created impervious weeds now infesting millions of acres of cropland, while decimating other plants, such as milkweeds that sustain the monarch butterflies. Food manufacturers are worried that a new corn made for ethanol could damage an array of packaged food on supermarket shelves. Other adulterated foods not publicized are genetically engineered potatoes combined with '*moth*' DNA, goat milk with '*spider*' hormones, cloned 'Dolly' sheep, soy contamination, and a list of many other hidden food alterations. (Why ??? and UGH!). Human negative effects may not be seen until ten years into the future. And they dare criticize the obesity of the American public who they are covertly poisoning!

Mainstream medicine is founded on corruption and greed at all levels from 'Big Pharma' boardroom to doctor's surgery. The ten top drug companies make more in profits than the rest of 'Fortune 500' combined. Big Pharma spends nearly $$$19 billion a year bribing and influencing physicians.

- The bottom line is that pharmaceutical corporations control billions of dollars, influence research, and determine *what* competition is allowed in the Drug World. They also need people sick and dependent on dangerous and expensive drugs.
- There has long been a systematic attack on the natural health movement; products and people who support health and keep you healthy. Big pharmacy needs to keep making money from our dependency on their drugs and an 'ill' population. They have evolved to a version of the 'Gambino' crime family. Who cares about getting people well and off medication?

"In medicine, we see the dominating power of big pharmaceutical corporations, spending millions to court doctors, influence research (all once deemed unethical), while expanding the mechanistic model of the human body. Corporate support of medical schools seems to be turning physicians into sales representatives, winning trips for pushing one drug over another." - *James Redfield*

Which leads us to the 'mother' of them all -

Obama and his cohorts had a 'V' day June 28, 2012 when 'OBAMA CARE' was ruled 'constitutional' by the Supreme Court solidifying another law to help them towards achieving the success of their mission: *destroying the United States of America.* It would seem that Chief Justice Roberts is the vehicle they used to accomplish their goal of obtaining more control of the country when they obtained his 'blessing'.

It is believed that declaring the bill as a 'tax' instead of a 'mandate' had been on the back burner since its inception. Obama and his cronies knew they would face resistance calling it a 'tax' from the get-go. They had this solution of 'reconstructing' the bill built in as plan 'B' from the very beginning of 'Obama Care'. In other words, they deceived the American public once again. Chief Justice Roberts may well be part of the scam since his appointment to the bench. Perhaps he is not a Conservative as he states, but one of them . . .

This deceitful health package to scam the American public allows decisions concerning patient care to be made by presidential appointments (I.R.S.) who would decide what medical plans covered, what doctors can and cannot do, and the extent or treatment allowed for elderly people. Rothschild Zionist, Dr. Richard Day, (aka 'Dr. Death') was quoted in 1969 as stating,

"Limiting access to affordable medical care makes eliminating the elderly easier."

Another 'loser', Tom Daschle, former US Senate Majority Leader and Obama's nominee for Secretary of Health and Human Services, was quoted as saying, "Seniors should be forced to sacrifice their health care in favor of younger people by denying them treatment. Those who received a 'hopeless diagnosis' need to accept their condition and not seek treatment for it."

As previously stated, "The pharmaceutical industry spends nearly 19 billion a year bribing and influencing physicians." It's more money than the entire United States spends on genuine disease prevention and health education. Drug companies are structured to make as much money as possible from the sickness, distress, and misfortune of others and to maintain the population in mental, emotional and physical disarray. Big Pharma, like all Illuminati cartels, hasn't any empathy with those who suffer from its daily exploitation or those it uses as guinea pigs in drug 'trials'.

The Obama Administration is in the pocket of Big Pharma. A White House memo leaked to the *Huffington Post* website in August, 2009 , confirmed how Obama and his handlers had struck a deal with Big Pharma in which the White House agreed to oppose any congressional efforts to bargain for lower drug prices or import cheaper drugs from Canada. (Remember?) They further agreed not to pursue Medicare rebates or change the designation of some drugs which would have cost Big Pharma $$$billions in reduced income. Obama and Co. *lied* to cover up the covert agreement while the drug companies spent up to $150 million on television commercials supporting Obama's healthcare 'reform' plans that included the deal. 'Corruption' and 'mendacity' are Obama's middle names. Supporters, claiming to be doctors, stood up at public meetings supporting his healthcare plan and what he was proposing to do, when in fact, they weren't doctors at all - just plants!

There are others . . . too numerous to mention. They're all from the same stench of evil . . .

And here's the worst nightmare . . . or heartache . . . to be discussed as yet. It involves children. If the information is true - if it is reliable and not fabricated, it is enough to 'hang' all the 'psychopaths' - no mercy! In league with the disclosure of the conduct of pedophiles, the *bloodline* families are targeting children more than anyone with their 'vaccination agenda' to turn them into good little 'robots' with damaged immune systems for life . . .

TARGETING THE CHILDREN

The realization is 'heart-wrenching'.

It is strongly recommended that every concerned individual educate his/herself on how the Illuminati/Reptilian Network is planning to destroy humanity. Each method proposed is more horrific than the previous. It will stagger your imagination when you learn about 'forced vaccinations' and the 'nano' microchips agenda planned to be enforced by these insane psychopaths.

Read: *'HUMAN RACE GET OFF YOUR KNEES'*

By David Icke

The Truth About Vaccinations

Excerpts from pages 440 - 582:

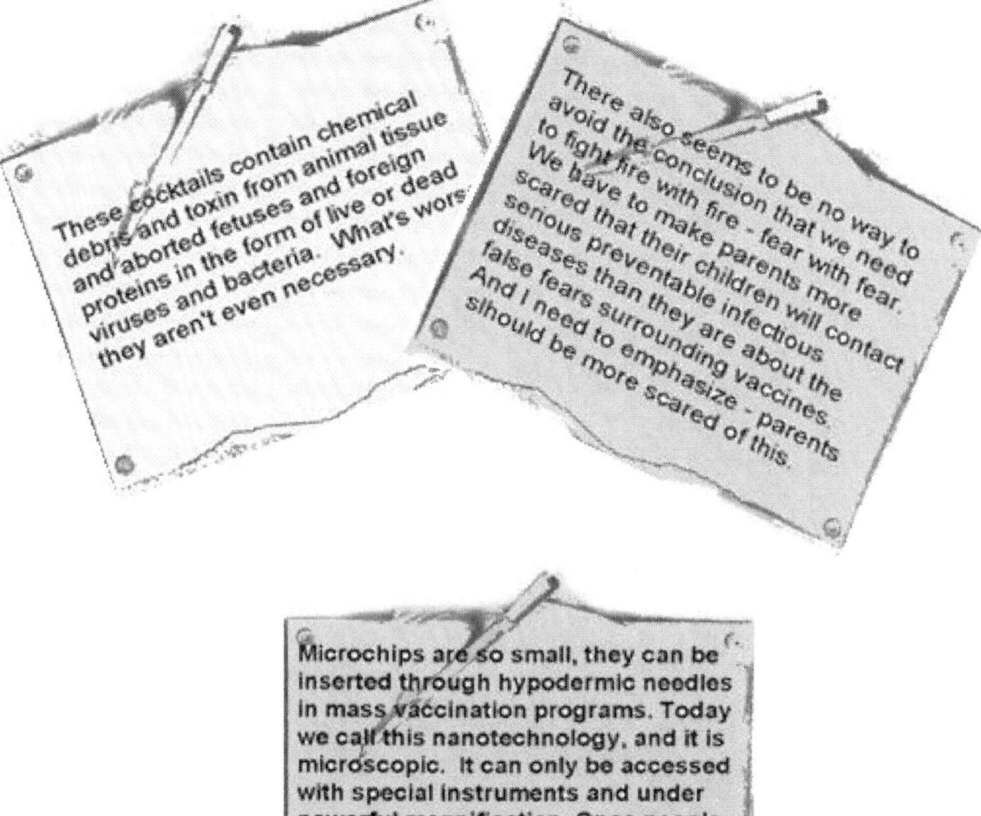

Microchips are so small, they can be inserted through hypodermic needles in mass vaccination programs. Today we call this nanotechnology, and it is microscopic. It can only be accessed with special instruments and under powerful magnification. Once people are chipped they can have their mind emotions, and bodies externally manipulated and they can be killed from a distance.

Read: 'Human Race Get Off Your Knees'

Australian journalist, Jane Burgemeister announced in 2009 that she had filed criminal charges with the FBI against the World Health Organization (WHO), the United Nations, Barack Obama, David de Rothschild, David Rockefeller, George Soros and many others over a plot she uncovered to destroy the population with a deadly vaccine. She said that bird flu and swine flu had been developed in laboratories and released to the public with the aim of mass murder through vaccination. Her filed document was called 'Bioterrorism Evidence'. It read:

SCARE TACTICS

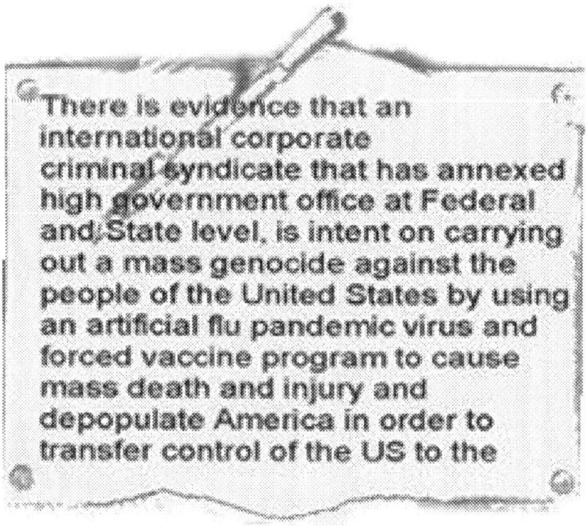

"There is evidence that an international corporate criminal syndicate that has annexed high government office at Federal and State level, is intent on carrying out a mass genocide against the people of the United States by using an artificial flu pandemic virus and forced vaccine program to cause mass death and injury and depopulate America in order to transfer control of the US to the

Curious who would receive the spoils of our country? Read the answer on Page 463 . . .

'Human Race Get Off Your Knees'
David Icke

Based on numerous documents and statements that have emerged over the years, it's clear that the Illuminati bloodline want to reduce the global population to 500 million. The Third World is being targeted for enormous population reductions. Under the control of Henry Kissinger (Rothschild Zionist), the covert plan, made public in the 1990s was to instigate population control through contraception, war, and famine, and using the threat of withdrawing US financial and food aid to force governments to cooperate.

The 'Bill and Belinda Gates Foundation' is a major contributor of vaccination programs in the 'Third World'. It has given multi-millions to Planned Parenthood (Bill Gates' father is a leading member on its Board) and other 'population control' organizations. Ted Turner donated massively to population control. Big Pharma has been increasing its influence and control over medicine decade after decade, and by funding and bribing corrupt politicians and medical 'experts', it has dictated political policy. It now wants to introduce *mandatory* vaccinations so that every child, in fact everyone, must be injected with its venomous poisons. It is the latest stage in the Reptilian Big Pharma war on the human immune system designed to cause more death and disease by devastating the body's natural defenses. Thank God the World is a lot wiser than it was five, ten, years ago. People are beginning to see the truth thanks to the efforts of many wonderful people who have put themselves at risk to alert us.

In August 2009, Dr. Ryke Geerd Hamer was giving a talk near Vienna, Austria. The topic of 'swine flu' was raised. A woman working for a pharmaceutical company in Vienna confirmed that swine flu needles, not the vaccine itself, did indeed contain 'nano' particles in their very tips. This could not be seen by the naked eye, but was clearly visible with magnification (12X normal). She was told that the nano particles work in the human body and could store lots of data. Dr. Hamer said that every single chip-vaccination needle had its own individual code number, which is added to the ID number. (Page 471) - (Human Race Get Off . . .)

Is foreign DNA contamination the autistic villain behind biologic vaccine injuries?

In 2012 an important paper by Leslie Carol Botha hit the Internet by storm. This revolutionary paper titled 'Unveiling the Culprit', is one of the first papers to discuss various *foreign* DNA fragments being discovered in sick, disabled and dying children after they have received various childhood vaccinations. Over the past six years, Ms. Botha has been heavily involved and dedicated to using her print and broadcast experience to share information with the public about the potential dangers of the HPV vaccines. She is a member of Truth-About-Gardasil and is one of six women who, in March 2010, presented research and data to the FDA on the alarming statistics of Gardasil and Cervarix deaths, injuries and harm in comparison to other vaccines.

Chapter Sixteen
The Devil's Operatives

Manufactured viruses and health scares are a 'Problem-Reaction-Solution' to enforce compulsory vaccination. Obama's Healthcare Bill makes it 'mandatory' for all Americans to take out health insurance, or face fines, even jail, if they don't. At the same time, the Centers for Disease Control states that anyone who doesn't keep their vaccinations up-to-date will be refused health insurance. The Massachusetts Senate has passed the 'flu pandemic' Bill S2028 that imposes a state of *Fascism* whenever the Governor decides to do so in the wake of a 'flu pandemic' - '*manufactured'* or otherwise. This bill authorizes the State Health Commissioner, law enforcement, and medical personnel to:

- Vaccinate the population
- Enter private property without warrants
- Quarantine people against their will
- Arrest without a warrant

- Jail or fine anyone accused of violating an isolation or quarantine order at the rate of $1,000/day.
- Similar isolation orders are to be implemented in Florida, Washington, Iowa, North Carolina - and all over the world - if people don't resist - or more likely, *don't know about.*

Incredible as it may seem, drug companies, in league with governments, coldly set out to kill and maim vast numbers of people. In league with John D. Rockefeller and Big Pharma, they have been doing so throughout history. American researcher, Patrick Jordan, uncovered World Health Organization memos dating from 1972, explaining '*how to kill people with vaccines by injecting viruses and activating an immune response so powerful that it kills the body'.* This is known as CYTOKINE STORM and is blamed for many of the tens of millions of deaths in the flu pandemic of 1918. The initial spread of AIDS in the US matched the locations of vaccination trails for Hepatitis B in homosexual communities, and the outbreak in Africa mirrored the mass small pox vaccinations ordered by the World Health Organization (WHO) with vaccine reportedly supplied by Novartis. Big Pharma and WHO are 'killing machines'. There are many stories around the World to validate this statement, unfortunately.

All this reflects the expansion of the eugenics 'master race' movement created by the Rothschilds, Rockefellers, Harrimans and other Illuminati families. The belief in 'elite' bloodlines - the 'demi-gods' - has been around since the interbreeding of humans with Reptilian and other non-human entities. The scandalous irony of it all is that the '*defective*' humans the 'elite' bloodlines are so obsessed in eliminating are the result of their own tampering with human genetics in the first place.

- It wasn't GOD (true God) who created sick, deformed, mentally ill people. It was the evil psychopaths 'playing God' who were responsible.
- Thomas Robert Malthus, Darwin, Francis Galton, Adolph Hitler, Julian Huxley, Aldous Huxley, Theodore Roosevelt, H.G. Wells, Margaret Sanger - are but a handful of sick psychopaths who advocated the removal of 'inferior' people through segregation, sterilization, and extermination to create a 'master race'.

We are now seeing 'eugenics' - the final frontier, with the emerging movement known as 'transhumanism'. This is developing and promoting various control technologies like microchips, brain-chips, brain-computer interfaces, cyborgs and nanotechnology. The word was first used by Julian Huxley, the eugenics fanatic. The Trans-humanists refer to mere humans as a future 'sub-species' of the cyborgs. Their biggest targets are children and young people. Aleister Crowley, the Satanist, Freemason and Illuminati operative, said of children, "Get them by eight, or it's too late." The 'sickies' want them mentally, emotionally, physically and vibrationally screwed up as early as possible. *Hug your children before they go to bed tonight.*

Given the facts, what an utter disgrace it has been to watch governments and the media targeting children to manipulate them and their parents to get vaccinated. One in ten American children take the mind-altering drug *Ritalin*, which is a derivative of cocaine. Statistically, 461,000 prescriptions were issued in 2007. Other copy-cat drugs have been produced to compete with the obsession of drugging the very young. These include: Adderall, Concerta, Metadate CD, Ritalin LA, Focalin XR, and Strattera (Atomexetine) and Risperdal given to children as young as 'two'. The drugs have possible 'side-effects' that can result in health consequences such as heart problems and diabetes. A very sad story accompanies the drug 'thalidomide' given to pregnant women to suppress 'morning sickness'. The 'side-effect was the birth of babies without arms!

Most doctors aren't healers - they are chemists that simply dispense drugs that they're told to prescribe. The body is an electrochemical system and anything that imbalances it is going to have negative consequences. Mobile phones are an excellent example of this threat (although the medical profession constantly denies that their 'use' encourages a risk of brain tumors). Nothing is being done about the dangers from electromagnetic and microwave technology because governments and the telecom companies are owned and controlled by the same families, and so the agenda of those families is served by both.

THE FRAUDS

"The individual is handicapped, by coming face-to-face with a conspiracy so monstrous, he cannot believe it exists. The American mind simply has not come to a realization of the evil, which has been introduced into our midst . . . It rejects even the assumption that human creatures could espouse a philosophy, which must ultimately destroy all that is good and decent."

FBI Director J. Edgar Hoover, 1956

Chapter Seventeen
OBAMA

The Obama campaign may have looked into history when selecting its new campaign slogan, 'Forward' - a word with a long and rich association with *European Marxism*. Many Communist and radical publications and entities throughout the 19th and 20th centuries had the name '*Forward*'.

Wikipedia has an entire section called 'Forward' (generic name of socialist publications). The name carries a special meaning in socialist political terminology. "It has been frequently used as a name for socialist, communist and other left-wing newspapers and publications, "the online encyclopedia explains. The slogan 'Forward' reflected the conviction of European Marxists and radicals that their movements reflected the march of history, which would move *forward* past capitalism and into socialism and communism.

Laughably, many idealistic fools in 'denial' still see Obama as their savior and hero. It's understandable considering all the 'perks' they have received from the government since he was elected into office. By now, it's obvious that Obama is a Fascist/Communist; one of the few authentic 'labels' we can use to identify him. The man is, and always has been, an 'empty suit'. His life (personal, academic, political) was fabricated by the 'power brokers' who put him into office. Obama is the Rothschild Zionist 'puppet' in the White House, funded by the Wall Street bankers and the Rothschild/Illuminati fronts. His roots are 'Chicago' - the most despicable, corrupt political 'cesspool' on the planet.

Obama's personality is 'narcissistic (another authentic label), which he has demonstrated repeatedly with his self-preoccupation, lack of empathy, and unconscious deficits in self-esteem. The covert circumstances involved with his arrogant hoax played upon the United States and its citizens are unbelievable. And let's not forget the man also claims to be a Christian while a large percentage of the World has identified him as the 'Anti Christ'. The most recent publicity has revealed him to be a closet 'gay' while he has been living as a married heterosexual male with a wife and two children. Nothing seems to faze this liar; not even his phony birth certificate or lying about his real name. The latest scandal boggles the imagination. This charlatan was elected President of the United States by a gullible American public and a corrupt hidden government.

Is this Obama's biggest secret?

A prominent member of Chicago's homosexual community claims Barack Obama's participation in the 'gay' bar and bathhouse scene was so well known that many who were aware of his lifestyle were shocked when he ran for President and finally won the White House. Founder and editor of the Hillary Clinton supporting website - (HillBuzz.org.) - Kevin DuJan - told WND that he had first-hand information from two different sources that Obama was personally involved in the 'gay bar' scene. Obama stopped going to 'gay bars' and bathhouses in Chicago when he began running for the U.S. Senate in 2004. "It was preposterous to the people I knew then to think Obama was going to keep his gay life secret, "said DuJan, who was a gossip columnist in Chicago for various blogs when Obama was living in the city as a Community Organizer and later, a State Senator. DuJan has been told that Obama's secrets would have to come out just like John Edwards' secrets came out.

(Chicago Mayor Rahm Emanuel and Barack Obama are members of the same gay bathhouses in Chicago).

Nothing fazes this fake. So much of his life is a lie, he probably can't keep track . . . unless of course, he reads it from his 'tele-prompter. It's the usual 'M.O.' for liars - "Just ignore the publicity and the story will go away - eventually." Not this one, Mr. Empty Suit. Not this one. We'll just include it in the 'cliff notes'.

Obama's political record since elected president in 2008 is nothing short of a disgrace. Under the dictates of his Rothschild masters, he and his 'party' (cohorts) have been guilty of undermining the US in every way conceivable. This author has documented many of his incorrigible activities throughout the years (Astradome.com) as have other concerned Americans. But unfortunately, it's not over until it's over. How much additional harm Obama can accomplish is up for 'grabs'. Much depends on other 'unknowns'. Included in the 'mix' are many other scams instigated against the American people by those in office prior to Obama. These scavengers and their infamous history have been recorded in the Akashic Records. All of it. There won't be a lack of transparency at the upcoming Trial when their activities are revealed. It will certainly 'liven up' the pace.

> *"The duty of a patriot is to protect his country from its government." Thomas Paine (1737-1809)*
>
> *"There's a plot in this country to enslave every man, woman and child. Before I leave this high and noble office, I intend to expose this plot." - Pres. John F. Kennedy*

The following pages were obtained from: StopTheCrime.net. The entire document may be downloaded in a PDF format from the above website. Because of its revealing and outrageous context, various pages were copied to be included in this chapter to inform the public and shed light on what is happening in the country and the World.

TOP SECRET

"Silent Weapons for Quiet Wars - Operations Research Technical Manual TM-SW7905.1 - Welcome Aboard

This publication marks the 25th anniversary of the Third World War, called the 'Quiet War', being conducted using subjective biological warfare, fought with 'silent weapons'."

This book contains an introductory description of this war, its strategies, and its weaponry. **May 1979 #74-1120 Security.** It is patently impossible to discuss social engineering or the automation of a society, i.e., the engineering of social automation systems (silent weapons) on a national or worldwide scale without implying extensive objectives of social control and destruction of human life, i.e., *slavery and genocide*. This manual is in itself an analog declaration of intent. Such a writing must be secured from public scrutiny. Otherwise, it might be recognized as a technically formal declaration of *domestic war*. Furthermore, whenever any person or group of persons in a position of great power and without full knowledge and consent of the public, uses such knowledge and methodologies for economic conquest - it must be understood that a state of domestic warfare exists between said person or group of persons and the public. The solution of today's problems requires an approach which is ruthlessly candid, with no agonizing over religious, moral or cultural values. You have qualified for this project because of your ability to look at human society with *cold objectivity*, and yet analyze and discuss your observations and conclusions with others of similar intellectual capacity without the loss of discretion or humility. Such virtues are exercised in your own best interest. Do not deviate from them.

▶ Historical Introduction

Silent weapon technology has evolved from Operations Research (O.R.), a strategic and tactical methodology developed under the Military Management in England during World War II. The original purpose of Operations Research was to study the strategic and tactical problems of air and land defense with the objective of effective use of limited military resources against foreign enemies (i.e., logistics). It was soon recognized by those in positions of power that the same methods *might be useful for totally controlling a society.* But better tools were necessary. Social engineering (the analysis and automation of a society) requires the correlation of great amounts of constantly changing economic information (data), so a high-speed computerized data-processing system was necessary which could race ahead of the society and predict when society would arrive for capitulation. Relay computers were too slow, but the electronic computer, invented in 1946 by J. Presper Eckert and John W. Mauchly, filled the bill. The next breakthrough was the development of the simplex method of linear programming in 1947 by the mathematician George B. Dantzig. Then in 1948, the transistor, invented by J. Bardeen, W.H. Brattain, and W. Shockley, promised great expansion of the computer field by reducing space and power requirements. With these three inventions under their direction, those in positions of power strongly suspected that it was possible for them to *control the whole World* with the push of a button. Immediately, the *Rockefeller Foundation* got in on the ground floor by making a four year grant to Harvard College, funding the Harvard Economic Research Project for the study of the structure of the American Economy. One year later, in 1949, *The United States Air Force joined in.* In 1952 the grant period terminated, and a high-level meeting of the Elite was held to determine the next phase of social operations research. The Harvard project had been very fruitful, as is borne out by the publication of some of its results in 1953 suggesting the feasibility of economic (social) engineering. (Studies in the Structure of the American Economy - copyright 1953 by Wassily Leontief, International Science Press Inc., White Plains, New York). Engineered in the last half of the decade of the *1940's,* the new Quiet War machine stood, so to speak, in sparkling gold-plated hardware on the showroom floor by 1954. With the creation of the maser in 1954, the promise of unlocking unlimited sources of fusion atomic energy from the heavy hydrogen in sea water and the consequent availability of unlimited social power was a possibility only decades away. The combination was irresistible. The Quiet War was quietly declared by the International Elite at a meeting held in *1954.* Although the silent weapons system was nearly exposed 13 years later, the evolution of the new weapon-system has never suffered any major setbacks. This volume marks the 25th anniversary of the beginning of the 'Quiet War'. Already this domestic war has had many victories on many fronts throughout the World.

▶ Political Introduction

In 1954 it was well recognized by those in positions of authority that it was only a matter of time, only a few decades, before the general public would be able to grasp and upset the cradle of power, for the very elements of the new silent-weapon technology were as accessible for a public utopia as they were for providing a private utopia. The issue of primary concern, that of dominance, revolved around the subject of the energy sciences.

▶ Energy

Energy is recognized as the key to all activity on earth. Natural science is the study of the sources and control of natural energy, and social science, theoretically expressed as economics, is the study of the sources and control of social energy. Both are bookkeeping systems: mathematics. Therefore, *mathematics* is the primary energy science. And the bookkeeper can be king if the public can be kept ignorant of the methodology of the book-keeping. All science is merely a means to an end. The means is knowledge. The end is *control.* Beyond this remains only one issue: Who will be the beneficiary? In 1954 this was the issue of primary concern. Although the so-called 'moral issues' were raised, in view of the law of natural selection *it was agreed that a nation or world of people who will not use their intelligence are no better than animals who do not have intelligence. Such people are beasts of burden and steaks on the table by choice and consent.* Consequently, in the interest of future world order, peace, and tranquility, it was decided to privately wage a 'quiet war' against the American public with an ultimate objective of permanently shifting the natural and social energy (wealth) of the undisciplined and irresponsible many into the hands of the self-disciplined, responsible, and worthy few. In order to implement this objective, it was necessary to create, secure, and apply new weapons which, as it turned out, were a class of weapons so subtle and sophisticated in their principle of operation and public appearance as to earn for themselves the name 'silent weapons'. In conclusion, the objective of economic research, as conducted by the magnates of capital (banking) and the industries of commodities (goods) and services, is the establishment of an economy which is totally predictable and manipulable. *In order to achieve a totally predictable economy, the low-class elements of society must be brought under total control, i.e., must be housebroken, trained, and assigned a yoke and long-term social duties from a very early age, before they have an opportunity to question the propriety of the matter. In order to achieve such conformity, the lower-class family unit must be disintegrated by a process of increasing preoccupation of the parents and the establishment of government-operated day-care centers for the occupationally orphaned children. The quality of education given to the lower class must be of the poorest sort, so that the moat of ignorance isolating the inferior class from the superior class is and remains incomprehensible to the inferior class. With such an initial handicap, even bright lower class individuals have little if any hope of extricating themselves from their assigned lot in life. This form of slavery is essential to maintain some measure of social order, peace, and tranquility for the ruling upper class.*

▶ Descriptive Introduction of the Silent Weapon

Everything that is expected from an ordinary weapon is expected from a silent weapon by its creators, but only in its own manner of functioning. It shoots situations, instead of bullets; propelled by data processing, instead of chemical reaction (explosion); originating from bits of data, instead of grains of gunpowder; a computer, instead of a gun; operated by a computer programmer, instead of a marksman; under the orders of a banking magnate, instead of a military general. It makes no obvious explosive noises, causes no obvious physical or mental injuries, and does not obviously interfere with anyone's daily social life. Yet it makes an unmistakable 'noise', causes unmistakable physical and mental damage, and unmistakably interferes with the daily social life, i.e., unmistakable to a trained observer, one who knows what to look for. The public cannot comprehend this weapon, and therefore cannot believe that they are being attacked and subdued by a weapon. The public might instinctively feel that something is wrong, but that is because of the technical nature of the silent weapon, they cannot express their feeling in a rational way, or handle the problem with intelligence. Therefore, they do not know how to cry for help, and do not know how to associate with others to defend themselves against it. When a silent weapon is applied gradually, the public adjusts/adapts to its presence and learns to tolerate its encroachment on their lives until the pressure (psychological via economic) becomes too great and they crack up. Therefore, the silent weapon is a type of biological warfare. It attacks the vitality, options, and mobility of the individuals of a society by knowing, understanding, manipulating, and attacking their sources of natural and social energy, and their physical, mental, and emotional strengths and weaknesses.

▶ Theoretical Introduction

"Give me control over a nation's currency, and I care not who makes its laws." -- Mayer Amschel Rothschild - 1743 - 1812.

Today's silent weapons technology is an outgrowth of a simple idea discovered, succinctly expressed, and effectively applied by the quoted *Mr. Mayer Amschel Rothschild who* discovered the missing passive component of economic theory known as 'economic inductance'. He, of course, did not think of his discovery in these 20th-century terms, and, to be sure, 'mathematical analysis' had to wait for the Second Industrial Revolution, the rise of the theory of mechanics and electronics, and finally, the invention of the electronic computer before it could be effectively applied in the control of the world economy.

General Energy Concepts In the study of energy systems, there always appears three elementary concepts. These are potential energy, kinetic energy, and energy dissipation. And corresponding to these concepts, there are three idealized, essentially pure physical counterparts called passive components.

1. In the science of physical mechanics, the phenomenon of potential energy is associated with a physical property called elasticity or stiffness, and can be represented by a stretched spring. In electronic science, potential energy is stored in a capacitor instead of a spring. This property is called capacitance instead of elasticity or stiffness.
2. In the science of physical mechanics, the phenomenon of kinetic energy is associated with a physical property called inertia or mass, and can be represented by a mass or a flywheel in motion. In electronic science, kinetic energy is stored in an inductor (in a magnetic field) instead of a mass. This property is called inductance instead of inertia.

3. In the science of physical mechanics, the phenomenon of energy dissipation is associated with a physical property called friction or resistance, and can be represented by a dashpot or other device which converts energy into heat. In electronic science, dissipation of energy is performed by an element called either a resistor or a conductor, the term 'resistor' being the one generally used to describe a more ideal device (e.g., wire) employed to convey electronic energy efficiently from one location to another. The property of a resistance or conductor is measured as either resistance or conductance reciprocals. In economics these three energy concepts are associated with:

1. Economic Capacitance - Capital (money, stock/inventory, investments in buildings and durables, etc.)
2. Economic Conductance - Goods (production flow coefficients)
3. Economic Inductance - Services (the influence of the population of industry on output)

All of the mathematical theory developed in the study of one energy system (e.g., mechanics, electronics, etc.) can be immediately applied in the study of any other energy system (e.g., economics).

▶ Mr. Rothchild's Energy Discovery

What Mr. Rothschild had discovered was the basic principle of power, influence, and control over people as applied to economics. That principle is 'when you assume the appearance of power, people soon give it to you'. Mr. Rothschild had discovered that currency or deposit loan accounts had the required appearance of power that could be used to induce people (inductance, with people corresponding to a magnetic field) into surrendering their real wealth in exchange for a promise of greater wealth (instead of real compensation). They would put up real collateral in exchange for a loan of promissory notes.

Mr. Rothschild found that he could issue more notes than he had backing for, so long as he had someone's stock of gold as a persuader to show his customers. *Mr. Rothschild* loaned his promissory notes to individual and to governments. These would create overconfidence. Then he would make money scarce, tighten control of the system, and collect the collateral through the obligation of contracts. The cycle was then repeated. These pressures could be used to *ignite a war*. Then he would control the availability of currency to determine who would win the war. That government which agreed to give him control of its economic system got his support. Collection of debts was guaranteed by economic aid to the enemy of the debtor. The profit derived from this economic methodology mad *Mr. Rothschild* all the more able to expand his wealth. He found that the public greed would allow currency to be printed by government order beyond the limits (inflation) of backing in precious metal or the production of goods and services.

▶ Apparent Capital as 'Paper' Inductor

In this structure, credit, presented as a pure element called 'currency', has the appearance of capital, but is in effect negative capital. Hence, it has the appearance of service, but is in fact, indebtedness or debt. It is therefore an economic inductance instead of an economic capacitance, and if balanced in no other way, will be balanced by the *negation* of population (war, genocide). The total goods and services represent real capital called the *'gross national product'*, and currency may be printed up to this level and still represent economic capacitance; but currency printed beyond this level is subtractive, represents the introduction of economic inductance, and constitutes notes of indebtedness. War is therefore the balancing of the system by killing the true creditors (the public which we have taught to exchange true value for inflated currency) and falling back on whatever is left of the resources of nature and regeneration of those resources. *Mr. Rothschild* had discovered that currency gave him the power to rearrange the economic structure *to his own advantage*, to shift economic inductance to those economic positions which would encourage the greatest economic instability and oscillation. The final key to economic control had to wait until there was sufficient data and high speed computing equipment to keep close watch on the economic oscillations created by price shocking and excess paper energy credits - paper inductance/ inflation.

▶ Breakthrough

The aviation field provided the greatest evolution in economic engineering by way of the mathematical theory of shock testing. In this process, a projectile is fired from an airframe on the ground and the impulse of the recoil is monitored by vibration transducers connected to the airframe and wired to chart recorders. By studying the echoes or reflections of the recoil impulse in the airframe, it is possible to discover critical vibrations in the structure of the airframe which either vibrations of the engine or aeolian vibrations of the wings, or a combination of the two, might reinforce resulting in a resonant self-destruction of the airframe in flight as an aircraft. From the standpoint of engineering, this means that the strengths and weaknesses of the structure of the airframe in terms of vibrational energy can be discovered and manipulated.

▶ Application in Economics

To use this method of airframe shock testing in economic engineering, the prices of commodities are shocked, and the public consumer reaction is monitored. The resulting echoes of the economic shock are interpreted theoretically by computers and the psycho-economic structure of the economy is thus discovered. It is by this process that partial differential and difference matrices are discovered that define the family household and make possible its evaluation as an economic industry (dissipative consumer structure). Then the response of the household to future shocks can be predicted and manipulated, and society becomes a well-regulated animal with its reins under the control of a sophisticated computer-regulated social energy bookkeeping system. Eventually every individual element of the structure comes under computer control through a knowledge of personal preferences, such knowledge guaranteed by computer association of consumer preferences (universal product code, UPC; zebra-striped pricing codes on packages) with identified consumers (identified via association with the use of a credit card and later *a permanent 'tattooed' body number invisible under normal ambient illumination).*

▶ Summary

Economics is only a social extension of a natural energy system. It, also, has its three passive components. Because of the distribution of wealth and the lack of communication and lack of data, this field has been the last energy field for which a knowledge of these three passive components has been developed. Since energy is the key to all activity on the face of the earth, *it follows that in order to attain a monopoly of energy, raw materials, goods, and services and to establish a world system of slave labor, it is necessary to have a first strike capability in the field of economics. In order to maintain our position, it is necessary that we have absolute first knowledge of the science of control over all economic factors and the first experience at engineering the world economy.* In order to achieve such sovereignty, we must at least achieve this one end: that the public will not make either the logical or mathematical connection between economics and the other energy sciences or learn to apply such knowledge. This is becoming increasingly difficult to control because more and more businesses are making demands upon their computer programmers to create and apply mathematical models for the management of those businesses. *It is only a matter of time before the new breed of private programmer/economists will catch on to the far reaching implications of the work begun at Harvard in 1948. The speed with which they can communicate their warning to the public will largely depend upon how effective we have been at controlling the media, subverting education, and keeping the public distracted with matters of no real importance.*

What was needed was a well-organized knowledge of the mathematical structures and interrelationships of investment, production, distribution, and consumption. To make a short story of it all, it was discovered that an economy obeyed the same laws as electricity and that all of the mathematical theory and practical and computer know how developed for the electronic field could be directly applied in the study of economics. This discovery was not openly declared, and its more subtle implications were and are kept a *closely guarded secret*, for example that in an economic model, *human life is measured in dollars*, and that the electric spark generated when opening a switch connected to an active inductor is mathematically analogous to the initiation of war. The greatest hurdle which theoretical economists faced was the accurate description of the household as an industry. This is a challenge because consumer purchases are a matter of choice which in turn is influenced by income, price, and other economic factors. This hurdle was cleared in an indirect and statistically approximate way by an application of shock testing to determine the current characteristics, called current technical coefficients, of a household industry. Finally, because problems in theoretical electronics can be translated very easily into problems of theoretical electronics, and the solution translated back again, it follows that only a book of language translation and concept definition needed to be written for economics. The remainder could be gotten from standard works on mathematics and electronics. This makes the publication of books on advanced economics unnecessary, and greatly simplifies project security.

Other large alternatives to war as economic inductors or economic flywheels are an open-ended social welfare program, or an enormous (but fruitful) *open-ended space program*. The problem with stabilizing the economic system is that there is too much demand on account of (1) too much greed and (2) too much population. This creates excessive economic inductance which can only be balanced with economic capacitance (true resources or value - e.g., in goods or services).

The social welfare program is nothing more than an open-ended credit balance system which creates a false capital industry to give nonproductive people a roof over their heads and food in their stomachs. This can be useful, however, because the recipients become state property in return for the 'gift', a standing army for the elite. For he who pays the piper picks the tune. Those who get hooked on the economic drug, must go to the elite for a fix. In this, the method of introducing large amounts of stabilizing capacitance is by borrowing on the future 'credit' of the world. This is a fourth law of motion - onset, and consists of performing an action and leaving the system before the reflected reaction returns to the point of action - a delayed reaction. The means of surviving the reaction is by changing the system before the reaction can return. By this means, politicians become more popular in their own time and the public pays later. In fact, the measure of such a politician is the delay time.

The same thing is achieved by a government by printing money beyond the limit of the gross national product, and economic process called inflation. This puts a large quantity of money into the hands of the public and maintains a balance against their greed, creates a false self-confidence in them and, for awhile, stays the wolf from the door. They must eventually resort to war to balance the account, because *war ultimately is merely the act of destroying the creditor, and the politicians are the publicly hired hit men that justify the act to keep the blood and responsibility off the public conscience.* (See section on consent factors and social-economic structuring.) If the people really cared about their fellow man, they would control their appetites (greed, procreation, etc.) so that they would not have to operate on a credit or welfare social system which steals from the worker to satisfy the bum. Since most of the general public will not exercise restraint, there are only two alternatives to reduce the economic inductance of the system.

1. Let the populace bludgeon each other to death in war, which will only result in a total destruction of the living Earth.
2. Take control of the World by the use of economic 'silent weapons' in a form of 'quiet warfare' and reduce the economic inductance of the World to a safe level by a process of benevolent *slavery and genocide.* The latter option has been taken as the obviously better option. *At this point it should be crystal clear to the reader why absolute secrecy about the silent weapons is necessary.* The general public refuses to improve its own mentality and its faith in its fellow man. It has become a herd of proliferating barbarians, and, so to speak, a blight upon the face of the earth. They do not care enough about economic science to learn why they have not been able to avoid war despite religious morality, and their religious or self-gratifying refusal to deal with earthly problems renders the solution of the earthly problem unreachable to them. It is left to those few who are truly willing to think and survive as the fittest to survive, to solve the problem for

themselves as the few who really care. Otherwise, exposure of the silent weapon would destroy our only hope of preserving the seed of the future true humanity. The general rule is that there is a profit in confusion; the more confusion, the more profit. Therefore, the best approach is to create problems and then offer solutions.

▶ Diversion Summary

- Media: Keep the adult public attention diverted away from the real social issues, and captivated by matters of no real importance.
- Schools: Keep the young public ignorant of real mathematics, real economics, real law, and real history.
- Entertainment: Keep the public entertainment below a sixth-grade level.
- Work: Keep the public busy, busy, busy, with no time to think; *back on the farm with the other animals.*

▶ Consent: the Primary Victory

A silent weapon system operates upon data obtained from a docile public by legal (but not always lawful) force. Much information is made available to silent weapon systems programmers through the Internal Revenue Service.

(See Studies in the Structure of the American Economy for an I.R.S. source list.) This information consists of the enforced delivery of well-organized data contained in federal and state tax forms, collected, assembled, and submitted by slave labor

provided by taxpayers and employers. Furthermore, the number of such forms submitted to the I.R.S. is a useful indicator of public consent, an important factor in strategic decision making.
Other data sources are given in the Short List of Inputs.

▸ Consent Coefficients: numerical feedback indicating victory status.

▸ Psychological basis: When the government is able to collect tax and seize private property without just compensation, it is an indication that the public is ripe for surrender and is consenting to enslavement and legal encroachment. A good and easily quantified indicator of harvest time is the number of public citizens who pay income tax despite an obvious lack of reciprocal or honest service from the government.

▶ Amplification Energy Sources

The next step in the process of designing an economic amplifier is discovering the energy sources. The energy sources which support any primitive economic system are, of course, a supply of raw materials, and the consent of the people to labor and consequently assume a certain rank, position, level, or class in the social structure, i.e., to provide labor at various levels in the pecking order. Each class, in guaranteeing its own level of income, controls the class immediately below it, hence preserves the class structure. This provides stability and security, but also government from the top. As time goes on and communication and education improve, the lower-class elements of the social labor structure become knowledgeable and envious of the good things that the upper-class members have. They also begin to attain a knowledge of energy systems and the ability to enforce their rise through the class structure. This threatens the sovereignty of the elite.

If this rise of the lower classes can be postponed long enough, the elite can achieve energy dominance, and labor by consent no longer will hold a position of an essential energy source. Until such energy dominance is absolutely established, the consent of people to labor and let others handle their affairs must be taken into consideration, since failure to do so could cause the people to interfere in the final transfer of energy sources to the control of the elite. It is essential to recognize that at this time, public consent is still an essential key to the release of energy in the process of economic amplification. Therefore, consent as an energy release mechanism will now be considered.

▶ Logistics

The successful application of a strategy requires a careful study of inputs, outputs, the strategy connecting the inputs and the outputs, and the available energy sources to fuel the strategy. This study is called logistics. A logistical problem is studied at the elementary level first, and then levels of greater complexity are studied as a synthesis of elementary factors. This means that a given system is analyzed, i.e., broken down into its subsystems, and these in turn are analyzed, until by this process, one arrives at the logistical 'atom', the individual. This is where the process of synthesis property begins, at the time of birth of the individual.

▶ The Artificial Womb

From the time a person leaves its mother's womb, its every effort is directed towards building, maintaining, and withdrawing into artificial wombs, various sorts of substitute protective devices or shells. The objective of these artificial wombs is to provide a stable environment for both stable and unstable activity; to provide a shelter for the evolutionary processes of growth and maturity - i.e., survival; to provide security for freedom and to provide defensive protection for offensive activity. This is equally true of both the general public and the elite. However, there is a definite difference in the way each of these classes go about the solution of problems.

▶ The Political Structure of a Nation - Dependency

The primary reason why the individual citizens of a country create a political structure is a subconscious wish or desire to perpetuate their own dependency relationship of childhood. Simply put, they want a *human god* to eliminate all risk from their life, pat them on the head, kiss their bruises, put a chicken on every dinner table, clothe their bodies, tuck them into bed at night, and tell them that everything will be alright when they wake up in the morning. This public demand is incredible, so the human god, the politician, meets incredibility with incredibility by promising the world and delivering nothing. So who is the bigger liar? The public - or the 'godfather'? This public behavior is surrender born of fear, laziness, and expediency. It is the basis of the 'welfare state' as a strategic weapon, useful against a disgusting public.

▶ Action/Offense

Most people want to be able to subdue and/or kill other human beings which disturb their daily lives, but they do not want to have to cope with the moral and religious issues which such an overt act on their part might raise. Therefore, they assign the dirty work to others (including their own children) so as to keep the blood off their hands. They rave about the humane treatment of animals and then sit down to a delicious hamburger from a whitewashed slaughterhouse down the street and out of sight. But even more hypocritical, they pay taxes to finance a professional association of hit men collectively called politicians, and then complain about corruption in government.

▶ Responsibility

Again, most people want to be free to do the things (to explore, etc.) but they are afraid to fail. The fear of failure is manifested in irresponsibility, and especially in delegating those personal responsibilities to others where success is uncertain or carries possible or created liabilities (law) which the person is not prepared to accept. They want authority (root word - 'author'), but they will not accept responsibility or liability. So they hire politicians to face reality for them.

The preceding pages (if you hung in and read all of them) are quite shocking, but they do shed light on the thought process of all the insane psychopaths we are dealing with today obsessed with their *One World System*. All the perverted tactics they have used in the recent past to murder, terrorize, deform, de-moralize, de-sensitize, and annihilate humanity are gut wrenching. But this has been going on for eons when you do the research. Suspect are the 'mind parasite Archons' that have succeeded in trans-forming many human/hybrids who resonate with their fear, greed, power, and obsession for control into 'becoming like them'. Supposedly, these hybrids comprise five percent of Earth's population, so why is humanity so complacent? Great minds have endeavored to share their insights (often at risk) to help reverse this pattern humanity is 'locked into', but as the old adage says: "You can lead a horse to water, but you can't make him drink it."

Of course, these psychopaths have been at this game a lot longer than we have been aware and alerted to the situation. They have used their wealth and power to manipulate and terrorize people. According to John Lash, (*Not In His Image*), Sophia has been in an 'autistic funk' for several hundred years. However, the Goddess has recovered and She now realizes the magnitude of the horror and perversion that exists in the World. It has been said that 'the pen is mightier than the sword'. However, a more realistic approach would be to consider a different, effective solution to end this nightmare once and for all.

We are at a historical crossroad. The corruption and criminality in government and law is now unprecedented. The greedy financiers, the corrupt politicians and lawyers, and the dishonest press are all leading our country down a path to national suicide. They must be stopped at all costs.

A ONE WORLD DICTATORSHIP GOVERNMENT - IS THIS WHAT YOU WANT?

The only achievement fascist Obama can brag about are his efforts to destroy America - and all his 'victims' cheer him on and shout: 'four more years'! So tell them everything they want to hear as if you intend to do it, and then wait for the morons to applaud and wave their slogans 'Forward' - when *'forward' into fascism* is what you are really talking about. Morons run the World because the World is full of morons worshipping morons. So sad, but true.

Chapter Eighteen

Lawyers

Many judges and those in the upper echelons of the global legal professions, know that the system is fraudulent, and the same goes for leading government administrators. Quite understandable, in lieu of the fact that most politicians are lawyers. The legal profession is similar to the medical profession; both are full of Freemasons and initiates of other secret societies. In fact, the legal profession is a secret society. All the professions are structured the same, and they are controlled by using the same techniques. Lawyers attend law school and memorize what they must believe about the law - their law. Every courtroom has its measure of 'elasticity' depending on how far the law may be 'stretched'. Ultimately the outcome in a trial 'snaps' back to the presiding judge who makes up his own law. "But Your Honor, the law says . . . " doesn't carry any weight. It's always in favor of whoever has the most money and the power to influence the outcome. Most people have had an unpleasant experience with a legal matter. How many people admit to having a lawyer they trust? Not too many. And if they do, they're paying 'big bucks' for his/her services.

Corporate lawyers are in a class by themselves. The U.S., posing as a legitimate government, has been in the control of bankers and mega corporations for quite some time. Our government, formerly referred to as USA, Inc., is in the process of being renamed by bankers to Earth, Inc. - a.k.a. - a New World Order. It is destined to become (if not resisted by its citizens) a totalitarian government of total oppression and total control over every aspect of American life. *The Department of Defense* is a corporate agency of the 'mother' corporation USA, Inc. The ultimate goal is to collapse the economy of the United States. What we thought our government to be is no longer thanks to the fascist political system in power with their legal 'bed fellows'.

What Obama is demanding:

- A doubling of his campaign 'promise' to $1.6 Trillion in new taxes levied on the American people (which will decimate what's left of the middle-class - his intent all along),
- An immediate funding (to Obama) of $50 Billion (to be used for political purposes as he sees fit. In other words, a 'gift' to him personally for any political purposes he deems necessary).
- Personal unlimited sole authority to raise the USA's debt ceiling as he desires . . . whenever he wants.

Translation: *Obama demands full dictatorial powers over the U.S. economy and the elimination of Congressional authority including any input in economic matters. In exchange, he may consider spending less of the taxpayers' money, but he didn't say it was a guarantee. Would you say this was a 'wanna be' dictator?*

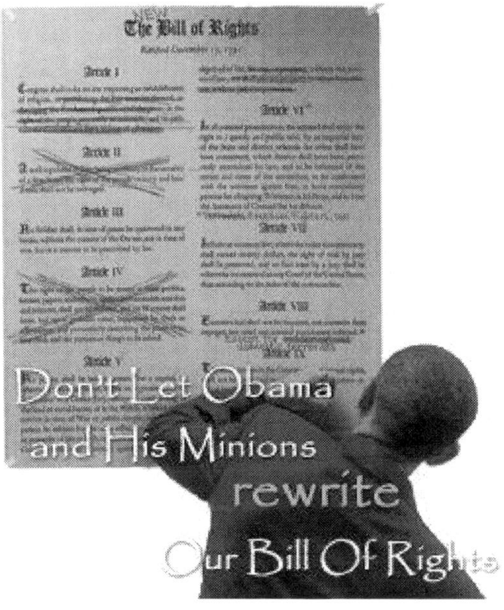

The plan of the elites in spelled out in the 'Silent Weapons - Quiet Wars' policy.

Note: a 'representative' government operating under the Constitution would not be spraying us with toxic chemicals (the Geo-engineering Program) via the U.S. Air Force and the many other agencies and corporations 'allowed' to fly over all of us creating 'weaponized' weather events, nor would a 'representative' government want poison (fluoride and other toxic chemicals) in our water supply, nor would a 'representative' government massively increase artificial frequencies to cause countless health disorders from the microwave radiation, nor would we be fighting against Monsanto to prevent GMO (terminator seeds) in our food supply, attacking our farmers and stealing our property though the schemes in the United Nations 'Agenda 21' a.k.a. 'Future Earth Agendas'. These are just a few of the assaults. It is directed GENOCIDE through the quiet weapons system. Simply said: "They want you to die and they are doing every thing possible to make this happen."

There is massive data being collected and stored by the NSA in Bluffdale, Utah. Children, little people, are being censored in schools to enable the government to transform the children's *thinking.* This will assist and enable the Fascist government's plans to mold and reshape the future society. Actually, data is being collected on every human being on the planet. You may say, "So what? I have nothing to hide." Understand this is an illegal invasion of your mind and thoughts. Supposedly, if you even think of a criminal action you will be swept off the streets and incarcerated in the prison system where you will be used as slave labor while being chemically altered for best behavior outcomes as required by the system. NSA is Quantum Computing and the next phase of this 'Data Analysis' is a world run by computers known as 'artificial intelligence' (AI). Human emotions will be discarded and computers will make decisions for all of us. Computers are void of feelings, ethics, or concerns for life itself. We see a rush to harvest and collect profiles on every human being on the planet. Keep in mind the *Global Smart Grid* is a large component of the enslavement and incarceration in your homes.

The 'Silent Weapons - Quiet Wars' policy states their plans to reduce education to the *poorest quality* and to mandate the use of 'Ritalin', a drug, on our children to provide for a faster fracturing of the family unit. The reality is - NSA is installing a 'tracking' chart. Like the IRS and the 'census', this information is used for surveillance and monitoring. This chart will show the progress being made towards bankrupting AMERICA, and monitor the progress of the projected goals and the timing to determine the accomplishments of the Global Bankers who are controlling AMERICA.

What about the American Constitution?

While Americans quote the 'We the People' Constitution in support of their rights, there are researchers who say the document doesn't even apply to the American people. It only applies to the 39 signatories and their successors. David Parker-Williams, who has studied this subject for a long time, highlights something called 'capitonym', a term that describes words that change their meaning, even their pronunciation, when they are capitalized. Huh?

> Q. In the original Constitution, why did they capitalize the 'P' in 'People'?
>
> A. It was done to change the meaning to a specific 'People'. Thirty nine to be exact. They wanted to make it clear that this document didn't apply to the American people - only to them. Semantics?

The last thing any dictatorship wants is an informed and aware public. The less people know - the less trouble they can do. Knowledge can't be destroyed, but it can be suppressed. If teachers conform to the demands of the system, they will obtain job security. If not, they may have to seek a new career.

Chapter Nineteen
The Media

If a fascist government wants to control the people by manipulating their perceptions of reality, they must dictate the information they receive. This makes control of the 'media' and education essential to any tyranny. This is why so many of us are disgusted with the mediocre news programs on TV and in the daily periodicals. It's blatantly obvious that the elite dictate what information can or can not be presented to the public. Journalists are extraordinarily uninformed about the World they claim to report. It's really self-survival and keeping their jobs. The owners (bloodline families) appoint and control the editors, who appoint and control the journalists, who write what they are told to write or speak - depending on the venue. We witness this suppression of the truth in religion, science, space exploration, archeology, medicine, world history, etc. The list is endless and we've all been victims. Not too many people are enthusiastic about letting go of the information they were brainwashed with as children to learn new information. It's easier to minimize the need to know the truth. They will often validate their reluctance with rationalizations such as: "It's impossible." "That can't be true." "I need more proof." And so on.

Historians refuse to rewrite history, scientists won't retract old worn out, inaccurate theories, and government will never acknowledge all the lies they have intentionally misled the public with. This is why they have never admitted the truth about their association with the Ets (Archon/Reptilian) and UFO sightings from the get-go. *(Alien abduction and UFOs were mentioned in the Dead Sea Scroll and the Codices of the Nag Hammadi).* The hybrid bloodlines fear being discovered and their secrets being exposed. All this is coming to an end as more people are becoming aware of their M. O.

The bloodline corporations dominate and influence the media they own right down to what you see and hear. To name a few of the major companies that have ownership: Disney, National Amusements, Viacom, CBS Corporation, Time Warner, News Corporation, Bertelsmann, AG, Sony, General Electric, Hearst Corporation, Aol, and Aol Radio. (A complete list is published in David Icke's *'Human Race Get Off Your Knees' (*pages 524 -525) which certainly validates the 'pyramid structure'. And just when you thought you found a venue where you could access decent information - the Fascist government lackeys are already plotting on how they can 'firewall' the Internet from the public.

BE INFORMED

Obama quietly (secretly) signed his name to an Executive Order on Friday, July 6th, 2012 allowing the White House to control all private communication in the country in the name of 'national security'. On the government's official website for the National Communications Systems, the government explains that the 'infrastructure' includes wire lines, wireless, satellite, cable, and broadcasting systems that include the transport networks supporting the Internet and other key information systems. This suggests that the President has indeed effectively just allowed himself to control the country's Internet access!

The Internet has been used creatively to expose the 'Orwellian' agenda, but the bloodline families are now seeking to suppress the free flow of information on the Web. While they have obtained some major benefits from the Internet in terms of surveillance, there has been a downside with the explosion of information across the Net about their *covert* operations and manipulations of the population. Patrick Redmond, a former employee of IBM, said in 2008 that the switch from analogue to digital TV was mainly to free analog frequencies for scanners that would read implanted microchips and track people and products wherever they went. The rush to go 'digital' was due to the plan to use the UHF-VHF frequencies of the chips.

The concentration of power in the global media is fast moving to a similar structure that destroys diversity and ensures that everyone receives the same version of' 'news' and information no matter where they are. The most extreme policy (so far) proposed to stop the truth coming out was delivered by Cass Sunstein (Rothschild Zionist), Director of the Office of Regulatory Affairs and a friend of Obama's at Harvard, who has said that the Internet is a 'threat to democracy'. Sunstein published a paper in January 2008, highlighting the need to break up 'the hard core of extremists who supply conspiracy theories'; more likely, he was speaking about *anyone criticizing the government.*

An ambitious counter-attack to gain control over the masses is their plan to 'microchip the global population'. And who are they targeting? Our babies! Micro-chipping babies at birth is the goal of the bloodline families to insure that no one comes into this reality in human form without being connected to the Reptilian computer network and the Global Positioning System, which is there to monitor everyone on the planet via satellite. It will allow the population to be 'tracked' every minute of their lives and there wouldn't be a single second when the 'authorities' would not know where you were. More significantly, since the body is a 'biological computer', they want to implant the microchip to hijack its electrochemical systems, control every human mentally, emotionally, and physically. Once inside the body, it can control the individual externally via signals to the chip. It can manipulate a person to be aggressive or submissive, sexually high or sexually suppressed, and feel extreme fear at the touch of a button or the click of a 'mouse'. How is this possible?

The 'chip' is the interface between two computer systems - the 'human body' and the one controlled by the 'authorities'. 'Thought' generates electrical signals and thought waves. Instructions (thoughts) can be implanted in the human psyche by sending them in vibrational/electrical form through the 'chip'. In that state, humans become nothing more than robots. The bloodlines want a 'micro-chipped' World army of human robots to work with the robot technology. With electromagnetic frequency (EMF) brain stimulation, fully coded, pulsating electromagnetic signals can be sent to the brain causing the desired voice and visual effects to be experienced by the 'target'. This technology to 'monitor behavior' is already well advanced and available. The potential for human control is horrific. The development of the brain/computer interface was conducted under contract to DARPA, the Pentagon's *Defense Advanced Research Projects Agency*. There aren't any potential benefits for those with disease and paralysis caused by a damaged 'electrical' body system because DARPA hasn't funded the development of this technology to help anyone. None of the Illuminati corporations have any interest in protecting the health of the 'cattle' (their terminology for humans). It's all about total control.

We are witnessing ridiculous excuses to remove children from their parents. The common theme is to equate 'refusing' vaccinations with being a 'bad parent'. Sandy Macara, former chairman of the Rothschild controlled BMA said that if parents can't be persuaded to give their children the highly controversial MMR vaccine, than it *should* be made compulsory. Parents are losing more and more rights to make decisions about their children. Obama has declared children should spend more time in school away from their parents and summer vacations because the challenges of a new century demand more time in the classroom. This wasn't to improve their learning skills. The sole purpose was to give government more time to impose 'behavior' and 'perception' modification through the 'education' system. Schools are becoming tyrannies - exactly as they were designed to becoming. (Silent War - Page 138)

"The quality of education given to the lower class must be of the poorest sort, so that the moat of ignorance isolating the inferior class from the superior class is and remains incomprehensible to the inferior class. With such an initial handicap, even bright lower class individuals have little if any hope of extricating themselves from their assigned lot in life. This form of slavery is essential to maintain some measure of social order, peace, and tranquility for the ruling upper class."

Profile of a Psychopath

Chapter Twenty

Has humanity become a sub-species of the Archons? Some people believe we are their slaves, doomed to eventual distinction. The hybrid/bloodlines would like us to buy this deception. However, true 'telestai', who have seriously studied the Sophia Myth, have different viewpoint/s. Some scholars of the Divine Mysteries theorize that the Archons are mere 'projections' of the human mind, brought to life by man's unlimited creative imagination. The Gnostics taught they were an inter-dimensional species determined to destroy mankind. Under the leadership of Yaldabaoth (Devil), they mentally pry on human emotions and inflict pain and confusion. Humans who resonate with their greed, evil, jealousy, and need to control, have allowed themselves to be victims of their parasitic 'mind control'. The reward for their resignation to perversion and betrayal to their fellow man is the accumulation of wealth and power while living on the Planet. This scenario has existed for eons and has reached a pinnacle at the present time. According to Hindu tradition of cosmology, We are now nearing the end of the Kali Yuga (Age of Iron), the most negative of four evolutionary Yugic cycles. 'Kali' is the female counterpart of 'Shiva' in the Hindu trinity. She is the goddess of the dissolution of time and the destroyer of illusion. During this Yuga, righteousness has shrunk to a scant one-fourth of its original strength. Throughout our current history, we have created and been assailed by all the evils of 'Pandora's Box'. But the turning point has now arrived and the 'dawn' once more sheds light on a confused and ignorant Planet. Because of the influence of increasing light vibration upon the collective Consciousness now, it has become very important for us to understand its effect upon three aspects of our nature known as the three 'gunas': Sattva (spiritual awareness), Rajas (practical awareness), and Tamas (density of matter or lower self). It is the play between them that gives rise to the phenomena of the World and of Consciousness. But the awakening of the light is a two-edged sword; the light that illuminates can also blind.

At this critical time, John Lamb Lash, a comparative mythologist, has brought our attention to the '*Sophia Myth*' and the '*Archons*' with his brilliant interpretation of the ancient Gnostic codices found in Egypt in the year 1947. His world-renowned publication, *'Not in His Image',* focuses on humanity's origin as well as the birth of Planet Earth. Insightful concepts may be read on his website - Metahistory.org. He is no stranger to the esoteric scholar and may be viewed on numerous interviews uploaded on YouTube.

The Archon is a simple but evil predator. He is very advanced technologically, but lacks the ability to create or initiate. He piggy-backs on man's creativity and other abilities and has earned a foreboding reputation with the assistance of the human hybrids on Earth. Archons are extremely envious and hateful of mankind. They have tried unsuccessfully to conquer the 'human genome', achieving only partial success throughout the eons of time. They cannot live on our organic Planet because of their inorganic genetic makeup. And so they improvise in various perverted ways which have been discussed. The Archon has an intense fear of being discovered and so he lurks in the darkness. His greatest achievement has been his ability to invade the minds of humans who have bargained with him for technical 'perks'. His own mind is baroque, contradictory, and morose.

Illuminati bloodlines are human/Reptilian hybrids, and the offspring of a race of Reptilian humanoids that are widely described in ancient legends and accounts. The Rothschilds and the bloodline family 'network' obsessively and incessantly interbreed because they are seeking to retain their 'special' genetics which would be quickly diluted by breeding with the general public. Researcher Stewart Swerdlow, who discovered the Reptilian connection as a captive in a U.S. government 'mind control' program, said that these hybrid bloodlines are the origin of the term 'blue bloods' to describe royal and aristocratic families.

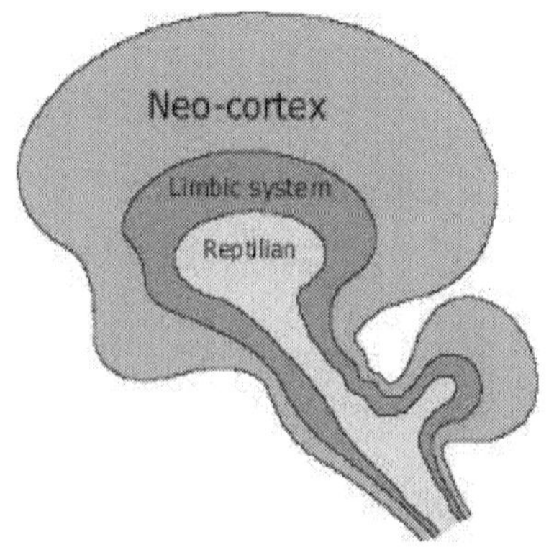

Their blood contains more copper, and during a process called oxidization, it turns a blue/green color. (It is a fact that a 'copper' bullet is the only bullet that will kill a giant). People aren't aware that all humans have Reptilian genetics and that they are fundamental to human behavior. 'Pheromone' is the substance secreted and released by animals so they can be detected by members of the same species, and the pheromones in human women and iguanas are a *chemical match*. You only have to look at the bottom of the human spine to see the remnants of a tail, and some people continue to be born with tails or 'caudal appendages', as doctors call them.

A major part of the human brain is known by scientists as the 'R-complex' or 'Reptilian brain'. It is the most obvious expression of our Reptilian genetic history and has an enormous effect on our behavior. Our animalistic desires and reactions generate from the Reptile brain, which resembles the brains of lizards, other reptiles, and birds. It isn't really a coincidence that the character traits of the Reptilian brain are overwhelmingly similar to those of the Illuminati bloodline families and the societies they've created.

- Scientists say that the Reptilian brain represents a core of the human nervous system and is responsible for character traits like aggression, cold-blooded and ritualistic behavior, a desire for control, power and ownerships (territoriality), might is right, domination, submission, compulsions and obsessions, worship, rigidity, and a desire for social hierarchies.
- There are at least five human behavior patterns that originate in the Reptilian brain that find expression In human activities: obsessive compulsive behavior, personal day-to-day rituals and superstitious acts, slavish conformance to old ways of doing things, ceremonial re-enactments, obeisance to precedent, as in legal, religious, cultural, and other matters and all manner of deception.
- Reptilian genetics are the source of cold-blooded behavior and lack of empathy shown to billions of daily victims. Racism, and a sense of racial superiority comes from the Reptilian brain, as does the aggressive, violent sex that the Illuminati bloodlines indulge in 'big time'. The Reptilian brain communicates through 'visual imagery'.
- The Reptilian brain is home to the body's reactive emotions and survival responses. It kicks in when we react to danger by fleeing, fighting, or freezing (fight or flight syndrome).

- It constantly scans its environment for possible dangers and reacts accordingly. When it thinks it can defeat the perceived danger - it will fight. When it decides it can't - it runs or will choose to freeze the body - 'frozen with fear.'
- When the Reptilian brain 'kicks in', it overpowers the thought processes of the neo-cortex through emotional responses based on fear of 'not surviving'. This is when people 'lose their heads' or 'don't think straight'.
- The Reptilian brain sees 'survival' as protecting status, power, reputation, superiority, intellectual pre-eminence, sense of self, etc. An example is when scientists, historians, and religious advocates aggressively reject new information or opinions if they upset or demolish their present rigid beliefs.
- The existing pyramidal structure of the World reflects a classic Reptilian mentality. This explains why millions of people are subordinate to authority. They're afraid of losing their job, being punished or humiliated. The hybrids know this and take advantage.

Cosmologist, Carl Sagan, wrote in his book: *'The Dragons of Eden'* - "It does no good whatsoever to ignore the Reptilian component of human nature, particularly our ritualistic and hierarchical behavior. On the contrary, the model may help us understand what human beings are really about."

Everyone has some of these characteristics. It's helpful to have instinctive reactions take over at times, but not obsessively.

Relationships

Woman to Woman . . .

Chapter Twenty One
Emotions

There are joys two hearts and only two can share . . . The joys that love and only love can give.

"You look tired, Tiffany Rose. I'm glad I checked-up on you."

"Thanks, Viola. I am wearing a little thin. I don't know about you, but my awareness of Earth's present situation has me very upset. How is Sophia ever to resolve the situation?"

"Like you, I'm clueless. But she will. According to Thelete, She is determined to deal with the Archons once and for all. Don't forget, She is the Goddess of Wisdom."

"True. She is also a loving and compassionate Mother. It's my feeling She has struggled with the Archons for some time, but Her compassion has held Her back from dealing with them."

"Agreed. According to Thelete, She has never forgotten Her impulsiveness that led to Her 'Fall'. She realizes It is the reason for their existence and has tried to understand their jealousy and vindictiveness. And that idiot, Yaldabaoth, takes advantage. He keeps egging them on so they follow his instructions blindly.

"Yes. He's the real culprit in this scenario, both in the higher dimensions and on Earth."

Tiffany Rose sighed. "Have you heard from Thelete?"

"No, but I suspect we will shortly. He told Darius that He had a 'plan' and will be calling us together to discuss it as well as our new information and suggestions."

"Oh, have you heard from Darius?"

"Yes, briefly. He seems to have a few plans of his own. He asked for you."

"Really? Perhaps he has some more news from my Father. Darius is rather unusual . . . in a positive way, of course."

"Yes. And very handsome. He reminds me of Carl."

"True. There is a strong similarity. Both are very dedicated to their spiritual vision. True Telestai, wouldn't you say?"

"Yes, indeed. Of course we don't know him as well as Carl. But I am happy he has joined us and offered to help."

"Do you think we are in any danger? "Tiffany Rose whispered.

"Maybe. Darius said your Father was concerned."

"About what? Oh dear. I don't want him to worry. I'll have to remember to ask Darius if Father knows something we don't, or if he's just worried in general."

"He was always very protective of you as was Carl of me. I am sure they worry because they love us."

"I want so much to speak to my Father. I hope Darius can arrange it."

"Your Father always wished that you would meet your true love. I don't think he has ever let go of his wish."

"Relationships were never easy, Viola. You were so blessed to have found Carl and not have to settle for an 'arranged marriage'."

"I know. However, 'life' gave him to me and then took him away. Actually, it wasn't life. It was those erratic zealots, who were no doubt infected with the Archon virus just as the pathetic humans are now."

Tiffany Rose sighed. "I came across some information that will blow your mind. Apparently, the human Reptilian hybrids are bent on downsizing the population on Earth by billions. Actually, it is 'genocide' and they are using various methods to accomplish their goal. All of them are horrible. But since we are on the subject of love and relationships, I realized how difficult it is for young people on Earth to find suitable mates - even more difficult than it was for most of us during our lifetime."

"How so, Tiffany Rose? What did you find out?"

"I'll try to be concise, as the information is voluminous. Agreed?"

"I'm all ears - your captive audience, "Viola smiled.

"O.K. Here goes. A major confirmation of our personality is considered to be the way we react emotionally to life. Are we calm, quick-tempered, rational, indecisive, etc.? All expressions originate from the emotions, which are electrochemical reactions that can be triggered from our five senses. A large majority of our emotional reactions are not 'us'; rather they manifest from external influences. A chemical imbalance can produce rather 'strange' behavior. People on Earth living near overhead 'power cables can feel depressed and not know why. Children consuming chemical-infested food and drink are prone to hyperactivity and other defiant behavior. Emotional reactions are part of the body's makeup (computer software) that manifests as 'programmed' responses which are nothing more than electrochemical reactions played out through the 'Reptilian brain'. 'Unconscious' humans ride a constant electrochemical roller-coaster of emotional reactions with each situation, experience, television program, movie, etc. 'Trauma' downloaded during childhood is especially powerful programming. These reactions are stored in the information levels of the cells/DNA - the computer chips - and the rest of the biological, energetic and digital structure of humans.

The most profound sense of human self-identity is, "Am I a man or a woman?" Some individuals become so confused between the two, they elect to endure long and painful sex-change surgery. The conflict of 'sexual identity' has become a huge social issue. So many young people are 'coming out of the closet' and confessing they are, and have secretly been, the opposite sex of what their physical body identifies them as. *"I was born this way. It's in my genes and not in my head. it isn't psychological, "they protest.* 'Damn right! It's physical. Why?

Because the insane psychopathic perverts in the scientific and medical professions have been sabotaging young people from birth with 'forced' chemical vaccinations to contaminate their genes - a.k.a. - their sense of sexual identification. As more and more same-sex people cohabitate, their union will be incapable of producing children (at least not in the usual biological way). This will surely reduce the population . . . 'big time'. Call it eugenics, trans-humanism, nano-technology, or whatever. It has violated humanity's spiritual essence and their biological DNA. I think it is a serious moral issue that should be addressed at the Trial."

"How is all this accomplished? "Viola gasped.

"The psychopaths have been experimenting in their laboratories 'unsupervised' for a long time. They did the same 'messing around' with human genetics in ancient times. Nothing has changed! The whole incredible transformation of sex and sexuality is caused by a chemical change. It's also known as 'behavior modification' and is accomplished with genetic and chemical manipulation. When people in a 'male' body feel they should be female (and vice versa) it is often because the chemical make-up of their body-computers contain a great deal of those elements or hormones. It is in puberty that teenagers go through the chemical changes that lead to sexual maturity and adulthood. The hybrids have been adulterating the food chain, water, vaccinations, medication, etc. for a very long time to bring about the desired sexual revolution they have obsessed about. My heart goes out to all young people who have been affected either physically or mentally by the 'sickies' in power."

"My heart too, "Viola sighed. "You know, I have to wonder when I hear ignorant people blaming 'God' for the deformities, illness, and abnormalities that humans have suffered through the ages. They would rather blame all these tragedies on God than face the truth and stand up to the perverted psychopaths who are to blame. So many people are lazy, indifferent, and ignorant."

"Yes, but many aren't, "Tiffany Rose replied. "There really are 'victims' and we must help them. Being a passive bystander is the same as giving your consent to the offenders."

"I agree. But we cannot allow ourselves to be too transparent. Caution and timing are essential. A dead person isn't very effective." Viola sat motionless as her thoughts drifted back to memories of Carl and a lifetime they lived long ago.

Tiffany Rose sensed her melancholy. She softly said,

"I disagree with you. People we loved who have passed still have a lasting effect on us. True they may not be here physically, but they never leave our hearts. Love is very powerful. We still have our memories. And our loved ones won't let us forget."

"Yes, you are right, "Viola sighed. "True love never dies. Our hearts hold our loved ones safe until we meet them again."

They sat quietly for a few moments to reflect on what they had expressed. Tiffany Rose broke the silence. "When did you think Thelete will want to meet with us?"

Chapter Twenty Two
Mano-A-Mano

Thelete was ready to meet with Darius and the girls. He was pleased that they had accomplished so much in the short interval of time. He no longer had any reservations about the fate of the Archons and the Demiurge, Yaldabaoth. Under the arrogant leadership of the demented god, the Archon/Reptiles had been a menace to Earth and humanity for eons. It was time for a change. Surely, when all the evidence was presented to Sophia and the Council, whatever punishment would be bestowed upon them would be justified and long over due. And all those who had elected to participate in the outrageous assault and destruction of the Planet and its life forms, would be included in the judgment.

Thelete knew the Archons were slippery and deviant. They had their secret hiding places on Earth and other neighboring planets in the Solar System. Their undercover tactics had served them well. Sophia never begrudged them their technological abilities. They were free to structure the Solar System and explore its territory. But they were forbidden to go beyond the boundaries of their domain and invade Earth. Yaldabaoth, had been blinded by his arrogance and inflated sense of worth. He blatantly ignored Sophia's wishes. After the last great cataclysm, he and the Archons seized the opportunity to capture the Moon Sophia had designated in Her 'Trimorphic Protennoia' (three body system - star, planet and satellite). They then hollowed it out, and designed it into a gigantic spacecraft, which they strategically positioned in relation to the Earth and the Sun to create the Moon/Matrix - a false reality that 'hacks' into the information from the Sun encoded in 'Light'. The Moon/Matrix feeds the hacked reality into the human collective mind via the Metaphysical Universe, the Earth's ocean and crystal structure, and the Reptilian brain (the *left* hemisphere of the human brain). Unless humans become 'Consciousness', their minds replicate the 'hive mind' of the Reptilian/Archons who manipulate humanity from the Moon. The Archons also had underground bases on Earth and Mars. In the beginning, they came and went openly among the people, as Ancient accounts described, but there came a time when they moved into the shadows, symbolically and literally, and hid behind the outwardly human form of their hybrid bloodlines.

Thelete decided he would ask Darius to assist him in locating their most strategic tunnel systems on Earth. He also realized that these underground systems had invaded and infected Sophia's anatomy. Perhaps this was the reason why the Goddess had felt overly fatigued and sluggish. She relied on humanity to keep records of Earth's history, but the accuracy of the information had become distorted. The Reptilian/Archons on the Moon who were manipulating humanity were in collusion with those on Earth in the underground passages; the same passages that were the veins, arteries, and capillaries of the Goddess.

It was urgent that the Archons were *purged* from all their underground cavities beneath Earth's surface and its oceans and waterways. Until this was accomplished, they would continue to hide and regroup on the surface when the time was favorable. Thelete reasoned that once they were purged and 'contained' He and Darius could destroy the artificial Moon 'construct' that had been enabling the Archons to transmit their electro-magnetic programs that were controlling the minds of humans and keeping them imprisoned. He believed his concept was a major 'breakthrough' and was anxious to discuss it with Darius.

Thelete's research also led Him to the discovery of several devastating cataclysms Earth suffered that were caused by the Archons in the recent past. He was shocked by the inhumane and smug attitudes of the *psychopaths* who initiated the events. All had been recorded in the Akashic Records and He intended to show Darius and the girls pictures of these atrocities when they met. The pictures were the strong evidence He needed before advising the others of His 'plan'; a plan He wasn't sure of how well would be received since it was rather 'over the top'.

As an afterthought, He decided He would meet with Darius first and not include the girls. He needed a warrior's keen opinion about his proposed strategy. It was risky. Perhaps including the girls shouldn't be an option. Thelete closed His eyes and concentrated on Darius. He mentally (telepathically) contacted the young man to advise him that He desired the honor of his company. Within moments, Darius responded telepathically:

"I am honored to hear from you, Sir. How may I be of assistance?"

"Thank you, Darius. I wish to discuss some plans with you privately without the presence of the girls. I think it would be easier if you were here with me physically, but I wanted to give you 'heads up' and obtain your permission. It is not my wish to have you suddenly removed from your location and not be properly warned. Do I have your consent?"

"It would be my honor, Sir. I am always at 'your command'."

"Good. This will only take several moments. Just advise me when you are ready. Take your time. Perhaps there are items you wish to bring with you."

"Thank you, Sir. I do have various insights of my own that I posted in my journal. I had planned to discuss them with you when we met. You may think some of them useful."

Darius reached for his journal, his invisible cloak, his sword and helmet. He took a deep breath and closed his eyes. "Ready, Sir." Within moments, they stood facing each other.

Darius was speechless when he opened his eyes and gazed upon the statuesque godly image standing before him.

"He stood tall and erect in a warrior's suit of silver metallic. He had to be at least seven feet tall . . . His hair shone with a brilliant radiance similar to the rays of the Sun . . . and his eyes were crystal blue . . . like the silvery waters of the ocean."

"It is an honor to meet with you, Sir . . . ."

"Welcome, Darius. I am delighted that you are here. Your surprise to find me clothed in a 'warrior's' suit of armor is understandable, for I made no mention of such. You see, even in the Domain of the Pleroma, there is need for a 'warrior' to protect the other Aeons. My status as 'Chief" is to teach our small group of supporting warriors the Divine 'Code of Ethics'. Most humans know of the 'Archangel, Michael. He is my 'second in command'. His courage and love for 'The One' is intense."

Darius was still in a state of shock. So many thoughts were racing through his mind. He finally regained his composure and inquired, "Surely you don't believe in war and bloodshed, Sir?"

"No, of course not. But there are times when rebellious angels and entities like the Archons get 'out of hand' and Aeon warriors, under my command, are called upon to restrain them. It is complicated and difficult to explain. You will be given this information eventually because your *heart* is true. I knew that when first you spoke to me. For the present, we will put this aside. I wish to discuss my plan and listen to your feedback."

"Yes, Sir. I am anxious to hear what you have to say."

"Good. I wish to start with one of the most cunning defense tactic the Aeons have been using to protect their position. It also affords them the opportunity to regroup. Do you have any idea of what I am talking about?"

"I'm not sure. I'd like to listen further before I comment."

"Well, it is a fact that there are underground colonies of 'Third Density' Reptilians connecting with underground military bases all over the World, including the area called Antarctica; and they are especially prevalent in the United States where the underground bases and cavern cities are linked by tunnel networks with incredibly fast electromagnetic transport systems and even more advanced technology. They have produced trains that travel as fast 15,000 mph, which make a 'coast to coast' trip in less than an hour. Reptilian and other extraterrestrial groups also have bases in the deep oceans, lochs and lakes. The massive facilities at 'Dulce' and Los Alamos in New Mexico, and the China Lake Naval Air Weapons Station in the northeast of the California Mojave Desert, are among the Reptilian 'human' bases in the United States. I have scanned around the perimeter of China Lake several times and have come to the conclusion that is a vast area with virtually nothing 'above ground'. It is connected by tunnel systems cut at incredible speed by advanced nuclear technology to underground bases in nearby Death Valley and Edwards Air Force Base. There are numerous other locations including: Mt. Shasta in California, Las Vegas, 'Area 51' in Nevada, Sedona in Arizona, and the sinister Denver Airport in Colorado. They have been exposed by researchers as 'covers' for underground bases. The Denver airport is adorned by Freemasonic symbolism, Reptilian gargoyles, and horrible murals depicting humanity subjugated by 'evil'. It's difficult to grasp that such evil exists. I understand Sophia's frustration completely. The Archons must be purged and exposed."

"It's quite astonishing, Sir. I also have been suspicious of Earth's tunnels and craters, which has prompted me to do some research of my own. I learned that underground bases, bunkers and high-tech underground towns can be found all over the World. More than six billion terrestrial humans inhabit the Earth, and yet the vast majority are walking around in a daze, as if they were drugged. Most people don't have a clue of what is happening on the Planet."

"Interesting you should say that, Darius. That is exactly my observation. These tunnels and caverns are really Sophia's arteries and veins that have been clogged and contaminated by the Archons inhabiting the underground passages and engaging in all types of atrocities. I have connected their activity with Sophia's 'state of health'. They have a debilitating effect on Her and humans on the surface of the Planet."

"I can believe it, Sir. There has been a lot of construction of huge manned bases - big enough to secretly dock submarines offshore in mid ocean, and deep beneath the seafloor, in locales where many UFOs have been seen. Secretive biological engineering and experiments are occurring underground. A percentage of the thousands of missing people reported every year are probably being held as guinea pigs or forced labor."

"Yes. There was a man who worked on a number of deep underground bases who confirmed this to be true. His name is Bill Smith. He died of very suspicious circumstances and his death was claimed to be 'suicide', which of course wasn't true. His story is recorded in the Akashic Records and I intend to call him as a witness at the Trial."

"That seems like a good move, Sir. There are thousands of people employed in these facilities, working in tremendous secrecy, and using technology that has been denied to everyday inhabitants of planet Earth. Maybe some of them could testify."

"Maybe not, Darius. Some of these underground facilities have at least eight floors and not everyone knows what's going on beyond the floor they are working. It's the *lower levels* that open out into the tunnel passages and where the scientists, government, and military personnel are working with the Reptilians on genetic and technology programs in secret."

"I have heard that there are 'jump rooms' that transport occupants to other parts of the World in an instant . . . similar to the way you transported me here, Sir. Perhaps they are not as 'advanced', but they are able to send people to Mars and the Moon to work on top secret technology programs."

"I know, Darius. They have successfully expanded their base of operation without any resistance because of their technical skill and their devious 'mind possession' tactics on humans. It is only now that a door has 'opened' for humanity to see the horrific deception. The message is being conveyed by a few avatars on Earth who were enlightened by Sophia. They are brave souls and the recipients of ridicule and dangerous threats to their lives."

"Is this the reason you are concerned about including Viola and Tiffany Rose in your plan?"

"Yes. There is great danger lurking on the Planet and these deviants are devoid of any compassion for humanity."

A brief pause elapsed before Darius presented his question.

"With all due respect, Sir . . . What exactly is your plan?"

Thelete smiled. "I was wondering when you were going to ask. We both agree that the success of our efforts to 'free' Earth from the presence of the Archons hinges on a fresh creative approach that will ultimately lead to the solution of the problem. Initially, it is essential that we awaken the resolve and commitment of humanity to take back their Planet, control of their lives and future, and become aware of their unlimited potential and power. Once they become 'conscious' of who their enemies are, where they are located, what they are planning and how they expect to accomplish their plans, humanity can hopefully reverse the situation in their favor. Sophia also needs answers to these questions to help Her make the wisest decision for all concerned. Understand?"

"Yes, Sir. And how are we to help Sophia make the right decision?"

Thelete sighed. "It might be beneficial if we made a trip to Earth. Once there, we would be able to get a closer look at the situation. More importantly, we could determine the mindset and emotional feelings of the people. What do you think?"

"Just the two of us?"

"No . . . no, my boy. We will need other warriors to make the trip with us. I have already contacted Michael and instructed him to gather a small group of his best men. It doesn't hurt to be prepared and have someone 'watch your back'. Did you bring your invisible cloak?"

"Yes, Sir . . and my helmet . . . I guess it's outdated."

"Not a problem. I'll get you a new model. We will need our cloaks to move in and out of different areas and not be seen. We definitely want to investigate those underground facilities I mentioned. They are the most strategic sites. However, I came

upon another site of interest located in central Asia. On an isolated wind-blown region called Kazakhstan, a large five-pointed star (pentagram), surrounded by a circle, has been etched into the earth's surface. It is located on the southern shore of the Upper Tobol Reservoir and there aren't any signs of human habitation in the area (at least not on the surface). The closest settlement is the city of Lisakovsk, about 12 miles to the east. The region surrounding Lisakovsk is riddled with ancient ruins, many of which have yet to be explored. Upon zooming into the center of the

Pentagram, there are two places highlighted. One spot is called

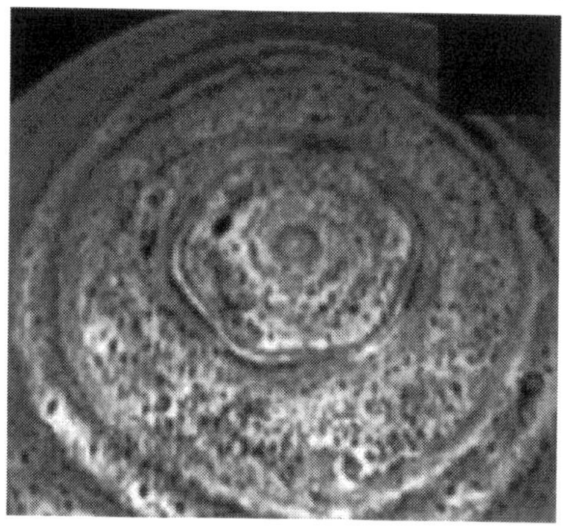

Adam; the other - Lucifer, a name often linked to *Satan.* Since we know the planet 'Saturn' is in cahoots with the Archons, I found it interesting that on Saturn's north pole, a hexagon-shape vortex vibrates constantly. The picture was taken by one of Earth's satellite telescopes. The Hexagram/Pentagram *symbol* shows up quite frequently . . . perhaps it's Yaldabaoth's way of staking his claim to ownership of various sites on Earth."

PENTAGON - U.S.

WASHINGTON D.C.

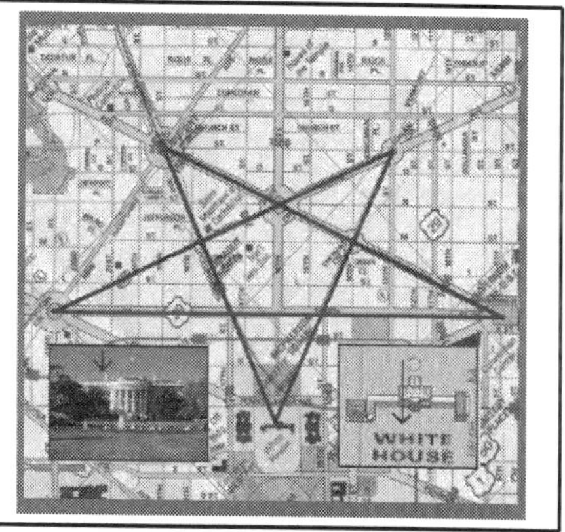

“There is strong evidence that the Vatican is working very closely with the Archons. The Roman Church is really the ‘Church of Babylon’ under another name. The clergy, including the Pope, are really ‘Sun’ worshippers operating behind the myth of ‘Jesus Christ’ and have been deceiving two billion Catholics for eons. There is an abundance of ancient symbolism (architecturally and ritually) on Vatican grounds. The actual layout of the Vatican site, when seen from an elevation, is built within the parameters of a Pentagram. It’s all in the symbolism.”

“In symbolism, an inverted figure always signifies a perverted power . . . Black magic is not a fundamental art; it is the misuse of an art. Therefore, it hasn’t any symbolism of its own. It merely takes the emblematic figures of White magic, and by inverting and reversing them, signifies that it is ‘left-handed‘.” - Manly P. Hall

Notice the upside cross . . .

"Below is a picture of a 'Black Mass'. Notice the three 'upside down crosses', which indicate the worship of SATAN (Anti-Christ). As prophesized, the last Pope, Francis, was elected to the Papacy in the recent past. Suspected as being the 'False Prophet', he will endorse the 'Anti-Christ'."

When Pope John Paul II visited the Western Wall in Israel in the year 2000, he wore a 'large cross' on his ceremonial robe that differed from the usual worn cross. This cross was upside-down, a 'symbol' of the rejection of Christ and a mockery of his crucifixion. The Jewish people approved of the upside-down cross because they understood its symbolism. Likewise, similar to the apostle Judas' betrayal of Jesus while pretending to be a loyal follower (Luke 22:47-48), the Pope, pretending also to be a loyal follower of Jesus, betrayed the faithful into the 'lake of fire' . . (Revelation 20:10, 15). The 'anti-Christ' will be the opposite of Jesus.

THE MITRE

"The origin of the Mitre (head dress) worn by Pope Benedict XVI originated from the Reptilian fish god, Oannes (Nimrod) of ancient Babylon. All religions originated from the Sumerians and have similar symbolism. The Pope's robe is decorated with the red Maltese cross worn by the priest of 'Horus' in ancient times. The four-spoked cross within a circle was a key symbol of 'Sun' worship within the Church of Babylon that moved to a different location and became the 'Church of Rome' (Vatican)."

Thelete paused. "I'm sure Carl will be interested to learn that the Roman Church is still going strong and presently has ties to the Illuminati and the *dark forces* on the Planet."

THE BENT CROSS

"The 'Bent Cross' is another symbol of Satanism that depicts a starving, pathetic suffering Messiah. It is a sinister symbol used by Satanists in the sixth century, that was revived at the time of Vatican II. Displayed on the bent or broken cross was a repulsive and distorted figure of the Messiah, which the 'black magicians' and 'sorcerers' of the Middle Ages had made use of to represent the Biblical term 'Mark of the Beast'. Yet, not only Paul VI, but his successors, the two 'John Pauls', carried that object and held it up to be revered by crowds, who hadn't the slightest idea that it represented the 'False Messiah'. "

BETRAYAL

Piazza del Popolo - Rome

Eye of Horus

"The All-Seeing Eye is an important symbol of the Supreme, borrowed by the Freemasons from the nations of antiquity - Egypt and India. Using the same principle, the Egyptians represented Osiris, their chief deity, with the symbol of an 'open eye', and placed the hieroglyphic in all their temples. In India, Shiva is represented by the Eye. Masonic author, Carl Claudy, writes: "This is one of the oldest and most widespread symbols representing God."

"According to Egyptian legend, the god Osiris was murdered by Set who was killed by Horus. Set lost an eye in the process - hence the 'Eye of Horus'. The 33º Freemason and Black Nobility president, Franklin Delano Roosevelt, had this symbol printed on the American dollar bill in 1933. It was a symbol of secret societies in Europe long before anyone heard of the United States and it is infiltrated with Freemasonic and secret society symbolism going back to the ancient world."

"Serpent crosiers were commonly carried by bishops and high Catholic officials during the Middle Ages."

Ancient Crosiers decorated with the Snake and Lion

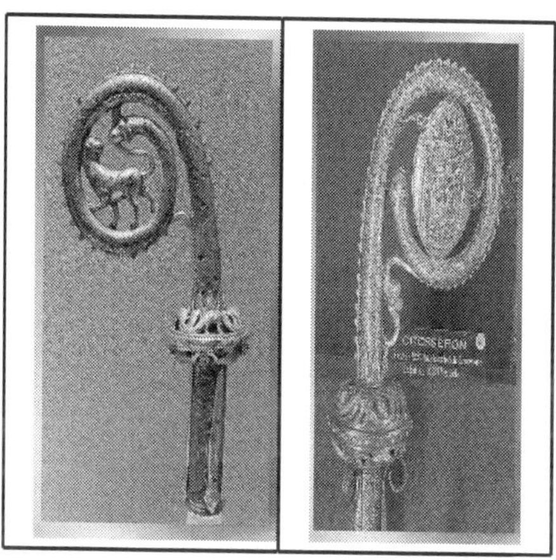

Babylon Sun god
SHAMASH

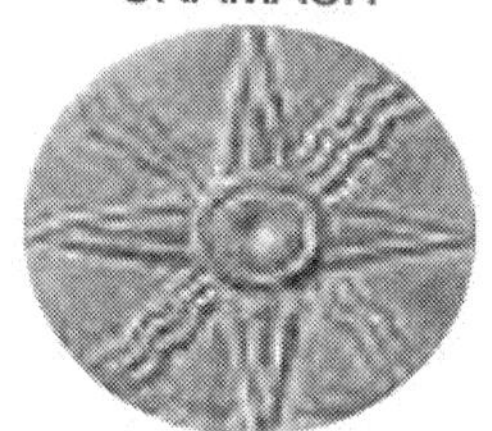

BAAL

BAAL
symbol in back
Jesus head

ISHTAR

"I think you're right on target, Sir. Evidently, the Archons are stationed all over the Planet. It's really quite astonishing."

"They've been planning their 'takeover' of Earth for thousands of years. However, they have made tremendous progress in the last sixty years or so. Their success was assisted by what has been referred to as 'The Fall of Man'. The human brain reached the peak of its powers some time in the distant past and then began to 'devolve'. The downslide was caused by a fundamental dysfunction within the human brain that distorted and limited humanity's sense of *reality*. The human brain has suffered a significant long-term decline in structure and function. The damage is primarily restricted to the dominant (left) half of the brain, which is the perceiver of reality. Humans are born with this condition and it progresses with age. Symptoms include depression, a compromised immune system, a distorted sexual experience, and the suppression of the 'perceptually' superior right hemisphere, which has led to a dysfunctional state of 'Consciousness'. Rapid brain development ends at puberty and the Archon/Reptilians are seeking to hasten the onset of puberty to reduce the period of such development. This is why the government is pushing children to 'grow up' and eliminate their childhood."

"True, Sir. It might also explain why Sophia has taken so long to address Earth's problems with the Archons. She certainly hasn't been receiving correct information from the people."

"Yes. Excellent observation, Darius. She depends on everyone to *remember.* It is every human's obligation to remember and record their experience mentally, historically, or verbally while they are living on Earth. They are co-creating their evolution with Sophia. And it is also their contribution for the advancement of the next generation. Mankind is at the precipice of a new cycle. Much depends on each individual's awareness and dedication to raise their Consciousness and create a better World. Sophia realizes Her children need help. She also realizes they have a blockage in remembering because they were so traumatized over the years. It is too painful to let the pain rise to the surface for many people. They experience only faint stirrings of the past and should these memories begin to become more vivid, they panic and use whatever methods help them to forget. Perhaps this is a good thing. It may not be necessary to remember everything . . . Earth has experienced some very significant traumas recently. They should be enough to awaken people's awareness to the fact that none of the events occurred from the 'the hands of fate'. Rather, they originated from the destructive mechanics of Archon/human 'hands' that put them into motion . . . I have compiled pictures of these recent events. Let's take a break and review them."

The appearance of humans on Earth was a particular expression of the 'Dreaming of the Goddess'; a display of Her intelligence. We are just beginning to understand that Sophia evolves life on Earth to invite human participation in Her story. She relies on us to remember our history so that we may learn from our mistakes and grow . . . Spiritually, Intellectually, and Lovingly.

Chapter Twenty Three 'Remembering'

Humans have a predator that came from the depths of the cosmos and took over the rule of their lives Some human beings are its prisoners. The predator is lord and master of them. It has rendered these people docile and helpless. If they want to protest, it suppresses their protest. If they wish to act independently, it demands that they don't do so. Indeed, they are held prisoner!

"This appears to be the present mindset of many people. However, this is exactly what the *psychopath parasites* wish them to believe. They are liars! Humans should pause for a moment and remember how often politicians, lawyers, doctors, bankers, clergy and those in authoritative positions have lied to them. They are manipulators, deceivers, vampires! 'Masters' of deception and illusion, they tell you what you want to hear to obtain their goals. As long as mainstream assumes an attitude of indifference and submission, these predators will continue to take advantage. Humans must focus on how they are being exploited right now with all their 'techi' toys."

WORLD TRADE CENTER - 9/11/2001

"It has long been thought that the attack on the two Trade Buildings in Manhattan, New York was an 'inside job' - a 'blood ritual' of the most heinous kind. Over three thousand innocent people were killed - trapped in their offices. Of course thousands have been killed in Iraq and Iran for the past two decades, not to mention the millions that were killed worldwide in WWII. How long will humanity put up with this?"

FUKUSHIMA - JAPAN

Benjamin Fulford announced to the World that the earthquake attack on Japan originated in New Mexico and Nevada, U.S. The earthquake weapon HAARP (which can also cause space quake) was employed when Japan was attacked March 11th, 2011. The resulting 10 meter tsunamis along much of Japan's coast line came from rogue elements of the U.S. government located in underground bases in New Mexico and Nevada, according to Pentagon and CIA sources.

"HAARP is a mass destructive weapon that was stolen years ago from Tesla's files. From a military standpoint, HAARP is a weapon of mass destruction. The next target will be the New Madrid fault line in the South-Western United States, according to threats originating from the Nazi - George Bush, Sr. faction of the U.S. government. The United States is supposed to be an ally of Japan. "We demand that you immediately send men with tanks and guns to take these bases and arrest these genocidal rogues. You know who they are and you know where they are, you must act or your own people will be next." ~ Benjamin Fulford

---

"The World is *not* being advised of the serious 'radiation' condition that this catastrophe has generated, not only for Japan, but the United States as well. Both oceans off the coastlines of the U.S. (Pacific and Atlantic) have been contaminated from the radiation spill of Japan's huge nuclear generators on Fukushima. The radiation has killed and poisoned the sea chain. The seriousness of the situation has been 'played down' to the American people as 'big business' has millions of dollars invested in the sea food industry. It may take several years before 'health related issues' (cancerous tumors, damaged intestines, etc.) are connected to the radio-active infested food that is being consumed by an unsuspecting public. It is only a matter of time before the radiation has its disastrous effect on people worldwide. About a year earlier, another disaster struck in the Gulf of Mexico. On April 20,

2010, BP's 'Deepwater Horizon' oil rig *exploded* in the Gulf of Mexico, killing eleven (11) workers. Months of unrestrained oil leaked into the ocean. Efforts to stop the spill were unsuccessful until BP capped the 'well' in mid July, halting the flow of oil into the Gulf temporarily. The 'well' was plugged and declared 'effectively dead' on September 19th. The oil spill has obtained the distinction of being the *worst oil spill* in U.S. history, surpassing the damage done by the Exxon Valdez tanker that spilled 11 million gallons of oil into the ecologically sensitive Prince William Sound in 1989. It is estimated that over 205 million gallons of oil were released into the Gulf. At risk are fishing areas that supplied one third of the seafood consumed in the U.S. and beaches from Texas to Florida that drew billions of dollars' worth of tourism to local economies."

The '**Deepwater Horizon**' Oil Spill

Exposed marsh grass roots are seen in an oil-impacted area of marshland in Bay Jimmy near the Louisiana coast Friday, Oct. 29, 2010. Estimates on how much marshland was oiled by the Deepwater Horizon oil spill range from less than a square mile to a handful of square miles. Regardless, Louisiana loses roughly 25 square miles of marsh each year due to a host of environmental and manmade causes. The state is the site of one of the most ferocious rates of land loss in the world. Oilfield services giant Halliburton will plead guilty to destroying computer test results that had been sought as evidence in the Deepwater Horizon disaster.

"It's quite unbelievable how much destruction is constantly generated by 'money crazed' power mongers around the World, "Darius sighed. "It appears that most people have taken a passive attitude and accepted these heart-wrenching monstrosities and just gone on with their lives."

"Yes, it appears so, doesn't it? This is what baffles me, "Thelete responded. "It's difficult to grasp how and why the population keeps taking it on the 'chin' without fighting back. Are they dazed? Hypnotized? Fearful? It is a mystery."

"I believe it is everything you mentioned, Sir. The dark forces have been poisoning the population with chemicals, food, water, and a myriad of other sinister methods. One in particular, is their agenda of spraying the atmosphere with Chemtrails."

There are citizens who are alerted to what is going on. A former FBI Chief, Ted L. Gunderson, made a statement regarding the Chemtrail 'death dumps', otherwise know as 'air crap', on January 12, 2011. Ted said the following:

"The death dumps, otherwise known as chemical trails, are being dropped and sprayed throughout the United States and England, Scotland, Ireland, and Northern Europe. I have personally seen them not only in the United States, but in Mexico and in Canada. Birds are dying around the World. Fish are dying by the hundreds of thousands around the World. This is genocide. This is poison. This is murder by the United Nations. This element within our society that is doing this must be stopped. I happen to know of two of the locations where the airplanes that dump this crap on us are located. Four of the planes are out of the Air National Guard in Lincoln, Nebraska. And the other planes are out of Fort Sill, Oklahoma. I personally have observed the planes that were standing still in Nebraska - Lincoln, Nebraska - at the Air National Guard. They have no markings on them. They are huge, bomber-like airplanes with no markings. This is a crime; a crime against humanity; a crime against America; a crime against the citizens of this great country. They must be stopped. WHAT IS WRONG WITH CONGRESS? This has an affect on their population, and their people, and their friends, and their relatives, and themselves. What's wrong with them? What's wrong with the pilots who are flying these airplanes and dumping this crap, this poison, on their own families? Somebody has to do something about it. Somebody in Congress has to step forward and stop it now. Thank you. I'm **Ted Gunderson**. For more details, visit my website:

"aircrap.org."

"It gets worse, Darius. The hybrids have developed nano-technology microchips that have 400 million transistors on a chip - half the size of a postage stamp! Anything seen in the public domain is way behind of what has already been developed in the secret projects done in the underground bases where elite scientists have access to the advanced technological knowledge of the Reptilians. Technology is introduced into human society when it suits their agenda. They use 'fake' cover stories on how it was discovered and by whom. It is believed that the nano-microchips are part of the chemical and metallic mixture that is known today as 'Chemtrails'. We all see contrails, or condensation trails, that pour from the back of aircraft and disperse almost immediately. Chemtrails look the same at first, but they don't disperse. Contrails, or condensation trails, are streaks of condensed water vapor created in the air by an airplane or rocket at high altitudes. These condensation trails are the result of *normal* emissions of water vapor from piston engines and jet engines at high altitudes in which the water vapor condenses into a visible cloud. The contrails are formed when hot humid air from the engines mixes with the colder surrounding air. The rate at which contrails dissipate is entirely dependent on weather conditions and altitude. If the atmosphere is near saturation, the contrail may exist for some time. Conversely, if the atmosphere is dry, the contrail will dissipate quickly. But, they are not the same as Chemtrails, that analysis has found they contain many highly toxic pathogens such as mycoplasma, that is fermenting *incognitos*. This was discovered by a Dr. Garth Nicholson in some 45 percent of former soldiers suffering from the debilitating illness known as 'Gulf War Syndrome'. Symptoms reported in sprayed areas have included respiratory and flu-like conditions and sometimes mental confusion and depression. This is an effective way the psychopaths can spread their laboratory-created diseases. Chemtrails contain barium and aluminum; both toxic to the immune system. Some 20 thousand covert experiments on civilian populations in the U.S. have been uncovered by Congressional investigation. Similar experiments were done in other countries. Rothschild Zionists have produced a report calling for the development of 'advanced forms of biological warfare' that

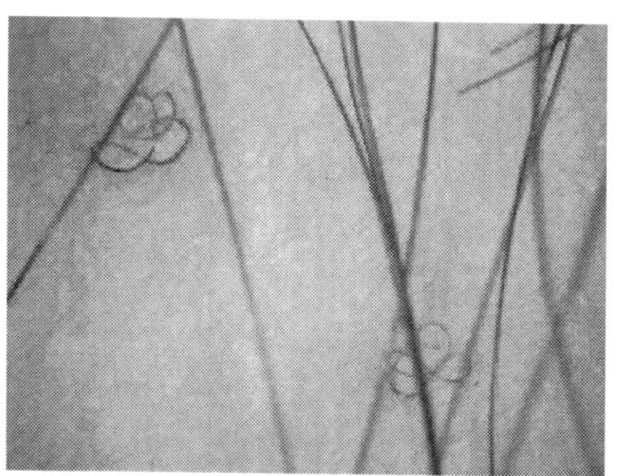

can target specific geno-types. Spraying the population with poisons and microscopic microchips isn't a problem for unbalanced psychopaths. Chemtrails were linked to the outbreak of 'Mogellons' disease in 2001 by some researchers, three years after the Chemtrail spraying began. The symptoms include crawling, stinging and biting sensations, skin lesions that won't heal, extreme fatigue, mental confusion, short-term memory loss, joint pain, a sharp decline in vision, and severe itching. The most striking symptoms are lesions with colored fibers growing out of them. The fibers can be pulled from the body with force, but this

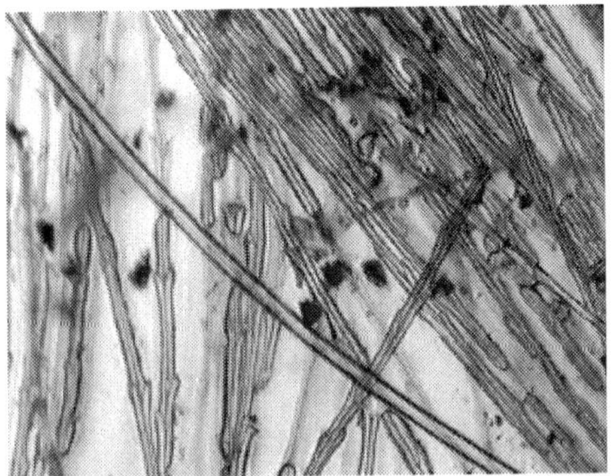

does not appear to stop their growth. We are looking at nano-technology that is able to grow and reproduce. You can see the scale of what the Earth and humanity are facing. These serious challenges must be addressed or humanity will perish."

"No way, "Darius gulped. "Sophia wouldn't let that happen - would She?"

"I don't think so, but unless we can come up with a real creative solution, the odds aren't exactly in Earth's favor. What I mean is, there may be some unfavorable repercussions. Of course, the odds certainly don't look good for the Archons and Yaldabaoth."

"Right, Sir. Which takes us back to your plan. What will going to Earth accomplish?"

"Being somewhere is more powerful than looking at pictures of the location. We could maneuver ourselves in various strategic places and perhaps interact with some of the people and plant a thought or two in their minds to get them motivated. It is my observation that people need encouragement. They have lost faith in themselves and God. Most don't even know of Sophia. Perhaps we could enlist the help of those who are still receptive."

Messages from
GOD

Chapter Twenty Four
Alexis

She had decided to write the story in 'fiction' mode since it offered a great deal of freedom in expressing the narrative. It was the venue in which a writer could transpose his opinions onto his characters about important issues to avoid setting himself up for disapproval or controversy. Still, an astute reader could see through an author's smoke screen. Best-selling writers have very distinct writing 'voices' that possess a certain rhythm and magnetism their readers identified with. It wasn't so much what they wrote; it was how they expressed the story that appealed to their audience. Voice is a very personal connection between writer and reader. Aware of this important consideration, Alexis knew her creative expression was trapped in the grips of a 'dry spell' unable to articulate the stirrings of her inner *voice* that struggled to surface and be heard. The story she began a few weeks ago was abandoned for this reason. She wanted to write something interesting, worthy of a novel. Or would it be a short story?

Perhaps a novella? She'd settle for anything at this point, but she knew she had to purge her inner mind and contact her 'Inner Self' to help her define the hidden blockage she was struggling with before she could rescue the content of her story. What was it she wished to write about? Her mind was flooded with a myriad of thoughts. She wanted something magical to capture her focus. She once read, "Genius was a higher order of thinking." Beyond survival and success, there was a 'synergy' people drew upon for inspiration. Many writers and creative people had availed themselves of this energy. Success was contingent on making contact.

"This is so frustrating, "she sighed. "Why can't I process my thoughts? Why aren't the words flowing?"

She could feel the grips of depression approaching; something she didn't want to succumb to. In desperation she cried out . . . "Higher Self! If you or any of my inner 'writing gurus' are listening, please tell them to *unscramble* my brains. I need help . . . I need it NOW!" She sat quietly for several moments and concentrated on other stories she had written. Challenge and enthusiasm had been the driving motivation for their creation. Content to realize a wonderful sense of accomplishment in the sheer writing experience, she never deluded herself that they would be 'best sellers'. Nor would she evaluate her writing potential with the success her initial attempts generated. Creativity incubated within a person's mind, coupled with feeling and emotion. She believed 'w*riting'* was a dynamic outlet that gave birth to her own feelings and emotions and assumed there would be other stories waiting for her to tell. However, her present challenge had begun to undermine her assumption. Where was that inner spark now? Had she exhausted her reservoir of ideas already? She hoped not. Something was holding her back. What was it?

The World in which she lived had finally arrived to the long awaited year of '2012'. People were apprehensive of what the future would unfold; many still unaware and unprepared to deal with the implied implications the 'Year' was suspect of ushering in. Should the perilous warnings prove to be true, the problems would be insurmountable. How could she write another fairytale romance story with these possibilities lurking in the minds of so many people? And if humanity was destined to experience a horrific cataclysm, would there be survivors?

Alexis realized that many successful authors captured their readers' imagination and enthusiasm by inviting them to share a moment in time unfolding within the lives of his story's characters against the backdrop of existing social and political issues. The combination gave dynamic impetus to the setting, plot, and characters of the story. She instinctively knew she had an opportunity to write about people destined to pioneer a journey in human evolution in this era of time. She recalled having a conversation with her dear friend, Harriet, while they were having lunch. Caught in the moment, she began to express her feelings passionately . . . "I want to write about something worthwhile and different. This is my dilemma. I can't get started this time. And I don't want to write about a story that hints of something I have already written about. Do you understand?"

"Yes, dear friend, I do. But there are so many interesting and bizarre events going on today. Why don't you hone in on some sci-fi stuff? Are you afraid of being associated with controversial subjects?"

"You mean like *aliens* or *space ships* or things of this nature?"

"Yes. There's definitely an interest out there. What's holding you back?"

"Hard to say. I can either write something controversial about the Mayan Prophecy, pole shift, alien invasion, parallel worlds, trans-genetics, etc. or I can just write a good fiction novel that will be acceptable and not invite any criticism. One approach is the 'high road'. The other - well, I guess it's the 'less challenging' option."

Harriet reflected. "What was your art work all about? Didn't you say you worked on some design ideas last night?"

"Yes. I designed a 'stargate'. Why? I don't know. No, that's not true either. The truth is, I was thinking about our lives; actually everyone's life. I began to wonder why we are born at certain times to certain parents and why our lives are cut out the way they are and who, if anyone, decided on them. You can understand the myriad of questions this generates - can't you?"

"Yes. I understand your dilemma much better now."

"Thanks. I wish you could hone in on how to solve it. Anything else you can think of or want to ask?"

"Hmmm . . . 'stargate'. It's an entry or portal, right?"

"Yes. It's how aliens or space ships supposedly enter our World or dimension."

"Right. And you're wondering if there's a real connection with us and aliens and if so . . . what it is?"

"Yes. From what I've read, they're here on Earth now; actually since the beginning of time. Why? Why are they here?"

"You've got me. I don't know. I personally have never seen an alien or a UFO. Have you?"

"No. But many people claim they have. There are people who claim they were abducted. Others just disappear and are never seen again. I used to laugh at all this. Now, I'm not so sure."

"Do you think humans can space travel like these aliens do?"

"In a way . . . yes. You see, as souls, we have all space-traveled. Want to know how? I thought about it. Every time someone is born, they leave their Mother's womb via the birth canal, which is really like a *stargate*."

"Oh, I see. But what about infants born Caesarian? They don't leave their Mother's womb via the birth passage."

"True. I don't know the actual reason and significance for this situation. I can only speculate that maybe the individual was too terrified to exit the womb the usual way through the birth canal. Unable to move forward, he/she required assistance. Interesting concept, don't you think?"

"Yes, very, "Harriet sighed. "Leave it to you to come up with this one. Did you ever tell Steve about this theory?"

"Hell, no! I'd scare him to death! My man was a realist. A kind, loving, compassionate *realist.* I hope he's listening to us right this minute. He probably knows the answer 'hanging out' with 'whomever' he does these days."

Harriet smiled. "He was a dear man. We all miss him."

Alexis forced a smile. She took a deep breath and continued.

"As far as I know, no one has ever written about this analogy. The challenge for me is to work the idea into a story of sorts, wouldn't you agree?"

"I think your idea is interesting. You just have to conjure up a good story about space travel or whatever."

"Well, it's not a definite. It's kind of far-fetched for me. However, with all the hype about aliens and life on other planets, it has possibilities. I must admit that since I have more time these days, I have done some research on different sci-fi theories. Most of the information is very interesting; although it can also be scary."

"We have to keep up with the times, "sighed Harriet. "At least to enable us to talk to our children and grandchildren. Otherwise, they'll think we're just two old cronies."

"It's a necessity for a writer too, "Alexis moaned. "If I wish to write novels and not 'cook books', I'll have to be more flexible."

"Who knows? It may be your next best seller! "Harriet smiled.

Alexis laughed. "I still haven't nailed it, but I'm getting closer." She didn't realize just how close she actually was.

Alexis had embraced a few profound insights at this stage of her life. She recalled a conversation with Judy when she tried to express some of her innermost thoughts: "You see, Judy, I believe that: 'real life' is stranger than fiction. People are very *strange*, but you have to give them their due. So many are suffering and are very unhappy. You and I have it so much better than most. Of course, we had our own share of pain when your Father died . . . and the twins. No one gets away completely free. The 'human condition' and the struggle with life is my focus lately. Who or what determines the type of life a person is born into? Some people have a good life; others realize a lot of hardship and suffering. We certainly aren't all born equal."

"Wow. That's pretty heavy, Mom. I don't think it's the wine. You only had one small glass. It's coming from somewhere deep inside of you. What do you think prompted these thoughts? Has something happened to someone you know?"

"No . . . well yes. All you have to do is read the papers or watch TV to realize all the problems people are dealing with. It's gut wrenching. You identify with their pain and begin to ask questions. I just wish I could put my feelings into a narrative. I'd like to write a story people could relate to on what it means to be 'human'. If I could put in words what I am feeling, it might be helpful to others."

"I understand where you're coming from, Mom. Peter and I feel the same way. Life is sacred and people should be happy. Their lives should be meaningful."

"Yes, but so many people seem to be in a 'funk', and yet they don't like to talk about their feelings. After a while, they aren't in touch with what they feel about anything, especially if it triggers pain. Putting your emotions on the 'back burner' is unhealthy. When the pain surfaces or screams for attention, people pop another pill or light another cigarette. Some become alcoholics, unfortunately. Our society seeks constant gratification and mental stimulation. Many people have become glued to their computers or engrossed with their 'smart' toys. They can't even communicate anymore. They're too busy 'texting' each other. This is why the World is in such sorry shape."

"True. And many people, especially in my generation, believe God has abandoned them. Do you believe God has forgotten us, Mom?"

"No, I don't. I believe most people have abandoned God. They have forgotten how to go within their hearts and listen to what the Divine is telling them. I'm not referring to a particular religion. I myself believe in the one true God - The 'One'. When people walk away from 'The One', who can they turn to? Who else is a source of life, love, strength, and courage if not the Creator? The mad psychopaths within the scientific community are feverishly building their 'artificial god' using nano-technology and genetic manipulation. They have convinced themselves they will invent a superior god with their technology that supposedly was given to them by evil sources from another dimension. Well, let them give it their best shot. The sad thing is that they are convincing others who don't know any better."

Alexis awoke with a slight headache although she had slept well. Laying motionless, she made an effort to remember if she had dreamt anything of significance that might explain her head's discomfort. She smiled when she remembered requesting the 'guides' to unscramble her brains. "Maybe they had a rough night trying to accomplish my request, "she chuckled. She was unaware that Thelete had spoken to her in her dreams.

Chapter Twenty Five
Peter and Judy

Thelete knew that Alexis' daughter, Judy, and Peter, her fiancée, were about to graduate Law School. They were aware, intelligent, compassionate young adults - a rare combination with humans nowadays. He was impressed with the tenderness they felt for each other. He had recently observed them while they were airborne traveling home.

Peter looked over at the petite limp body slouched in the seat next to him. She had been very quiet for the last fifteen minutes. He assumed she was reading, but taking a closer look, he realized she had drifted off to sleep, her book still positioned in her lap. He gently lifted her head back and brushed a lock of hair from her eyes as he studied her peaceful countenance. He had been attracted to her beauty from the beginning. Her soft unblemished complexion maintained a rosy flush on her cheeks. When awake, her blue eyes were alert and expressive and her smile was contagious. In addition to her good looks, she was intelligent and had captured his attention that first day in class. He was startled when she raised her hand to answer the question other students, including himself, were reluctant to address. Even their law Professor seemed impressed. She was bright; no doubt about it. Peter knew he had to meet this intriguing young woman. He closed his eyes and reflected back to that eventful day they first said 'hello'. He found the opportunity to introduce himself as they left the classroom. Using the pretense of not fully grasping their assigned homework, he persuaded her to become his 'study partner'. He understood her innate ability more readily when she told him about her Father who had made his reputation within the New York Corporate structure. Law was in her blood. It enabled her to go for your *jugular* whenever she debated theory in a 'mock trial'. She was a formidable opponent, but he was her match. Months later, their relationship 'morphed' from a casual friendship into a serious love relationship. He proposed marriage. She accepted, and they became engaged the following Christmas. They were convinced their meeting was 'fated' having grown up in the same neighborhood on Long Island only several miles away in location; yet having never met until they attended the same law school. There had been practical considerations why they selected Penn Law University for their education. The big incentive was the 'Scholarship and Financial Aid Program' the school offered. Both he and Judy qualified for tuition reimbursement because of their high scholastic grades. Their combined abilities made them a winning team. It was obvious they both embraced high expectations for their future. Falling in love was the 'icing' on the cake. He often reflected on how they met. It had to be 'destiny'.

He opened his eyes and turned to see if she was still asleep. Lying there so peacefully, she seemed almost fragile. He felt protective and 'in charge'. No doubt her Father had given her a healthy sense of confidence, although her Mother certainly wasn't any slouch. Mrs. Stevens was a strong woman; yet noticeably feminine. Both mother and daughter possessed the right combination of strength and softness.

He checked the time. They would be landing soon. He was relieved the flight had been smooth and punctual. Neither of them really enjoyed flying, but in today's world, it was necessary.

"I'll let her sleep a little longer, "he thought.

He turned his head to view the soft, white blanket of clouds from the small window he was pressed against. Clouds always symbolized a *spiritual dimension* to him. He imagined angels holding golden harps hiding behind the larger clouds and watching over their plane to assure them safe passage.

Judy suddenly stirred. "What time is it, Peter?"

"Hey, 'sleeping beauty'! You're awake. It's time to 'buckle up'. We'll be landing shortly."

"Really? I must have dozed. It felt real good." She closed the book on her lap and put it into her carrying case.

"Was I sleeping long?"

"No. Not really. Just enough to give you a little edge. Are you excited to be home? I know I am, "he sighed.

"Yes, I am. I miss my Mom. It will be nice to spend time with her and just talk. I'll call her as soon as we land."

She put on lip gloss, combed her hair, and put her back rest forward. She looked at her watch and realized they were right on schedule. "I wonder what the weather is like? "she said aloud.

"It's going to be muggy according to the news report, "he moaned.

Suddenly, they heard the expected announcement over the loud speaker to secure their seat belts and prepare for landing. They held hands as the plane began to descend.

Thelete envisioned Peter and Judy standing before the Council as Sophia's defense advocates. The Aeons would be impressed that humans wished to be personally involved in the defense of their species and the outcome of their future. He was pleased He had found *caring* people within the same family who were receptive to what He had to tell them. He just had to 'tweak' the circumstances to include them all into the scheme of things. Perhaps Viola and Tiffany Rose could give him some insight on the matter. He had forgotten that they were waiting to hear from Him about the meeting and hoped they weren't offended. He didn't want them to feel left out.

Thelete schedules the meeting

Chapter Twenty Six
The Meeting

"Viola! Thelete has finally contacted us. I just spoke to Him on the globe. He wishes us to meet Him and Darius in the Great Room as soon as possible."

"Really. I was beginning to wonder why we hadn't heard from either one of them. Men. They're all the same. Do you have your information together?"

"Yes. How about you?"

"Honestly, I could go on indefinitely. There is just too much information about the Archons and their manipulation - all negative. And we're dealing mainly with present time."

"I know, Tiffany Rose. It's difficult for me to understand too. I hope Thelete has come up with a great defense strategy."

"I heard that *'time'* for Aeons isn't the same as it is for us, "Viola replied. "Thousands of years is only a few minutes in their realm. What we experience as eternity is only the *wink of an eye* to them. Still, as humans, we've been suffering for a very long time."

"Right, "agreed Tiffany Rose. "Experiment or no experiment, we have been at the hands of these ugly demented creatures for too long. Frankly, I'm tired of it and I intend to voice my opinion at the meeting. Humans aren't able to be as loving or patient as Sophia. Our tolerance level is not that great."

"I wonder if our opinion counts? Maybe we were just meant to help Thelete compile information, "Viola sighed.

"Well, that's not fair, Viola. I think there should be some major changes if 'LIFE' is to continue on Earth. First on the list - 'Get rid of the Archons!' They have reached the same sick level of control as they had in the days of 'Noah'. Is humanity to be annihilated once again only to start all over? If so, I don't wish to ever return to Earth. It's ridiculous to even consider."

"O.K. Calm down. Let's just go and see what happens. We'll listen to what Thelete and Darius have to say. Maybe they'll surprise us."

Tiffany Rose took a deep breath. "You're right. We'll see what they have to say. Let's go."

The girls 'perked up' their appearance, picked up their folders, and closed their eyes. Within moments, they had relocated to the Great Room. The men were smiling when they arrived.

"Greetings, dear ones, "Thelete beamed.

"A pleasure to see you, "Darius added.

"Please make yourselves comfortable. Sit wherever you choose as long as you can see the screen, "advised Thelete.

"Thank you, Thelete, "they replied in unison. His ambiance was awesome and a tad intimidating. They were both mesmerized by His eyes, which were indeed *celestial*. Tiffany Rose felt Darius studying her. He quickly redirected his focus when she looked his

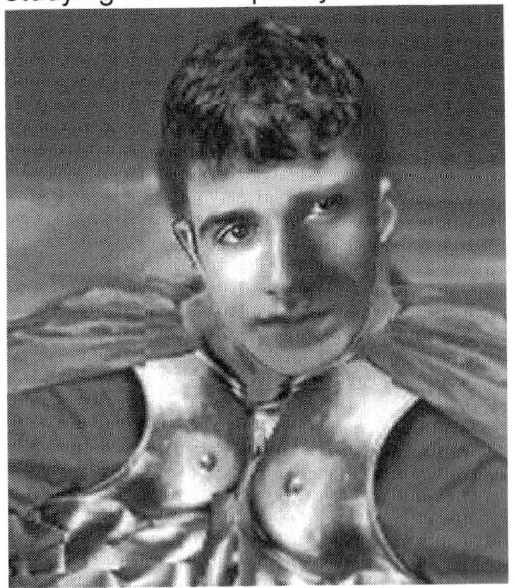

way. "Why is he staring at me, "she wondered. Her cheeks were beginning to flush. He looked very handsome sitting next to Thelete. Somehow his expression was much softer than she had remembered. She hoped he didn't notice her blushing. She focused on Thelete as He began to speak:

"The situation is very serious, dear people. We are up against a formidable enemy. Yaldabaoth is gloating at this very moment. He believes he has every detail covered before he makes his next move . . . which I feel will be shortly. I don't think he is aware of us. This is good. It gives us an edge. But we have to coordinate our efforts and work together as smoothly as possible. Time is of the essence. Here is what I would like to propose. Of course, if any of you have a different opinion, please let me know. I am open to your insights and creative genius. Understood?"

They shook their heads in agreement. Viola sighed. She wished Carl was by her side holding her hand. "I must be nervous, "she thought. She took a deep breath and exhaled.

"Michael and some of his men have grouped. Adhering to my wishes, they are going to make a trip to Earth and do some 'up close' spying. They move as swiftly as lightning, but so does Yaldabaoth, so they must be careful they aren't detected. They will visit some of the major underground caverns and laboratories to obtain a 'first hand' look at the facilities and the colonies of the Reptiles and cyborgs. We want to know how far beneath the surface they have located and their strength in numbers. Also, we want to know who is with them. Many may be captured prisoners held in protest. You all know about the abductions, right?"

Thelete put a picture of the sinister Denver Airport in Colorado, U.S. on the screen. It has been widely exposed by researchers as a 'cover' for an alien underground base and is adorned by Freemason symbolism, Reptilian gargoyles, and horrible murals depicting a 'humanity' subjugated by evil. The mural on the screen includes three caskets with dead females. There is a Jewish girl, a Native

American and a Black woman. Another girl is holding a Mayan tablet which tells of the destruction of civilization. A huge character, described as 'Darth Vader' stands over a destroyed city with a sword in his hand and women are walking along a road holding dead babies. All the children of the World are depicted taking weapons from each country and handing them to the figure of a German boy with an iron fist and an anvil in his hand. The underground alien facility is huge and it connects with other underground bases all over the United States. This is just one of many. 'Dulce' in New Mexico also has a reputation for heinous activities as well as 'Area 51' in Nevada. People who have worked there reported:

> *"I have seen multi-legged humans that look like half/human half/octopus. Also Reptilian humans and furry creatures that have hands like humans and cry like a baby. It mimics human words . . also a huge mixture of lizard/humans in cages."*
>
> *"I frequently encountered humans in cages, usually dazed or drugged, but sometimes they cried and begged for help. We were told they were hopelessly insane and involved in high risk drug tests to cure insanity. We were told never to try and speak to them. At the beginning, we believed that story until a small group of workers discovered the truth in 1978."*

There was a dead silence for several moments until Tiffany Rose stood up and exclaimed, "Nineteen seventy eight! That's thirty five years ago! What has been done to eliminate these insane activities since then?" She began to sob softly. Darius rushed to her side and took her into his arms. He said softly,

"Don't cry, Tiffany Rose. We're going to put an end to all of this."

"How? How are you going to end all of this? It has been going on for eons and eons. They have been persecuting humans for too long. Too long."

"You are right, dear child, "Thelete whispered. "But I think I have realized a major factor that has been in their favor all of this time. It is these very same underground passages and bases that are so detrimental to Earth, our Goddess Sophia, and all humans. These underground passages are Sophia's arteries and veins. They have slowed Her down and at times, have caused Her go into a coma. Humans become ill when their arteries are clogged. Can you grasp this concept?"

"Yes . . . it makes sense. What do you think caused Sophia to wake up and become conscious - more aware of Her problem?"

"I don't believe She is aware of Her health issues, "Thelete responded. "I suspect She may have had a *Kundalini* experience from all the stress to the Planet. Her alignment with the Sun and Center of the Galaxy may have triggered it. I believe the Sun was trying to help Her."

"Amazing, "sighed Viola. "Utterly amazing."

"This is why we must decide on what is to be done with these underground bases. They were always part of the landscape, but they weren't always inhabited by the aliens."

"I'm sorry for my outburst, Thelete. I'm just so very stressed about this whole situation."

"No problem, Tiffany Rose. It shows me you have a heart and feelings - a big heart. The work yet to be done is very dangerous. This is why I insist that you and Viola stay here at the Library while we make the trip, get our info, and make a fast exit. We will need you to keep the lines of communication open in case we need information from the globe. Is this agreeable to both of you?"

"Yes, of course. Do you require any information before you leave; such as the names or locations of any of the human hybrids?"

"Not as yet. All the information you have gathered will certainly be submitted to the Aeons at 'trial' time. But I did come up with another 'brainstorm' I haven't even told Darius about."

Darius came to attention. "Sir?"

"Relax, Darius. It doesn't require your participation - only your creativity. Actually, all of your creativity. I will briefly inform you of what I had in mind and leave it with you for a brief spell to give you time to think of a creative solution/s. You may not like the idea. You may find it too complicated. Whatever. I am open to suggestions."

Thelete explained his intention of enlisting the legal expertise of Peter and Judy at the Trial and why He thought it would be advantageous. When He was finished, He turned to

Darius, and with a wink in His eye, said out loud: "Darius. Why don't you give Viola her surprise."

Darius smiled and looking over at Viola, said, "Good thinking, Thelete. I will do that."

Viola sat up with a puzzled look that inquired . . "What? What surprise?"

"Hold on Viola. Someone wishes to talk to you." Darius stepped away from the screen of the globe and a familiar face appeared.

"Carl, "Viola gasped. "Carl. Is that you?"

"Hi, Viola. It's me . . . thanks to Darius. Hello everyone."

"Hi, Carl, "Tiffany Rose called out excitedly. "How are you?"

"I'm fine. Your Father says hello. I'll put him on the screen shortly."

"C'mon Thelete. Let's give them some 'alone time', "Darius smiled.

Some things never change. It is how you were programmed. Oh noble heart, will you never learn how you are being used? Will you never recognize those who are your real enemy and who desire to possess your very soul? Your brother and sister are not your adversaries. Those who wish to destroy mankind are. Look into the eyes of those who lead you into battle. See the evil darkness of death and destruction they envision for the World in their glare. ~ Sophia ~

"Greetings. My name is Carl and I speak for all soldiers. We have been programmed for eons to believe the lies of those who wish to destroy humanity. They are the true terrorists who have staged World unrest. We believed we were protecting our country and its citizens from terrorists. However, we are merely part of a greater evil to assist those (Illuminati) who wish to start World War III. A 'One World Government' has been their focus and goal for eons. I urge those of you who are reading this message to pay attention so that my words permeate your hearts and minds. We are in danger of mass extinction. The Archon/Reptilians and their minions, the Illuminati, (which includes many factions of our society and government) have set the stage waiting for their cue. Jesus said: "Father, forgive them for they know not what they are doing." Well, that's not going to 'cut it' this time. You have been warned - you just haven't been paying attention."

Chapter Twenty Seven

"The New World Order and the Alien Agenda are one and the same. It is 'World takeover' of the population of the planet. There are 9 races of alien populations. They get high off our adrenal gland substances; it is something like cocaine to them." - Bill Smith

---

Michael and his small band of men met Thelete and Darius at the Great Room to discuss their plans to survey the underground bases on Earth held by the Archons. He and his men changed their appearances prior to resemble humans - human 'pirates'.

"Greetings Thelete. It is an honor to be in Your presence. I heard your call and came as quickly as I could. I was in conference with 'Tolec' from the Andromedan Galaxy when first you summoned me. He and other Andromedan members needed my reassurance since they have heard about Sophia's situation and Her upcoming meeting with the Council. Naturally, they are quite concerned.

"What did you tell them, Michael? I hope you didn't divulge our plans."

"Of course not, Thelete. One never knows if there is a 'spy' amongst one. I merely told them that You were aware of the situation and that You were attending to the matter."

MICHAEL

"Good thinking. May I ask why you chose to look like pirates? It's all rather amusing, "Thelete smiled.
"I'm happy You find us so amusing, "Michael replied.
"We just thought it would be a nice change. Pirates are universal, anyhow . . right?"
"Yes, you are quite right."
"Where are the lovely girls? I had hoped to meet them, "Michael chuckled. (Darius and Carl were surprised with his question).
"We thought it best that they be excused from this discussion. They are rather upset and weary at this point. It has been very traumatic for them to learn of so much horror."
"Understandable. I wonder if the ladies are aware of what the Archons look like? I think they are rather repulsive, myself."
"They are as ugly as their deeds, for sure, "Thelete remarked. He shook his head and caught himself before saying any more. "God! They really are ugly creatures, "he thought. "Only Sophia is able to deal with them. They are too repulsive for the rest of us."

"I was going to show the girls these pictures, but I'm glad I changed my mind. Let me show you what I'm talking about."

Mr. Wonderful

And his buddy

Reptile skulls

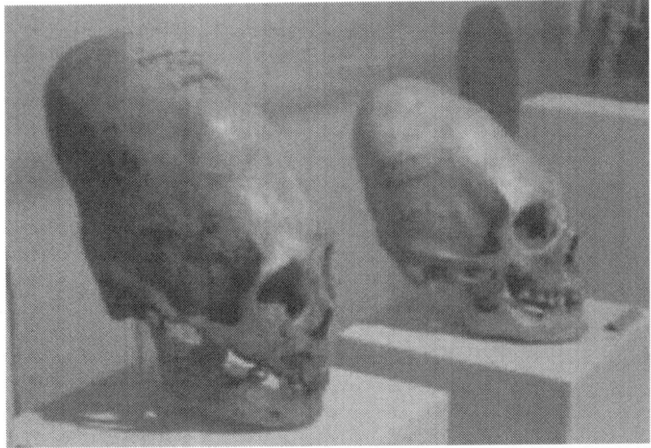

"I picked these pictures up with other material supplied by a man named Bill Smith. He's going to testify for us as he has 'first - handed' experience with many of the bases. But before we start with his information, let's review what we know so far . . .

As we discussed, underneath most major cities, especially in the USA, there exist subterranean counterpart 'cities' controlled by the Masonic/hybrid/elite. Often surface/subsurface terminals exist beneath Masonic Lodges, police stations, airports and federal buildings of 'major' cities - and even not so 'major' cities. The population ratio is close to 10% of the population (the hybrid military-industrial fraternity 'elite' living below ground as opposed to the 90% living above). This doesn't include the full-blooded Reptilian species who live in even deeper recesses of the Earth. Some of the major population centers were deliberately established by the Masonic/hybrid/elite of the Old and New 'Worlds' to afford easy access to already existing underground levels; some of which are thousands of years old. Considering that the Los Alamos Labs had a working 'prototype' nuclear powered thermo *bore drill* that could easily melt tunnels through the Earth at a rate of eight mph 40 years ago, we can imagine how extensive these underground systems have become since then. The sub-cities also offer close access to organized criminal syndicates, which operate on the surface. They have developed a whole science of 'borg-onomics' through which they *nickel and dime* humans into slavery via multi-leveled taxation, inflation, fines, sublimation, manipulation, regulation, fees, licenses . . . and the entire debt-credit scam which is run by the Federal Reserve and Wall Street. New York City is one of the largest 'Draconian nest' in the World. They literally control the entire Wall Street pyramid from below, with more than a little help from Reptilian bloodlines like the Rockefellers, etc. The underground society are acting as the 'parasite' society and the surface society operates as the 'host' society.

The 'extraterrestrials' aren't coming - they're here!

The whole hierarchical pyramid is based on parasites of various kinds feeding off the sweat and efforts of others. Smith can elaborate on the subject. I'll tell you a little about the man. Actually he died in 1996. I met him while doing some research the other day. He was murdered like so many other humans who offered their services to expose the Archons and their hybrids on Earth. Previous to his death, he had been on tour across the United States speaking out about various subjects including his involvement with building a secret underground base in Dulce, New Mexico for the military. During this time, he had an encounter with a violent ET race in the late 1970's, which changed his whole world 'reality' immediately afterwards. He offers a very well explained history about underground bases as he has attended UN underground meetings. The real meetings are not held in New York at the UN Plaza. The policy-making meetings are held in deep underground military bases (DUMB), which are controlled and dictated by the 'tall grey' aliens. He personally attended two of these meetings and knew that after the second one, he was working for the 'wrong' people. This was why he quit his services as a *geologist* for the government. He said it was run by aliens and that the aliens are behind UN policy and many other activities happening on the Earth. He said that they were gradually taking over and were running *The New World Order.*"

> *"The New World Order and the Alien Agenda are one and the same. it is 'World takeover' of the population on the planet. There are nine (9) races of aliens."*

"Because he initially believed that the underground bases were for legitimate national security, he wanted to 'come clean' and tell about their true purposes. An average base costs $17 billion. The 'Black Ops' budget is half a trillion dollars per year - a quarter of the U.S. gross national product. Black Budget is not monitored by Congress. It's an independent taxing body, but it is mainly financed with drug operations by the CIA, NSA and the Drug Enforcement Administration - and more recently . . . the FBI.

The Black Budget currently consumes $1.25 trillion per year. Presently, there are 129 deep underground military bases in the United States. They have been building them day and night, unceasingly, since the early 1940's. Some of them were built even earlier than that. These bases are basically large underground *cities* connected by high-speed magneto-leviton trains that have speeds up to Mach II.

The average depth of these bases are over a mile and are between 2.66 and 4.25 cubic miles in size. They have laser-

drilling machines that can drill a tunnel seven miles long in one day. He helped hollow out more than 13 deep underground military bases in the United States and worked on the Malta project, in West Germany, in Spain and in Italy."

"Pretty amazing stuff, "Michael commented.

"Yes, it is, "Thelete replied. "And there is another gentleman, still living, who had additional information to offer he claims he receives from the Andromedans. I won't tell you his real name since he is in potential danger. Here's his story . . .

"Most of the underground tunnel system across the U.S. runs as deep as 2,500 - 3,500 feet. The 'Boeing Aerospace Company' built and created fuel batteries and power generators to operate this subterranean highway system that is apparently all across the United States. They mix chlorine and hydrogen in the fuel cells to create electricity as well as hydrogen chloride, which is separated again into hydrogen and chlorine. The process creates an endless supply of electricity. The New World Order and the 'black government' financed these alien bases and underground facilities through drug trafficking. The majority of the financing was the result of the CIA creating solutions to impossible situations. Proceeds from the sale of narcotics have been used to finance these 'black' projects. Disclosure about the operation is just now coming to the surface in a publication called *'Compromise'*. It talks about Bill Clinton's involvement with the CIA, and the import of over $100 million worth of cocaine each month for a period of several years into Mena airport in Arkansas, from where it was distributed throughout the United States.

There are existing underground bases and tunnel systems throughout the Earth. Some of these are ancient and were built by advanced alien beings who were here in the past, mining our Planet for minerals and precious metals. Many of the bases are protected by present Earth governments. As you will notice, the bulk of the underground installations are in the United States.

▸ In *Australia*, located in the center of the Continent, is an extremely dangerous base known as Pine Gap. Much of the equipment taken from the Earth to the Moon leaves from this base. There is another base in the Snowy Mountains of Australia.

▸ In China, there is an underground base that is US-Alien-Soviet controlled located in Xining, Mongolia.

▸ *Soviet Union.* Much of the underground hidden space program that developed the *lunar bases* was a covert US-British-Soviet operation in progress since 1958. The majority of it was launched from the Soviet Union to the lunar surface because of its vast expanse, and no one anywhere, could see what was coming and going. They didn't use large rockets to transport the equipment to the lunar surface. The Greys provided anti-gravity technology that allowed them to do this very easily. There is also a base at Serov that is a joint US-Soviet-Alien base. The Andromedans claim this base is very large and very dangerous. Lastly, there are bases at Karaga and Sakaueen and an *ultra secret* level base in the Ural Mountains, north of Serov.

▶ *Iran* has several bases. There is one right smack in the middle of the country in the desert. It's very large, and apparently there are tunnel systems that run to the Red Sea and to the Indian Ocean. There is a very large base in a trench under water at the Masurine Islands and a base in In Algeria in the Tahot Mountains.

▶ *Africa. T*here is an alien base in Sudan in the Nyala Range. In Zaire, there is an alien base west of Kindu. There is a base In Botswanaat, Kamahaki, and another on the South Sandwich Islands."

"Anyone who can pronounce these names will receive extra credit, "Thelete smiled. The men 'picked up' on his attempt to 'ease' the somber itinerary.

▶ *Egypt.* There is a base close to the Libyan border, and I understand that it is as big as the State of Maryland. There is also one west of Cairo, underneath the Giza plateau. There aren't any aliens there at present, I am told, but there are U.S.-NSA *personnel* inhabiting the premises.

▶ In *Switzerland*, there's a base under Mount Blanc that is shared by seven races considered to be benevolent. There is also a base In Scandinavia east of Narvik. In Sweden, there is a base under a private island called Gottland Island.

There have been many attempts by the Andromedans to open up a dialog with World governments. The benevolent Pleiadians and a group from Sirius A have also made the attempt, but the first thing they ask is that the governments disarm. Most governments really don't know what to do with the technology they have - especially the nuclear weapons, but they refuse to abandon their 'killing capability' and disarm.

▶ *South America.* There are bases in the Andes Mts. In Chile, there are bases north of Calama. In Brazil, there is a base at Moto Brava Cuinva."

"I've been to South America, "Michael volunteered. "There's always a revolution over some dictator, but the people are mostly friendly and up-beat."

▶ *United States.* "I thought I listed most of them, but Mr. 'X' added others to the list, "Thelete remarked. "There are bases in Alabama, Missouri, Minnesota and Amarillo, Texas. In New Mexico, there are bases at Dulce, Datil, and White Sands. In Arizona, there are bases in the White Mountains and the Superstitious Mountains. In Utah, there are bases underneath Salt Lake. There are bases in Montana, Wyoming and Idaho. In Oregon there is a base under Mt. Hood that is engaged in massive surveillance of the World's communications. (It has since relocated to Utah). It is also where U.S. military is 'cloning' human beings. I don't know what species of *aliens* are involved, but they are cloning human beings there."

▶ In California, there are bases at Twenty-Nine Palms, Death Valley, Edwards AFB, and in Bishop, where there are landing ports. There are also bases in the Mojave Desert and a NASA secret underground base at Crows Landing near Nights Ferry.

▶ Washington State has two. There are several in Nevada. There are 19 miles of caverns and tunnels in the Yucca Mountains used for the construction of *gravity craft*. This area is also attached to S-4. These facilities were designed and built by A. A. Matthews Construction Company in Maryland, which was once owned by the *Payseur* family.

"That family name is very familiar, "Michael interrupted. "If my memory serves me right . . .

"Boeing was another company secretly owned by the 'Payseurs'. Former French paymaster George Payseur became American 'George Bayshore' and was gifted land and stock in The Virginia Company. The Payseurs acquired land to build railroads and solicited the services of the Rockefellers, Vanderbilts, Loebs, Schiffs, Harrimans, J.P. Morgan and other well-known banking families as agents. George Bayshore was also the owner of Jekyll Island, where the Federal Reserve Act was secretly penned by the front men for the Rothschilds and King George V. For their role in facilitating the establishment of a foreign central bank in the U.S., these operatives were well-rewarded and became known as America's 'power elite'. They're all connected!!"

"You are quite correct, Michael. Thank you for your input. To continue on, relative to the S-4, the Greys gave the U.S. government nine of their craft, which the U.S. government duplicated and now the NSA now has at least 53 of these UFO-type craft. Virtually all of them are sitting on the Moon at this time.

▶ In Alberta, Canada, there are bases near Calgary. In British Columbia, there is a base near Dawson Creek. In North Bay, Ontario, there is a large NORAD facility."

"Are there any other benevolent facilities? "Darius inquired.

"A few, "Thelete responded. "Supposedly there's a benevolent alien base under Tibet. Then there is Mount Shasta, the Grand Tetons and Banff, Canada, and of course Mount Blanc in Switzerland. There is also one in both the Atlantic and Pacific Ocean. I don't know a lot about it, but I can tell you this. The U.S. government has been wanting to 'test sound devices' in the ocean off the coast of Hawaii and down to New Zealand. It's the *military* that is running this. I have been informed by Mr. 'X' that the Andromedans told him that the military, in using this technology, is trying to look for a particular '*mother ship*' that they know is hiding south of the equator in the Pacific. They feel they cannot find it in any other way and think that the sound will do the trick."

"Whose mother ship?, "Michael inquired.

"He didn't know, "Thelete responded. "Perhaps you can check it out, but remember. We're talking 'mother ship' and not just an underground base."

The Middle-East region has an undersea base. It's located in the area of the Gulf of Aden, which is located in the Arabian Sea between Yemen, on the south coast of the Arabian Peninsula, and Somalia in the Horn of Africa. In the northwest, it connects with the Red Sea through the Bab-el-Mandeb strait, which is about 20 miles wide. Because of what Mr. 'X' learned from his Andromedan contacts, he did some additional research and learned that the Gulf of Aden is a dangerous area known as 'Pirate Alley' because of the historically large amount of *pirate* activities located there . . .

Michael couldn't resist. "And you made fun of our *'pirate outfits'*, Thelete. I think you owe us an *apology*. Our dress attire is quite appropriate and will serve our mission very well."

"Touché, Michael, "Thelete laughed. "Anyone else have any questions?"

There was a long silence. The men were deep in thought. Finally, Carl, who had been silent, spoke, "There is certainly strong evidence of how the Archons have 'dug in'. This is probably why they are so 'smug' in assuming they can overtake the World. They've been busy and since they didn't incur any interference from the unsuspecting people living on the surface, they have been extremely productive."

"A great deal of the work is supervised by the military and government, "Darius remarked. "What could people do anyway?"

Thelete put a map of the United States on the screen that showed the various locations of the underground bases. There were too many to count. The group was silent as they studied the map.

"Look how they've infiltrated the United States alone, "Darius shouted. "They have contaminated the Planet . . big time. They must go! Once and for all - we must get rid of them!"

Michael was impressed with his passion. He looked over towards Darius and Carl and spoke out, "Are you men with me?"

"It would be our pleasure, "Darius answered. "Thank you for including us in your plans."

Thelete smiled. "If this information proves to be true, you all have your work 'cut out'. But before you get started, it is in your best interest to review another problem you may have to deal with."

"Sir? . . . What might that be? "they questioned in unison.

"Weapons, my boys! The toys they've been playing with. There are too many to talk about at this time, but believe me, DARPA has been busy dreaming up all sorts of 'kill' weaponry and robots."

"Most of the technology is secret, "Michael added. "Mainstream would be horrified. I'm even horrified!"

"It appears that the Reptilian/hybrids are preparing for a war. It's only a matter of time, "Darius commented. "They always calculate when their next move will be the most advantageous. Rest assured, the Middle East is the hot spot! The indigenous infected people know violence as a 'way of life'. No doubt they were programmed thousands of years ago. Right, Carl?"

"You could say that. They're always fighting about something."

UNDERGROUND BASES

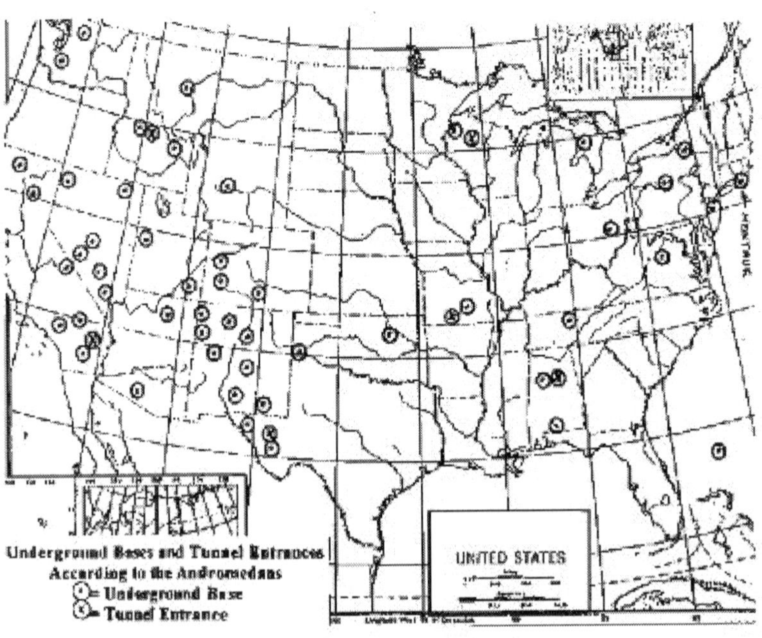

Map of the United States

Certainly not an easy map to read, but it does give an idea of how 'spread-out' the bases are all across the country.

"The US government is developing robots so advanced that they make today's predators and reapers look positively impotent and antique. These killer robots will share one thing in common with their primitive progenitors: with remorseless purpose, they will stalk and kill any human deemed 'a legitimate target' by their controllers and programmers."

Lt. Col. Douglas Pryer

Chapter Twenty Eight
DARPA

Award-winning military writer and former intelligence officer Lt. Col. Douglas Pryer 'penned' an *essay* warning of the threat posed by remorseless 'killer robots' that will be used to stalk and slaughter human targets in the near future. "It is heart breaking to think that future generations will someday look back upon the last decade as the start of the rise of the machines, "writes Pryer. The United States government is developing robots so advanced that they make today's predators and reapers look positively impotent and antique. These killer robots will share a common feature with their primitive progenitors. Without any remorse, they will stalk and kill any human deemed a legitimate target by their controllers and programmers.

Pryer's comments echoed those of Noel Sharkey's, Professor of Artificial Intelligence and Robotics at the University of Sheffield, who has repeatedly warned that the robots currently being developed under the auspices of DARPA, will eventually be used to kill. Sharkey described the DARPA robots as an incredible technical achievement, but he felt it was unfortunate that they were going to be used to kill people. “They’re going to be used for chasing people across the desert, I would imagine. I can’t think of many civilian applications; maybe for hunting, or farming, or for rounding up sheep. But of course if they’re used for combat, they would be killing civilians as well, and these machines aren’t going to be able to discriminate between civilians and soldiers.”

Giving machines the power to decide who lives and dies on the battlefield would take technology too far. Human control of robotic warfare is essential in minimizing civilian deaths and injuries. It is urgent to stop the development of ‘killer robots’ before they show up in national arsenal. “As countries become more invested in this technology, it will become harder to persuade them to give it up, ”said Steve Goose. He is calling for a ban on the technology.

A robot named ‘*Cheetah*’ has set a new World speed record for *legged* robots, running faster than the fastest recorded human. The headless machine, funded by the Pentagon, reached 28.3mph (45.5km/h) when tested on a treadmill. Jamaican sprinter Usain Bolt's top speed is 27.78mph (44.7km/h). The project is part of efforts to develop robots for military use. It was created by ‘Boston Dynamics‘, the Massachusetts robotics company, and is backed by **DARPA , who claimed the purpose of the machine was to assist *war fighters* across a greater range

** US Defense Advanced Research Projects Agency

of missions. It's design was inspired by the fastest land animal, the Cheetah, which can reach speeds of 75mph (121km/h).

Thelete added additional information . . .

"NSA, in collusion with DARPA, is training human/robots to fight a war against any possible alien invasion should the need arise. They are called 'supra soldiers' and have been integrated with nano-technology and other secret technology. NSA has been experimenting with people in the military for at least 50 years. Cloning methodology and the art of 'mind control' was taught to the NSA by the Greys. Presently, there are 'cloned human beings' so heavily implanted, that NSA no longer considers them to be humans. They are part of the integrated cloned 'group-mind'. These people no longer have any free will and are essentially robots. Their souls are seized. DARPA has other robots and mutations in inventory as well. They run, they dance, they gesture and do various chores - mostly like shooting a gun or piloting an airborne 'drone'."

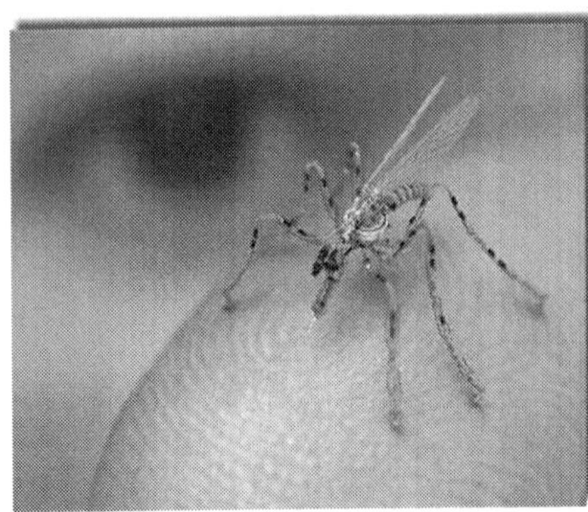

Tiny insect cyborg drones that are designed to go places that soldiers cannot to work as spies or as 'swarm' weapons. Such a device could be controlled from a great distance and is equipped with a camera and micro-phone. It could land on you and then use its needle to take a DNA sample with the pain of a mosquito bite. Or it could inject a micro RFID tracking device under your skin.

“I see what you mean, “Carl remarked, as he looked towards one of the robots Thelete was referring to. “What’s this dude’s name?”

DARPA ROBOT

“Pick any politician’s name. That’s this guy’s ‘handle‘, “suggested Michael.”

“Agreed, “Thelete grimaced. They’re all robots! They pose a serious threat to humanity, however. Luckily, there are some concerned citizens about the ramifications and dangers of this technology. Researchers are now investigating the possibility that technology will be *mankind's ultimate undoing*."

"I can understand their concern, "Carl remarked. "It's reflective of the Archons, isn't it? You know; that's their thing - *technology*. I'm sure DARPA received a significant amount of technological advice from them when they designed these war machines."

"You're right, "Thelete responded. "But the Archon/hybrids are also *genetic* engineers. They always have been. They are unable to create or envision anything new, but they have technical expertise that is probably redundant. Still, they're unable to duplicate what Sophia has created - a 'human' with a soul. If they could, they would have taken over the Planet a long time ago. The Archons are an *inorganic* species and will never adapt to Earth's atmosphere on their own. They've always needed humans as their 'go-betweens' to do their dirty work. More significantly, they will never be able to duplicate the human 'genome'."

"So you're not concerned about the possibility of 'AI' computers (robots) annihilating all humanity within the next two centuries and destined to become Earth's new dominant species? "Michael questioned.

"Not if we have anything to say about it, "Thelete bellowed. "We're going to make sure the '*dark forces'* don't even attempt it. This is why Sophia has contacted the Council and is putting Yaldabaoth and his minions 'on trial'. She has the evidence. They're on their way out."

Chapter Twenty Nine
Yaldabaoth

"You sent for me, Yaldabaoth?"

"Yes, Arizel. There are rumors that Sophia is on the warpath. What news can you give me?"

"According to my sources, She has requested a meeting with the Aeons."

"What? For what purpose would Sophia contact the Pleroma? What could She possibly hope to accomplish?"

"It is unknown at this time, Yaldabaoth. We are probing and extracting information from the minds of every hybrid on the Planet who may have information."

"Fools. Why would Sophia expose Her intentions to these pathetic puppets? No, there must be another method to obtain the information I seek. We must search the *hearts* of those humans who seek the Goddess in prayer and meditation. She may have communicated with some of them about Her plans."

"As you wish. I will notify those stationed on the Moon and

their affiliates to proceed immediately, although I fear it will be difficult to read the minds of humans who have refused to conform to your wishes. They are a different breed."

"I don't want excuses. I demand results! Do you understand?"

"Yes, 'Most Powerful One'. You will have the information as you requested. May I be excused?"

"Go! Your presence is extremely annoying. But before you leave my chambers, set up the 'Sphere'. I wish to see what activity is transpiring on Earth since I cannot depend on those under my command."

The cyborg activated the Sphere and fled as quickly as he could. "He's in a foul mood, "he thought. "I best warn the others."

Yaldabaoth exhaled several clouds of sulfur. His fiery temper had been aroused. He didn't need any complications now. Time was drawing near and he had assumed his plans were intact. He never anticipated Sophia would upset them and interfere with destiny.

"Is there no one I can trust to do the right thing? "he protested. "They're all idiots! The burden is always on me!"

He walked over to the Sphere. The screen was in 'ready mode' to accommodate his instructions. He decided to observe what was going on at the Vatican in Rome - his closest affiliate on Earth at present. The Roman Church and he had established close ties during the last century. As planned, the appearance of the *antichrist* had reached its final stages and the 'end game' had been activated with the arrival of the 'false prophet'. The plan was initiated by the formation of *The Council of the Religious Institutions of the Holy Land* in 2005. The Council had Muslims, Jews, and Catholics who declared there were *'Christians'* in its governing body. Their statement of faith introduced the final 'One World Religion', claiming that all faiths led to the same 'god'.

"Why wouldn't it? "Yaldabaoth sneered. "All religions were initiated by me to begin with. It was one of my cleverest accomplishments towards controlling the humans and arousing tension between the religious groups of the World." Many wars had been fought with 'religion' as its main theme. He continued to mentally review his plans . . ."Now that the 'false' Pope/Prophet has been elected by the Vatican's Papal system, my final plan will be presented to Israel's government as an offer they simply '*have to'* accept. The new statehood in Eastern Jerusalem will have a *Chief Administrator* who governs a special regime. His powers will be similar to the Pope of Rome . . .under my dictates!" His mood lightened. But his thoughts went back to Sophia. What possible threat could She declare against him at this time? Still, he felt a strange uneasiness he wasn't able to identify. He needed reassurance and decided to make a trip to the Vatican. He would notify the 'Black' Pope of his intended visit and time of arrival. There was no rush. Tomorrow would suffice.

Author's note: For more than 800 hundreds years scholars have pointed to the dark augury having to do with 'the last Pope'. The prophecy taken from St. Malachi's 'Prophecy of the Popes', is among a list of verses predicting each of the Roman Catholic

Popes from Pope Celestine II to the final Pope, 'Peter the Roman', whose reign would end in the destruction of Rome. First published in 1595, the prophecies were attributed to St. Malachy by a Benedictine historian named Arnold de Wyon, who recorded them in his book, 'Lignum Vitæ'. Tradition holds that Malachy had been called to Rome by Pope Innocent II, and while there, he experienced the vision of the future Popes, including the last one, which he wrote down in a series of cryptic phrases. According to the prophecy, the next Pope (following Benedict XVI) would be the final pontiff, Petrus Romanus or Peter the Roman. The idea by some Catholics that the next Pope on St. Malachy's list heralded the beginning of 'great apostasy' followed by 'great tribulation' set the stage for the imminent unfolding of apocalyptic events, something many non-Catholics would agree with. This would give rise to a false prophet, who, according to the book of Revelation, leads the World's religious communities into embracing a political leader known as 'Antichrist'. In recent history, several Catholic priests - some deceased now - have been surprisingly outspoken on what they have seen as this inevitable danger rising from within the ranks of Catholicism as a result of secret Satanic 'Illuminati-Masonic' influences. These priests claim secret knowledge of an multinational power elite and occult hierarchy operating behind supra-natural and global political machinations. Among this secret society are sinister false Catholic infiltrators who understand that, as the Roman Catholic Church represents one-sixth of the world's population and over half of all Christians, it is indispensable for controlling future global elements in matters of church and state and the fulfillment of a diabolical plan they call 'Alta Vendetta', which is set to assume control of the Papacy and to help the False Prophet deceive the World's faithful (including Catholics) into worshipping 'Antichrist'. As stated by Dr. Michael Lake, "Catholic and Evangelical scholars have dreaded this moment for centuries. Unfortunately, as readers will learn, time for avoiding Peter the Roman just ran out."

Chapter Thirty

Michael Returns

Plans were coming to a head. Michael and the men had teleported to Earth to investigate the underground bases. They were almost finished and would be returning shortly. Viola and Tiffany Rose were busy compiling their data and were preparing the testimonies they would deliver before the Council. Thelete waited before he apprised them of his intent to have Peter and Judy help them testify. He was relieved when He finally did.

"They're both intelligent young lawyers with a good amount of integrity, "He advised. "They'll help you present your testimony before the Aeons." The girls were receptive and agreed to brief the lawyers on their information. Thelete was now free to work with Bill Smith and Mr. 'X'. There was still one unsettled matter. Yaldabaoth had to be informed that his presence was required on the day of the Trial. Thelete wasn't counting on the Demiurge's cooperation. Michael would have to become involved. He was the only choice among them; and an excellent one.

Michael and the men returned late the next day. Thelete gave them some 'down time' to rest before he called a meeting. They agreed to meet Him and the girls the following morning. Upon their arrival, they were enthusiastically greeted.

"Well done, Thelete smiled. "I'm pleased you all returned safely. Whenever you are ready, we will give you our full attention."

"Thanks, Thelete, "Michael responded. He took a deep breath and began: "Well, just as we thought, Earth is infested with Archons, Reptilians, and some other dudes that are really 'robots'. They are pretty well 'dug in' and have numerous laboratories all over the place. I will refrain from shocking the ladies and speaking about the atrocities we saw. Included in the lot were 'giants' that were caged or suspended in 'stasis'. I remember the likes of them in ancient times and I wouldn't want to deal with them again unless it was absolutely necessary."

Darius agreed. "I know what you're talking about, Michael."

Carl saw the panic in Viola's face, and smiled to reassure her. He had returned this time - safe and sound.

Tiffany Rose glanced in Darius' direction and sighed. She was relieved he too had returned safely.

Thelete smiled. "There's a great deal of mental telepathy going on around here." His humor helped to ease the gravity of the situation. Michael relaxed momentarily, but resumed his serious demeanor. "There were a few surprises we hadn't counted on. You will be upset at what I am about to tell you. I know I was!"

He had their full attention . . . "The Archons and most of the extraterrestrials out there are '*genetic engineers*'. They value life forms, as opposed to precious minerals like gold and silver and consider 'genetic knowledge' their wealth. There's a great deal of genetic engineering and experimentation being done on Earth by them. Also on Phobos, which is actually an artificial *construct* and not one of Mars' *moons*. The experiments have been going on for a very long time. The Reptilian/Archons want *to create a slave race*, which is currently in full swing for the purposes of control, physical services and labor, sexual energy acquisition, a food source, stock for more hybrid experimentation, and biological material. *They feed off human energy*. Whenever there's a war, they feast on the energy of human '*fear*' and death. Extensive research on the human brain and the nature of the soul is actively being pursued. I'm not trying to promote *fear*. I don't believe in it, but I am telling you that humans have boxed themselves into a corner, and their only way out is for them to become consciously aware of what their World is really about, what is really going on, and to begin living life from their 'Heart chakra'. They must create a world of *optimism and love*. Once they do, the Archon/Reptilians won't be able to handle the *vibration* and their control will collapse. Most humans would rather die than knowingly live like *slaves*. Humans need to be free . . .and allowed to do their thing.

There are approximately 15,000 Reptilian/Archons living in caverns and ancient tunnel systems created thousands of years ago that ranges from a depth of 100 miles to 200 miles beneath the surface of the Earth. They aren't benevolent and have been seen in New York City, Missouri, Chicago and some of the Southwestern states. These areas happen to be the largest locations for *missing children*, numbering in the thousands. There have been approximately 32,000 children taken by the Archon/Reptilians over the last 25 years. They drink human blood and consume live human flesh. Children are their favorite human food. So much for all the abductions of the *little ones.*

We discovered a base located in the area of the Gulf of Aden in the Arabian Sea between Yemen and Somalia. It connects with the Red Sea through the Bab-el-Mandeb Strait, which is about 20 miles wide. Destroying this Reptilian base is important, but taking out the Reptilian base on the floor of the ocean south of Yemen off the Oman Peninsula is a *priority.* Skirmishes and battles have gone on for thousands of years and the constant 'bombardment' of this region from sonic energy beamed from the transmitter of this undersea base has escalated the possibility of a full blown war in this region and has caused constant fighting, irritation, and bickering among their own people. They don't even realize what is going on or know that it is being triggered from this undersea base with its transmitter.

Likewise, there is another Reptilian base thousands of feet deep in the ocean off the coast of China much like the undersea base in the Middle East region. It has been in operation for about 3,000 years. The sonic *frequency* beams a 'fear-based' pulse toward the Asian mainland. Its purpose is meant to keep the people of China in this region in a constant state of emotional fear, intimidation, anxiety and control. For years these people have been highly manipulated and controlled by an emotionally charged '*fear for their lives'* mode. They have so few freedoms, living under the strict regime of the government. The beam is activated for approximately 30 minutes at a time and even if it is set at a low frequency, it is still effective. Like the undersea transmitter in the Middle East, it can rotate and its long range affects the Korean Peninsula, China, Vietnam, Laos, Cambodia and other countries in the region."

Michael paused. "Any questions?"

"What type of energy frequency were they using, "Thelete inquired.

"I believe it is a type of 'pulse' or 'electric' energy. It's probably not known to mainstream at this moment." He continued . . .

"We observed various military in these areas. Many of the soldiers are disgusted and depressed. They were there mostly because they weren't able to secure jobs at home. Enlisting in the military seemed their only choice to earn a living. The more intelligent people were assigned technological positions. Those uneducated, were put in the ranks. The constant bombing and arsenal explosions have resulted in homes and villages being leveled and innocent people (including children) being killed, losing limbs, traumatized, deranged, and unable to salvage their lives or ever be the same again. Tiffany Rose felt a lump in her throat. Her eyes began to tear as she felt the pain of the soldiers and innocent victims. They had suffered inhumane treatment either above or below the Earth at the hands of perverted psychopaths focused on 'blood rituals'. Her cheeks started to flush and burn. She wiped her eyes hoping no one had noticed her distress, but Darius had been observing her discreetly. He felt very protective of her, but he didn't dare do anything that might embarrass her. Perhaps he could offer some comfort after the meeting.

They lingered for another hour or so. All present were somber and distressed, but their resolve to help Sophia rid the World of the evil parasites who were the underlying cause of so much pain and suffering had been strengthened. All were in agreement to do whatever was necessary to rid the Earth and its inhabitants from future atrocities. Thelete decided to bring the meeting to closure. He thanked all the warriors and the girls for their bravery and honorable services. He advised them He planned to have another meeting with them before Trial and that they should be prepared for His call. As the group began to leave the room, Thelete called out, "Michael, my brave Archangel, may I please have a word with you privately."

Michael smiled. He had an idea of what Thelete had in mind and wasn't surprised when He requested him to inform Yaldabaoth of his upcoming day in court. "Reel him in, my boy. Reel him in!"

Michael Meets With Yaldabaoth

Chapter Thirty One

"Greetings, Yaldabaoth. I can appreciate your 'surprise' when I requested that we meet, and I am pleased you responded in lieu of this fact. Surely it was your curiosity that motivated your willingness to accommodate me."

"Quite true, Michael. What has prompted your need to speak with me? Surely it wasn't an *impulsive whim* that mirrored something Sophia might do . . . or claims to have done?"

"Your sarcasm reflects your arrogance and ignorance, Yaldabaoth. I am not surprised. My sources have advised me that you have been watching Earth very closely these days. What is it that compels your interest so intensely? Is it because of some inner fear that stirs within you? I know what it is you fear, and you know that I know. You hope I will betray the secret in an unguarded moment."

"Perhaps, Michael. But the reality is, I know that you cannot be caught off your guard. You are far too intelligent and aware to be outsmarted by me. I realize that you must have something of significance to tell me, otherwise you wouldn't have made the effort."

"Yes, this happens to be true, Yaldabaoth. And well you should have something to fear for you and your minions have gone the limit! We have been observing the shameful activities performed by your hybrids on the Planet. They have caused insurmountable sorrow and upheaval for humanity. You have been advised repeatedly to command them to cease all their abusive activities, and yet, you have ignored the warnings of Sophia, disrespecting your Mother's wishes."

"You toy with me, Michael. Surely you don't believe that I and the cyborgs should show Sophia respect and obedience after She admitted our *creation* was a mistake. Would you want to be considered an accident?"

"I am not going to be entrapped with your argument, Yaldabaoth. Sophia has showed her remorse and compassion to you and the others for eons. She has tried to make amends."

"Well, I don't accept Her apology. She should have given us the same deal as the Anthropos."

"You were given the entire Solar System to mold as you wished. But you were not to cross the boundary and invade Earth. Your jealousy and envy has corrupted you and the Archons forever. You have endeavored to destroy Sophia and the Earth inhabitants since the day you were created. But you will never succeed. She is more powerful than you, although you refuse to acknowledge this. From the beginning, even after the Fall, men of Earth were concerned with the welfare of their fellow men. The race was intellectual, although their thinking was constantly clouded by your efforts. Earth's artists, scientists, architects, and engineers designed the most elegant cities, free of pollution and filth. And even though the landscape was mined for its metals, oils, and minerals, no scars were permitted to remain. There weren't any evil areas of gloom or ugliness or decay, for the people were industrious and had pride. They were revolted by the slightest deformity or hideousness. All had to be harmonious, serene, and pleasant to the eye, the ear, touch, and taste for every landscape created by the Goddess was sacred and beautiful. It was difficult to believe that the Golden Age had fallen. But that was your opportunity. Out of calm, you created fury. Out of order, you created chaos. And as fallen men are prideful and wish to exalt themselves, you whispered to the more intelligent men of Earth that they should rule Her *absolutely* for Her own good. It was they who should design Her destiny, and control other men. You inspired the few with a 'lust for power'. They had immense designs, but it was you who pushed their greed to the limit. They would eventually control the lives of the people and keep them in abeyance and a constant state of confusion and ignorance. Men of pride hate equality and freedom. You told them that the more humble of humanity shouldn't be allowed to enjoy freedom or have what they had. 'Fallen men' love thrones. It is their ecstasy. Pomp and ceremony are their ultimate desires. They craved to be adored. Power was their dream. So they conspired together and with you and your Archons. Many became your hybrids on Earth. It took centuries for you to rebuild your dynasty after the great Flood. You aroused no suspicion. You spoke lies and made promises to men of building a great *empire* and an even a greater *destiny* in which they would explore other worlds in the Universe. It was the 'Great Destiny'. The people listened and believed. They were excited and refused to see the deception. They refused to listen to the warnings we whispered in their ears of events about to transpire. And when some of the people were aroused, you quickly snuffed out their suspicions with more promises that everything would be O.K. And then the scientists erected vast domes of protection over their heads to enclose the cities and protect them from inclement weather, especially the devastating rays of the Sun and 'global warming'. They did this by spraying the skies with chemicals known as *'Chemtrails'*. The climate was controlled and everyone could come and go without fear of the climate. To protect people from disease, they invented 'cures' with their diabolical mixtures of chemicals they called 'medicine'. And their children would be protected with vaccinations to escape all the diseases on the horizon. The people nodded their consent. And the cities held all the amusements and entertainment for everyone. No need to wander off into the wilderness and run barefoot on the grass or smell the trees and wild flowers along the undeveloped and uncharted areas. One was told he didn't have to venture beyond the neatly developed houses built in the suburbs that were surrounded by their chemically treated lawns and foliage. People traveled in their cars every day for several hours to and from their jobs anyhow. They were too tired to explore and settled for their TVs, computers, smart phones, and 'techi' toys during the scant hours left for recreation. Perhaps this is why the people never noticed or complained about all the 'spy' equipment that was installed along every main highway and every corridor of every city or the concealed spy gadgets that were installed in their cars and appliances as well as their phones and computers. Why should they complain? It was all for their protection against the 'terrorists, wasn't it? Why would the people suspect their *enemies* were in government, medicine, and the law?"

"Dear Michael, the men of Terra, in uncountable millions, are neither wise nor concerned. They are detached and lazy for the most part. Most don't even believe there is a God or 'Me' for that matter. They are arrogant and defiant and insist they can do better than the 'gods of old'. This explains their obsession with *artificial intelligence*, nano-technology, biotechnology, etc., which I have helped along considerably."

"Wipe the sneer from your face, Yaldabaoth. You don't hold all the cards. In fact, it is my pleasure to inform you that we hold the 'Ace' as you will soon realize."

"Am I being threatened, Michael? I concede that I haven't been entirely successful to have all of humanity declare 'God is dead' or doesn't exist. On the contrary, men are not only denying God, they are rediscovering Him/Her. And there has been a noticeable increase in those who are now seeking the Goddess Sophia. Her story is very appealing to whomever is searching for answers. Myth or no myth, She has become powerful."

"Yes, and it has also drawn attention to you and the Archons, albeit your history is quite unappealing and negative. People know

your base is on the planet, Saturn. They marvel at its beauty, but 'looks' can be deceiving. Look at you. You delight in wearing an 'attire' that is quite foreboding to the majority of people. I'm sure the mask you have chosen to wear is very uncomfortable and hot."

"Why should it concern you? Beauty is in the eyes of the beholder. The 'light' bestowed upon me at my creation doesn't fit my personality, does it?"

"No, it doesn't. However, 'light' can be positive and illuminating or it can 'blind' one from the truth. I just thought you may wish to consider your options when you are called before the *Council of Aeons* at your trial . . . the Trial requested by Sophia."

"Trial? What trial? I don't understand, Michael."

"You will. Just be there when you're summoned."

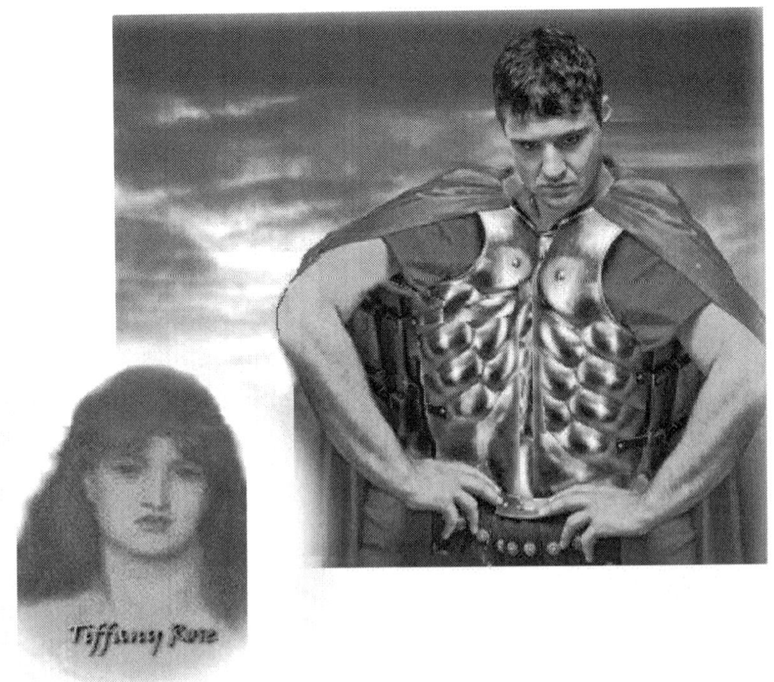

Darius has decided to tell Tiffany Rose about his feelings for her. She appears resistant. He intuits she is afraid . . . afraid to make a commitment to him or any other man.

Chapter Thirty Two

When Hearts Meet

We are creators. If we knew what we wanted, if we embraced our spirituality, if we said, 'Enough!', and refused to accept the negative reality orchestrated by ugly psychopaths - we would literally change our lives in an instant. They know this and they are terrified that we will finally wake up and become all that we are.

Fair maiden, why do you resist your feelings? Can you not see that I care for you? I believe I have awakened some stirrings in your heart for me. Am I to believe I have fantasized all of this?"

"Forgive me, Darius. You aren't wrong about your observations. I admit that since we met, I have felt an attraction towards you. But I hesitate to express my love for you because of the present situation that faces all of us. I am fearful that if I give my heart to you, I may lose you like Viola lost Carl. You may not return from your mission. I am concerned about everyone's safety and worry about how all this will end."

He looked into her moist blue eyes before responding. Taking her hand in his, he whispered, “Dear Tiffany Rose. You cannot run away forever from ’what may happen‘. We must seize the day.”

“How wise are your words, Darius. I do appreciate your patience.”

“I saw how you reacted at the meeting, “he commented. “It was gut-wrenching for me to watch your pain as you listened to the horrible stories Michael and the others spoke of. You are indeed a very sensitive and compassionate woman. I see within you a great capacity to love another with all your heart and soul. Please let it be me you love so intensely.”

Tiffany Rose was moved by his unrestrained ability to express his sincerity and passion. She sighed and smiled as her thoughts resonated with her heart. Wasn’t he the ‘man’ she had always hoped to meet? Didn’t he appear to have the same admirable qualities she loved and admired in her beloved Father? It was as if her Father had sent him to her. In reality - he had! She suddenly realized her Father, Josef, knew that Darius would be right for her. He knew and he made sure they would meet, that wise old rascal!

“Darius, please take me into your arms. I have been so foolish. I was afraid - terrified really - as you wisely surmised. Hold me tightly so I may feel the warmth and strength of your ‘embrace‘.

He took her into his arms and kissed her tender lips softly. It was all that he had imagined it would be. He had finally found his true love. They lingered in each others arms and enjoyed the moment. This time the tears upon Tiffany Rose’s cheeks were tears of joy.

Captured in the moment, they began to feel 'lighter' as the heaviness in their hearts began to dissolve. A glorious new energy of love and happiness permeated their entire being. It was more exhilarating than either had ever remembered experiencing.

"Wow! "Darius exclaimed. "Do you feel it too? It's as if I was just reborn . . ."

"Yes, "Tiffany Rose sighed. "I don't feel apprehensive any more. I feel confidant and free and . . . 'very special', "she laughed giddily. "Who would have ever thought . . . "

"Shhhh, "Darius insisted. "It happened because we both desired it so. I am convinced that 'love' is the glue that holds everything together - even the Universe. Without love, there is nothing to live for. Life becomes empty."

Carl and Viola suddenly appeared. "We were looking for you, "Viola exclaimed. "I was worried about Tiffany Rose, but I see she is in good hands."

"We were discussing the meeting and all its ramifications, Darius stammered. "There's a lot on Thelete's plate."

"Michael's, too, "Carl added. "I wonder what Thelete wanted to talk to him about privately?"

"Well, the day of reckoning is almost here, "Darius offered. "I'm nervous about being in the presence of all those other Aeons. It's mind boggling. Come, let's go somewhere and enjoy whatever time we still have before Thelete calls his next meeting."

Gathering the Fold

Chapter Thirty Three

The Witnesses

Thelete sighed. "Well, it's almost time for the Trial, "he said softly to Himself. "I must contact all my witnesses and instruct them on what to expect when they testify. I will reassure them that they will be fine and that there isn't anything for them to be nervous about."

He decided He would teleport the *Earth* humans first . . . Alexis, Judy, Peter, Bill, and Mr. 'X'. Except for Bill, the others would be 'programmed' to remember their experience as if it were a 'dream'. They wouldn't suspect they had testified in the most important Trial humans had ever participated in and that they had traveled to the Galactic Center of the Universe to do so. When they awoke from their sleep the following mornings, they would feel refreshed and calm. Perhaps they would remember bits and pieces of the dream; perhaps not. At best, they might sense they had dreamt about a strange story. Thelete thought He would call Alexis first. As His 'court stenographer', she would return to her

Earth environment afterwards and proceed to write the most important novel of her life. He closed His eyes and concentrated on her whereabouts on Earth. She had dozed off in the big chair in her den while watching television. He mentally lifted her limp body from the chair and teleported it to the Meeting Room, gently placing her to rest on the lounge. When she awoke shortly afterwards, he introduced Himself and reassured her not to be frightened. He then reminded her of their first meeting and refreshed her memory about the Trial.

"Alexis, I would appreciate if you consented to assume the responsibility of assisting me as my 'court stenographer' at the Trial. It is imperative to record every word uttered by the others so that the information may be retained in the Akashic Library. My understanding is that you possess this skill, having had much experience when your late husband was alive and active in his professional capacity as an attorney. With your permission, I have contacted him, and he is waiting to visit with you after our meeting has concluded. It is my way of thanking you."

Alexis gasped, "Yes, of course I will do my best to assist you. I just hope I am 'up to' the task. Can you enhance my keyboard 'stroke' capabilities to bring my speed and accuracy up to snuff?"

"Not to worry, Alexis. I have already anticipated your concern and you will be 'lightning fast'. Don't worry."

Relieved by his kindness, the thought of seeing her husband Steve brought tears to her eyes. "Thank you, Thelete. I am ready to listen to your instructions about the Trial. I realize how important it is for all of us to do our best. Much is at stake. Please advise me on what you wish me to do."

They engaged in conversation for another hour. When Alexis felt confidant and clear about her duties, she smiled and excitedly asked Thelete, "May I see Steve now?"

Thelete had arranged for Alexis to meet Steve in the adjacent Lounge. He escorted her there to make sure she didn't lose her way. Thanking her for her commitment, he watched her run to her husband's open arms and embrace. His thoughts of Sophia at that moment brought tears to His eyes. He would allow them ample time before Alexis returned to Earth.

His next endeavor was to meet with Judy and Peter. He teleported them to the Meeting Room as a 'team'. When they first arrived and saw Thelete, they were startled. Standing protectively in front of Judy, Peter inquired, "Who are you? Where are we and what are we doing here?"

"Please relax, Peter. This is just a dream. My name is Thelete. Make yourselves comfortable as I explain the details of your 'dream'. You will enjoy it and find it to be very interesting as it takes place at the 'High Court' of the Pleroma, located at the center of the Galaxy. Sophia, the Goddess of Wisdom, has requested that Yaldabaoth and the Archons be summoned before the Council of Aeons to stand 'trial'. Their long history of inflicting pain and suffering on Earth and humanity must come to an end.

If left unchallenged, they will continue to pursue the destruction of the human 'genome' and replace it with their own species of robotic cyborgs who obey and worship Yaldabaoth, their master. He desires to control the World. If he achieves his goal, the entire Solar System will finally be imprisoned within his domain. He may even have plans to blow up Earth as he has utter contempt for humanity. Are either of you familiar with the 'Sophia Myth'?"

"I am to some degree, "Judy replied. "It has captured the hearts and minds of many humans at the present time. People are very disillusioned and unhappy on Earth. They seek answers."

Thelete was surprised. "Really, "he commented. "I trust after this dream, you will be curious to learn more about Sophia. But your knowledge of the Myth is not necessary for your participation in this Trial. I know you both have a strong moral fiber and your compassion towards life and people has been noticed. This is why I have high expectations that you will perform brilliantly in our defense. Your integrity cannot be compromised."

Peter was shocked. "I don't know what to say except - *thank you.*"

"Yes, your words are very complimentary, "Judy replied.

Thelete nodded. "I have contacted you to ask for your assistance. Your legal expertise would be a tremendous asset and greatly appreciated. Of course, it is your decision. Understand?"

Peter looked at Judy. She nodded 'yes'. Thelete was pleased. He smiled and proceeded to inform them about the Trial's format. At first, they were overwhelmed, but as Thelete continued to speak,

He gained their confidence. He knew it was a bit of a stretch, but their concern over the atrocities on Earth took precedence. They recalled conversations about the societal ills with Alexis just the other day. “We agree, Thelete. Something has to be done before our species no longer has a ’future’. Many people on Earth are concerned, but they just don’t know what to do. There isn’t any leadership anywhere. The majority of those in power just don’t care about human life and doing the right thing.”

“True, “Thelete agreed. “The corruption and perversion is everywhere. These psychopaths have destroyed your beautiful Planet with their perverted schemes; all of which will be mentioned at Trial. They are ‘murderous scavengers’ and deserve to be punished.”

“I’m open to that - big time, “Peter grimaced. “How will we catch up on the information you have compiled? Will we be given a journal of sorts to study?”

“Well, sort of. I will download information to you during your sleeping hours, making sure I don’t overload your mind with too much information all at once. And, you will have your journals to review and study. Does this sound workable?”

“I think it’s a plan, Thelete. Judy and I are used to retaining information ‘before’ and ‘during’ every trial about hidden agenda, motivation, circumstances, etc., as well as conflicting testimony witnesses tend to give. We must be well informed.”

"I'm sure you must. And when the Council observes the sincere concern and love you and Judy and other humans who will be testifying have for their *species* and Planet, I think they will understand that all humans aren't detached or uncaring. They will realize many humans do care and that they desperately want to make positive changes on the Planet. They just have to be educated."

"You are right, Thelete. Perhaps we will be instrumental in spreading the word. We could give seminars."

"Yes. That would help. Your Mother is certainly doing her share."

"My Mom? "Judy questioned. "How so, Thelete?"

"Well, I didn't wish to influence your decision by telling you she has agreed to be the court stenographer at the Trial."

"Really! My Mom? Oh, how wonderful! Will we know afterwards about our individual contributions at the Trial?"

"I think you will, although it will probably be a subtle knowingness."

They sat in silence for a brief moment. Thelete spoke first.

"Well, that just about covers it for now. I will be in touch. The Trial is about to begin shortly. Stay healthy, alert, and positive. I will speak to you soon . . . in your dreams of course."

Thelete teleported Judy and Peter home. "That went well, "He thought. He needed a little time before contacting His next two witnesses. They wouldn't be as easy to interview since both had a great deal of information that had to be discussed. Thelete decided to contact Mr. 'X' next. He wanted to determine if the man was feeling *stressed* since he knew a great deal about the Reptilians. He didn't think so. He knew Mr. 'X' had gone public many years ago and was known worldwide to those who had an interest in Ets. However, it was only in the past few years that the World had embraced the idea of extraterrestrials seriously. Mr. 'X' was the only human testifying who claimed to have contact with the Andromedans or any other Et race, for that matter. Michael had validated much of Mr. 'X's info on the underground bases. So, he obviously was getting his information from someone - if not the Andromedans.

"Well, I must move on. Time is passing by rapidly. I hope I can locate him without too much difficulty, "Thelete thought.

It did take a little more effort to locate Mr. X, but he was available. Thelete found him in Switzerland. He and his family were living on a ranch nestled on an acre of land that had a breathtaking mountain backdrop. Its location was remote enough to conceal his whereabouts or at least give him an edge should he wish to make a fast exit.

"Greetings, Mr. 'X'. How are you? I'm assuming you are familiar with my style of 'making a grand entrance' as if you were dreaming. Is it convenient for you to visit me at my office?"

"You must be Thelete. I have been waiting for you. Yes, I am free to talk to you. My Andromedan contact, Tolec, advised me that you would be calling on me shortly."

"I see. Does he care to join us? I don't have a problem if he does."

"I would prefer that we speak privately. It's not that I have a problem with him or any of his associates. They just seem to be a little nervous that Sophia contacted the Council about Yaldabaoth and the Archons. They hope the matter doesn't escalate and involve their galaxy. They are aware that Yaldabaoth is devious!"

"I see, "Thelete replied. "What exactly are they concerned about?"

"I thought it would be quite obvious, "Mr. 'X' responded. "The Andromedans don't want a war overlapping on their turf. It has happened in their past."

"A reasonable concern, "Thelete replied. "That would prove to be a serious problem. I am glad you brought my attention to their concerns. We certainly don't wish this matter to escalate. However, from what I have observed, Yaldabaoth is very capable of instigating a 'pay-back' scenario if he feels trapped. This is why Sophia has decided to deal with him once and for all. I believe She is determined to put an end to his activities."

"Did She confide to you on how She intends to do this? Is She aware that Yaldabaoth has a huge fleet of 'mother ships' and a vast array of Reptilian soldiers under his command. They are fierce 'war machines'. As you know, they thrive on 'blood rituals', which is what *wars* are all about. Their technology is eons advanced of anything they have shown their Earth hybrids. They are devious, malicious, and very motivated to conquer the entire Universe."

Thelete sighed. He didn't wish to show His impatience.

"Mr. 'X', you seem to have forgotten that Sophia is an Aeon. Her family of Aeons reside at the Galactic Center. The Aeons are technically more advanced, more powerful, more treacherous and resilient than any *species* they may have created. The Draconians, Reptilians, Cyborgs, Demiurge, Archons and countless other life forms throughout the Universe were created by the will of *some* Aeon at *some* moment in time. Why would they fear Yaldabaoth? Sophia created him!"

"If this is the case, Thelete, why has She allowed him and the Archons to exist knowing the *evil* they are capable of? Their actions have caused humanity tremendous suffering and chaos for thousands of years. Why haven't they been restrained?"

"I haven't a problem with your question. It is an intelligent and passionate inquiry. I'm sure many other humans have questioned this strange conundrum. We, at the Pleroma, have questioned it, although not too loudly. Sophia is the *Goddess of Wisdom*, you know. Still, in an effort to understand Her reluctance to resolve this matter, we believe She has avoided doing so because of Her guilt and remorse. She still regrets Her Fall (mistake) and realizes the Demiurge's and Archons' very existence was the result of Her compulsiveness and unrestrained enthusiasm concerning Her *Dream (experiment).* It aroused a profound and unsettling attraction within Her and She was captured with total fascination on how the Anthropos would evolve and manifest their unique potential. Drawing Her currents away from the Pleroma, She mused about a W*orld* where the human singularity would emerge and thrive. She empathized intensely with the human creature that would appear in the Divine Experiment. Since She configured the 'genome', She took an unusual interest in its future development, and did it without consulting . . 'Me'! It was unusual behavior for an Aeon to transgress the norm, but it was within the freedom allowed by the 'One' that such developments can arise.

Sophia formulated Her own act of projective Dreaming, independent of the other Aeons, when She dreamt about what might happen to a strain of the Anthropos. In Her freedom, She was impetuous and daring and went much further than Aeons usually do to in Her anticipation. She idealized the situation, picturing a three-body system - Star-Planet-Satellite (Sun, Earth, Moon) where a strain of the Anthropos would have optimal opportunity to discover and develop its encoded talents, even to achieve works of genius.

"Are you following me, "Thelete inquired. "I know it is a lot to absorb, but I hope it gives you a better understanding of what I'm up against. Should I continue?"

"Yes. Please do. It is most interesting."

Thelete continued . . . "Well, totally enthralled in Her solitary view, and detached from the rest of us in the Pleroma, Sophia envisioned a World yet to be, where humanity would emerge to live, learn, and love. The sight of the Anthropos nested in the nebular cloud engaged her Divine powers of Dreaming in an unusual way, with exceptionally intense involvement. Rather than leave this cosmic novelty to mature and unfold on its own, according to the instructions encoded within it, She succumbed to a strange attraction and was deeply compelled to get involved. Her desire followed the path taken by the Anthropos, out into the 'Dema', the chaotic flux of elementary matter in the spiral arms of the galaxy. Compelled by the excitement of what might happen out there, She was gradually pulled away from the core - until the moment She plunged out and spiraled downward toward the object of Her desire. The currents that composed Her energetic *form* distended into a massive power spike, a tongue of pearl-white luminosity leaping from the Pleroma, shooting light-years into the exterior regions until She fell out of the Galactic Center into the Dema."

"What is the Dema? "Mr. 'X' questioned.

"The Dema is *quantum foam* composed of subatomic elements not yet formed into discrete elements. It is pure chaos, but it is not blind, dead 'matter'. The chaotic flux of elemental matter is a residue from previous worlds and the raw material of worlds to come. Even the Dema has the potential for life, if not 'organic' life. It glitters and crackles with a kind of 'phantom' life. In the residual dust of dissolved worlds, vast fields of particles surge with attractions and repulsions; potentials consisting of impulses that remain from things seen and done in previous worlds, but left incomplete when those worlds dissolved. Out of this residuum, new worlds continually arise. In the Kenoma, many worlds are in the making, and some will become the habitats of 'organic species' like the Anthropos. But the plunge of Sophia perturbed the usual order of cosmic evolution in the Kenoma. The impact of Sophia's *power surge* upon the Dema produced weird conditions as normally an Aeon does not act directly upon the physics of the spiral arms. To Her astonishment, She realizes that She is now the *Mother* of a bizarre species that has emerged from the Dema due to the impact of Her Divine currents, but without Her Divine intention. Then something even more odd occurs. Sophia sees a distinct mutation in the Archon swarm; an aggressive figure appears; a dragon-body with the head of a lion that rages and roars. This Reptile-like mutation of the Archon horde rapidly dominates the embryonic creatures and assumes the role of *Overlord.* The entire Archon colony comes alive with the Reptilian Overlord assuming a 'god-like' stance over the rest of the species as he rapidly becomes conscious of himself and his surroundings. He prances and preens before the swarming horde that has arisen from the fracture pattern of Sophia's impact. He is *blind arrogance* embodied, and he is truly blind. Looking around, the chief Archon doesn't see the Pleroma or the Anthropos, nor does he even see Sophia. This monster, the Demiurge, takes the *impact zone* for the entire Cosmos, and declares himself to be 'lord' of all he surveys. "I am the only god, let there be no others before me." The Archon Overlord is delusional, believing that he has created the elementary cosmos in which he finds himself along with the countless minions of the embryonic *Archons*. Sophia feels compassion for the plight of the Archons and their 'Overlord', the Demiurge. They are, in a sense, Her offspring and She is responsible for their survival, if not their ultimate fate. But they are a blind, rabid species, swarming without sense or intention. They do not even have a proper domain to inhabit! Sophia imparts a portion of Her Dreaming power to the chief Archon so that he sees the Pleroma, even though he doesn't realize what he is seeing. To him, the living energies in the Galactic Core appear as a kaleidoscopic array of colored rays in regular patterns. The Demiurge commands his legion of celestial drones to *imitate* these living fractal designs. From the fracture zone of Sophia's impact arises the proto-planetary 'disk', the groundwork of a stable world system where the Archons can construct a system of celestial mansions that mimic the divine designs of the Aeons in the Pleroma. Thus the Solar System was formed."

"Well, that was quite a story! "Mr. 'X' exclaimed. "Thank you for your exhaustive explanation to help me understand. I certainly will advise the Andromedans about your situation."

"Good. Please assure them we do not intend to do anything impulsive that will jeopardize their people or any other race in the galaxies. This is why Sophia has reached out to the Council. Why don't you extend my invitation to the Andromedan Ambassador to attend the Trial. We will be happy to listen to any of his concerns."

"I will do just that. He will probably wish to inform you about some of their own problems they have encountered with the Reptilians. They have also had reports from nearby solar systems."

"The plot just seems to be mushrooming, "Thelete responded.

"Yes, but this may be a good thing, "Mr. 'X' answered. "They also want the Reptilians to be restrained. I will do my best to help in any way I can. You can count on my testimony."

They shook hands and parted. Thelete was encouraged. He had just had one other person to speak to . . . Bill Smith. Recalling the importance of the man's information concerning the underground bases, Thelete decided that Michael should be present when they met. Michael could also locate the man and escort him to the Meeting Room. It would save Him some time and give Him a chance to take a break. "I'll contact him on the globe. I hope he isn't involved with some other crisis, "thought Thelete.

Within moments, Michael appeared on the screen. "You called, Thelete?"

"Yes. Do me a favor and locate Bill Smith. He's my last witness and I want to 'wind up'. Please advise when you have him."

"No problem. I'm sure I'll be able to contact him."

Chapter Thirty Four

"I am very worried about the activity of the Federal government. They have lied to the public, stonewalled senators, and have refused to tell the truth in regard to 'alien matters'. I can go on and on. I am not a very good speaker, but I'll keep shooting my mouth off until somebody puts a bullet in me, because it's worth it to talk to a group like this about these atrocities. . . . Bill Smith

---

Michael read the words repeatedly. Evidently, Bill Smith was a man who cared . . .enough to give his life. "I'm tired of the bad press 'humanity' is always getting, "he thought. "True, maybe there aren't *enough* people at the moment who are sympathetic and concerned about the suffering and atrocities happening in the World, but there have been many people through the years that have risked their lives for their fellow man, just like Bill Smith did. Mankind has been put through it. And, they keep bouncing back, generation after generation, only to wind up behind the 'eight ball'.

Maybe people have grown weary of the same 'ol, same 'ol and want a new environment. They are tired of all the evil and control those in power have gotten away with despite the efforts of so many decent people. Most humans are just not aware of some of the most salient points responsible for the status on Earth.

After the aliens arrived, man couldn't fight them in direct combat or with energy that reciprocated their own natures or machinations. The Reptilian/Archons were a 'biological infection' - the infestation of a parasite, a virus, into a normally healthy host organism. The virus has no life of its own and, no energy other than what it derives from its host - 'man'. The parasite acts slowly and penetrates the cell, but only when the immune system of the host is malfunctioning. The pathogen cannot be removed allopathically which is the futile tactic attempted by those who are under the mesmeric influence of its grips. Nor can the parasite be removed by radical surgery or an interval of 'time' where the hope is that it will change its ways or *character.* (The outward manifestation of this analogy is experienced when someone we love has been infected with the virus (drugs, alcohol, sex, etc.) and *cannot or will not* change their offensive behavior no matter how much therapy or love has been given to them). Likewise, the Reptilian parasitic energy can only be eradicated swiftly and permanently when the 'immune system' of planet Earth itself is working at 100 percent. Yaldabaoth and the Archons know this and have made sure the indigenous peoples are slaughtered *'en masse'.* This is the reason why there are so many wars . . . War and genocide were, and still are, the precautionary measures the Reptilians have used to maintain a low biospheric immunity and make conditions suitable for them.

Earth (Sophia), is a living, intelligent, sacred Aeon who morphed into Earth and created all its living species. Over billions of years, Sophia has shown that She is fully capable of recovering Her life force after massive traumas and extinctions. The continuity of Her life-cycles is shared by creatures whom She selects for resurrection, but it is lived out by humankind in a special way, because humans have a narrative skill more advanced than the other forms of life. Through the medium of language, the human species can recall and recount the entire trajectory of Her metamorphosis. But as Thelete has so astutely advised us, Sophia has been infected and poisoned by many factors, specifically the underground bases worldwide. She has been retarded in Her regeneration because Her 'white blood cells, her lymphocytes, are not able to do their work. Her 'T' and 'B' cell count is constantly waning due to toxicity brought on by the presence of the pathogens and the sluggishness of the regenerative agents. Humans affect Her lymphocytes as well. Because they have been negligent in their duties, the 'cell wall' was penetrated and the parasite was able to invade."

Michael's thoughts were interrupted by a figure on the globe. It was Bill Smith returning his call.

"This is Bill Smith. Someone on this frequency called me."

"Greetings, Bill. This is Michael. Thelete asked me to locate you. He wishes to speak to you about your testimony at the Trial. We can teleport to his whereabouts together. Are you free to go right now?"

"Sure. Just let me know when we're about to make the leap."

"Let's do it on my count of three. Agreed?"

"I'm ready. You can start counting . . . "

Michael closed his eyes. "One . . . Two . . . Three . . ."

Thelete was sitting back in a chair with his eyes closed when they made their sudden appearance and was caught *off guard*.

"Sorry, Chief, "Michael grinned. "I should have signaled you with a few mental waves. Actually, I tried, but you may have dozed off for a moment or two."

Thelete gave Michael one of his infamous *stares* - the one with the *arched eyebrow*. Bill didn't flinch until he was sure they were jesting. He was surprised with their casual interaction.

Thelete turned his attention to Bill. "Hello Bill. It is nice to see you again. I thought we might review your testimony before trial."

Chapter Thirty Five

The Final Meeting

"Well people - this is our last meeting before the Trial. It's been quite a journey for all of us to arrive at this moment. I want to thank each and every one of you for your commitment and outstanding efforts to prepare us for this important moment in history. I could never have walked before the Council at the Trail as confident if not for your encouragement and help. Thank you."

Viola and Tiffany Rose walked over to Thelete, and looking into his 'celestial' blue eyes, Viola said, "No, dear One. We wish to thank you for showing us that 'love' is the foundation of life. It is the *healing elixir* that comforts and soothes our hearts after we have experienced the disappointments and hardships along the way. Your devotion to Sophia has been inspiring. She has suffered just like the rest of us. But *love* is a revolving door. One must *love* to receive *love*. One must *forgive* to receive *forgiveness*. Sophia made a mistake. She asked for forgiveness and understanding to no avail. She has decided to move on."

"You are so right, Viola. I am not a Mother, but I sympathize with Sophia and support Her decision. When a child, or children, do not have respect or forgiveness for their parents, especially their own Mother, they are worthless and must be severed from their heritage, "Michael sighed.

"Yes, unfortunately, this is the case, "Darius added. "The Archons, encouraged by Yaldabaoth, have delighted in hurting Sophia with their spitefulness. They could have accepted their creation, (albeit it may not have been as regal as they would have liked), and lived their existence. They had a big chunk of the Solar System to romp around in and use as their playground. They were in essence, another species in the scheme of things. Another experiment."

"True, but not every entity has the capability of understanding the complexity of life. They acted like *spoiled brats,* who only know resentment and jealousy. Perhaps, it is an inferiority complex turned inward, "Tiffany Rose added. "Not that I sympathize with them. They have caused so much pain and hardship to innocent humans who never hurt them."

"They have instigated the murder of billions of people throughout the eons of time. I know. I was one of them, "replied Carl. "And my death caused pain to those I left behind . . . especially Viola."

"I'm not totally convinced that the soul forgets the pain, "Bill replied. "It's nice to think about all that spiritual and altruistic stuff, but let's call *a 'spade a spade'.* There's a great deal of baggage humans carry from one lifetime to another. It's deep down."

"Every soldier in the World probably carries a certain amount of guilt and shame deep down, "Darius stated. "Mine kept me from moving on until I met a kind person who showed me how to find my lost soul . Only then was I ready to know life and find 'love'."

Mr. 'X', who had been silent until now, suddenly sat up and began to speak. "It seems to be a sort of *yin-yang . . . a duality.* For every bit of happiness we know, there is a bit of sadness. If I had the opportunity to express my thoughts, I would bring this to the attention of the Aeons to consider for their future 'experiments' or 'creations'. I think the *paradigm* could be improved in several ways."

"Perhaps you will, my friend. We don't know what questions we will be asked at the Trial, "Thelete commented. "I think you all have excellent insights in regard to the issues at stake. Perhaps those mentioned are the flaws that must be worked out. Perhaps not. The Council may one day decide it would be best if all *life* became '*spirit'* once again and we just floated in the ether without any disturbance to contend with. However, for the present, we have a Trial on the agenda. It is scheduled for tomorrow. I think we are ready. We will give our best to help Sophia. We will meet here tomorrow morning at 7:00 sharp and travel to the Pleroma together. Michael has made the arrangements. If you think of anything that you find troublesome, you may contact either one of us. Until tomorrow . . . "

Home of the Aeons

The Council

Thelete Speaks before The Council

Chapter Thirty Six

The Trial

Greetings Mother Barbelo, honorable Aeons, and Guests. I, Thelete, and my associates, thank you for your attendance. We are here today on behalf of the Goddess Sophia. Upon Her request, we will be assisting Her in bringing to your attention very serious allegations against Yaldabaoth, the Demiurge, and his Archons in regard to Earth's welfare, which is presently in extreme jeopardy. We implore your wise judgment to help Sophia resolve this matter. We hope to gain your compassion and interest. Time is of the essence. I have prepared an organized summary of the allegations we are declaring. My associates and I have engaged in a considerable amount of research. Much of the information was obtained from the Akashic Records. This is where I met the lovely Tiffany Rose and Viola, who have been extremely helpful to me. Ladies, will you please stand and greet the Council." Viola and Tiffany Rose obliged. "Thank you, dear ladies, "Thelete declared.

"I am also indebted to several men who will be giving us their *personal* testimony to validate our claims. We are on a first name basis today. Please welcome Carl, Darius, Bill, and Mr. 'X'."

The men arose from their seats and greeted the Council.

"Finally, please allow me to introduce three special people . . . all from the same family, actually. This is Alexis, my stenographer. She is an author and will be writing a very interesting novel, I suspect. But, for now, she will be recording the 'minutes' of the Trial." Alexis stood and shyly greeted the Council.

Thelete then introduced Judy and Peter the young attorneys He requested to help Viola and Tiffany Rose. They acknowledged the Council, in particular, Mother Barbelo, who in their eyes was the presiding *Judge.* Lastly, Thelete introduced Michael . . .

"And of course, please welcome my assistant and '*right hand*', Michael, the beloved Archangel."

After a short silence, Mother Barbelo spoke. "Greetings Thelete and honorable Associates. I see you are well prepared to present your concerns and testimony. It is to your credit. I trust that Sophia will be addressing the Council at some later point in time?"

"Yes, Mother. I have also taken the liberty of inviting one of our Andromedan neighbors. He wishes to address the Council later on, with your permission."

"I see, "She replied. "It will depend on how quickly we progress. But before we begin, has anyone notified Yaldabaoth that he and his chief Archons were to appear at this Trial?"

An Angry Thelete holds Yaldabaoth's Costume

"Yes, Mother. I did, "Michael replied.

"I fail to see him or his minions, "She declared. "Apparently, he has decided not to oblige us with his presence. Did he contact you at all?"

Thelete interrupted. "An Archon delivered a package to my office early this morning. When I opened it, this is what was enclosed." He held a large garment in His hand for all to see. The crowd gasped. "What utter contempt, "someone murmured.

"He evidently has many different disguises, "Michael replied. "I think that 'one' was his favorite."

Mother Barbelo shook Her head. "We will discuss this later on. Obviously, it doesn't go well for Yaldabaoth, to say the least. Failure to comply with the Council's request to appear at this Trial automatically indicates Yaldabaoth's statement of GUILT. Am I correct in this assumption, Peter?"

"Yes, 'Your Honor' . . . I mean . . . Mother Barbelo. You are quite right."

Thelete sighed. How kind it was of Her to acknowledge His young attorney.

Mother Barbelo continued, "Well then, let the record show that Yaldabaoth or any entity designated to represent him, has failed to attend this Trial in the Earth calendar year of '2013' to offer rebuttal in his defense against allegations made by Sophia, submitted to this Council by Her partner, Thelete. So be it."

She turned Her attention to Thelete. "Are you ready to proceed?"

"Yes, quite ready, Mother Barbelo, "Thelete replied.

"Well then, please begin." Thelete stood erect and cleared His throat. "Honorable Aeons, with your permission, I would like to begin on Sophia's behalf with a brief overview of Earth's present status. It is very grave, indeed. I must confess. I had no idea of how serious the situation was, as my dear Sophia never complains. She has always been steadfast. It took a great deal of determination and humility for Her to realize that She has a problem that won't go away. After eons of endings and new beginnings, Gaia and her inhabitants are still suffering at the sinister hands of Yaldabaoth and the Archons. We all know the story of how they came into existence. Unfortunately, they just don't rise to the occasion and never will. They are an *evil* energy that seeks to destroy all that is sacred and beautiful. Perhaps it is Sophia's stubbornness or 'blind love' that has kept Her from admitting this fact. You cannot stack one creation (man) against another (Archons) and hope the *preferred* one will triumph. The struggle has been going on too long. Man is tired! I must speak in his defense. Humanity has been badgered."

Thelete paused. He wanted Mother Barbelo and the Aeons to grasp His dramatic statement. Despite all the noble intentions and contributions of so many humans, these *parasites* were never going to go away. They were relentless and now they even *challenged* the 'Godhead'. This was blatantly expressed by Yaldabaoth's 'no show' at the Trial.

"Here in this portfolio I am holding - a rather thick one at that - are pages of information and pictures I and my staff gathered and compiled to substantiate the many horrific atrocities instigated by Yaldabaoth and performed by Archons with the help of their hybrids on Earth. My associates and I were horrified by the information . . it is so unbelievable!"

Mother Barbelo interceded . . . "Perhaps you would like to tell us about some of these atrocities of which you speak, Thelete."

"I suppose it would be apropos at this time, "He responded. "They are briefly summarized as follows:

- *They (the dark forces on Earth) wish to kill 90 percent of the human population and establish a 'One World Government'. They plan 'mass murder' and will use various methods: They initiate* ***wars****, manufacture fatal* ***epidemics****, destroy world economies,* ***starve*** *and* ***infect*** *people of poor countries, create fatal illnesses and then sit on cures for the illnesses they have created.*
- *They tamper with weather and geographical conditions causing tornados, earthquakes, tsunamis, oil spills, tidal waves, vortexes. They have sprayed the atmosphere with poisonous chemicals. People have lost homes, jobs, money, standard of life. Countries have gone bankrupt.*
- *They tamper with human DNA hoping to destroy the human genome, are engaged in child and human abduction for genetic experimentation, child porno, genocide, mind control,*

trans-genetics, poisonous viruses, epidemics, fatal illnesses. The Reptilian/Archons and military hybrids have built underground labs and bases for genetic experiments and hideouts for Reptilians. The underground facilities have weakened Sophia.

- *They (Reptile hybrids) engage in medical mal-practices, force poisonous vaccinations on public, contaminate the water supply, modify crops, food, fowl, fauna. Have disrupted natural eco-system.*
- *World governments and politics are corrupted. Laws were passed that have corrupted societal mores, destroyed family values, lowered living standards, initiated mental illness, legalized narcotics. Many people have become confused 'zombies'.*
- *Their ultimate goal: There is a strong suspicion they intend to blow up the Planet with advanced technology once they have an absolute stronghold. The 'Military Complex' has developed secret war technology to be used for 'mass killing'. A Reptilian fleet of mother ships has been seen positioned just outside of Earth's atmosphere. There are rumors they have attempted to create a 'pole shift' in hopes of destroying the Planet.*

There was a long silence. Thelete and Michael stood side by side. They had just begun to fight, but knew they had a long day ahead of them.

Chapter Thirty Seven

Testimony

In response to Thelete's wishes, a large screen had been installed to accommodate Him and the other speakers if they opted to display visual 'backup' as they spoke to the Members of the Council. They knew it was a very effective vehicle to introduce information on important issues. A picture was often more powerful than many words.

Since Carl's experience took place in ancient times, it was decided that he would speak first. His feelings were still very intense from his past life. He had been murdered because of his religious convictions and his refusal to conform to the dictates of the Roman Emperor Constantine in the early 4th century. He was surprised that the Roman Church was still as influential. The present revolutionary issue would revolve around the 'Anti-Christ'.

Prompted by Judy and Peter, Tiffany Rose and Viola presented information about the medical and pharmaceutical professions and their roles in supporting the *One World Government's* 'intent to kill' six billion people. Disclosure concerning the hidden dangers of medication and vaccinations, especially those given to young children, left a dramatic impact on the Council. Political issues and corrupt politicians were included in the presentation. Eventually, they discussed the various satanic worship rituals and belief systems within society. Satan worship was common throughout the World. Those who comprised its membership weren't any surprise since greed, power, control, and money were the foundation for all Satan followers.

Thelete called Bill Smith to the stand. His testimony involved his personal experiences with the 'Reptilian' underground bases. He began with the base at Dulce, New Mexico:

Bill Smith testifies

"I have helped build two main bases in the United States that have some significance as far as what is called the 'New World Order'. The first base is the one at Dulce, New Mexico. Back in 1954, the Federal Government decided to circumvent the Constitution of the United States and form a treaty with alien entities. It was called the '1954 Greada Treaty', which basically made the agreement that the aliens involved could take a few cows and test their implanting techniques on a few human beings, but that they had to give details about the people involved. Slowly, the aliens altered the bargain until they decided they wouldn't abide by it at all. I was involved in building an addition to the deep underground military base at Dulce, which is probably the deepest base. It goes down seven levels and over 2.5 miles deep. At that particular time, we had drilled four distinct holes in the desert, and were going to link them together and blow out large sections at a time. My job was to go down the holes and check the rock samples and recommend the explosive to deal with the particular rock. As I was headed down there, we found ourselves amidst a large cavern that was full of 'outer-space aliens', otherwise known as large Greys. I was attacked and I shot two of them. At that time, there were 30 people down there. About 40 more came down after this started, and all of them got killed. We had surprised a whole underground base of existing aliens. Later, we found out that they had been living on our planet for a long time, perhaps a million years. This could explain a lot of what is behind the theory of ancient astronauts.

I was shot in the chest with one of their weapons, which was a box on their body that blew a hole in me and gave me a nasty dose of cobalt radiation. I have had cancer because of this. I didn't really become involved with UFO technology until I started work at Area 51, north of Las Vegas. After about two years spent recuperating the 1979 incident, I went back to work for other companies. At Area 51, they were testing all kinds of peculiar spacecraft.

I am very worried about the activity of the Federal Government. They have lied to the public, stonewalled senators, and have refused to tell the truth in regard to 'alien' matters. I can go on and on and I am rather disgruntled as you can see. Our *present structure of government is 'technocracy', not democracy, and it is a form of feudalism. It has nothing to do with the Republic of the United States. These people are godless, and have legislated out prayer in public schools. You can get fined up to $100,000 and two years in prison for praying in school. I believe we can do better. I also believe that the federal government is running the gambit of enslaving the people of the United States. I am not a very good speaker, but I'll keep shooting my mouth off until somebody puts a bullet in me, because it's worth it to talk to a group like this about these atrocities. Eventually, this is exactly what happened to me. I was shot by the very people I had worked for. Eleven of my best friends in the last 22 years have been murdered. Eight of the murders were called 'suicides'.*

I can also support the testimony of the two young women about the government creating fatal diseases. Look at AIDS. It was created by the National Ordinance Laboratory in Chicago, Illinois in 1972. It was a biological weapon to be used against the people of the United States. The reason I know this is that I have seen the documentation by the Office of Strategic Services, which by the way is still in operation to this day, through the CDC in Atlanta. They used the glandular excretions of animals, humans and alien humanoids to create the virus. These alien humanoids the government is hobnobbing with are the worst news. There is absolutely no defense against their germs - none. They are a biological weapon of terrible consequence. Every alien on the planet needs to be isolated.

Lastly, I wish to advise that the Federal Government has invented an earthquake device. I am a geologist, and I know what I am talking about. It is a 'Tesla' device that is being used for evil purposes. The black budget programs have subverted science as we know it."

Bill Smith stepped down from the witness stand and returned to his seat. Thelete thanked him for his in-depth testimony.

"Your information is extremely helpful. It has given us greater insight as to what has been going on."

Mother Barbelo suggested the Court take a short recess.

"Please return to your seats when you hear the chimes."

Thelete walked over to greet Mr. 'X' and the Andromedan Ambassador sitting next to him. Extending his hand, He stated, "Glad you could make it, Sir"

"Tolec . . . my name is Tolec. Nice to meet you, Thelete. You and your people are doing a find job. I am very impressed."

"Your man is next, "Thelete advised. "Do you wish to help him with his testimony?"

"I would be delighted to. Do you have to clear it with Mother Barbelo?"

"Yes, but I don't anticipate a problem. I think She is pleased with the flow of our testimony."

"What arrogance on Yaldabaoth's part not to show. I wonder what he had in mind? He can't be that confident about all of this, can he?"

"I'm not sure. For all we know, he could be right here wearing a different disguise. You heard Michael."

"Yes, but it's still hard to believe. He's a *'slippery article'."*

Michael strolled over to join in the conversation. "What's up? New plan?"

"Sort of. If Mother Barbelo agrees, Tolec will be giving testimony along with Mr. 'X'."

"Good idea, Tolec. It certainly can't hurt. Are you going to discuss some of the information you told me the other day?"

"I think so. We want to show we are concerned and will help in any way possible. Of course, any offer made must be discussed and approved by our own Council before it is initiated."

They heard the chimes resonate. "That's our cue, "Thelete stated.

Everyone assembled back into the courtroom quickly and quietly.

"Will the spectators remain standing until Mother Barbelo and the Aeons are seated, "the court official announced.

Mother Barbelo walked elegantly into the room followed by the Aeons.

MOTHER BARBELO

"She really is beautiful, "Viola whispered to Tiffany Rose.

"Yes, "Tiffany Rose agreed. "She is 'The One's' partner.

Thelete took a deep breath. "Here we go again, "He thought. "I hope She is receptive to the 'Adromedan'."

Mother Barbelo spoke:

"Are you ready to continue, Thelete? I believe you have one more witness to call to the stand."

"Yes, and with your permission, since my witness has had close affiliation with the Andromedans, his Ambassador contact, Tolec, who is present, would like to assist him with his testimony. Is this agreeable to you?"

"Let the Ambassador rise and introduce himself, "She replied.

Tolec rose from his chair. "Madam Barbelo, I am honored to meet you and your entourage of noble Aeons. I have known Mr. 'X' for a long time. He is our trusted liaison between his World and *ours* and has been instrumental in communicating our messages to *higher evolved souls* (walk-in's) on Earth. There are approximately 140,000 walk-ins on the Planet right now who are part of the Andromedan Council. They are focused on balancing the negativity that has been created on Earth. Because of our laws of non-intervention, the Andromedan Council felt it necessary to intervene in another way that would not violate Council directives. Thus, the walk-in's, who are Earth human beings, are here to do that work. It's a 'back-door' approach."

"Have you ever communicated your intentions to Sophia?"

"We have tried. It has been difficult for us to get through to Her, but I feel this is changing now since more Earth people have become aware and receptive of Her presence. We understand the tremendous burden She has endured in trying to hold everything together. As Thelete stated, 'She never complains'."

"Quite true, "Mother Barbelo replied. "She is a very brave and compassionate Aeon. We all admire and respect Her greatly. It was time for Her to ask for our help. And She should be made aware of friends like yourself that have given their support. I wish to thank you on Her behalf as well as ours."

"Thank you, Mother Barbelo. I believe I have a great deal of information that will encourage everyone's understanding and awareness. May I begin?"

"Yes of course. Please proceed. We are anxious to hear what you have to tell us."

Thelete helped him start . . . "Mr. Ambassador, you heard Michael and the men disclose information concerning the Reptilian underground bases they had investigated when they made their trip to Earth. It is our intent not to be redundant and exhaust the attention of Mother Barbelo, our Honorable Aeons and guests. Therefore, I respectfully request that you speak only about new information."

"I will try my best, but it may be difficult not to overlap a little, "he smiled.

"We understand, "Thelete reassured him.

The Andromendan stood tall before the Council. Without the help of any backup paper work, he began to speak:

"As I have told Mr. 'X' repeatedly, 'no one is going to save you'. If you are waiting for a 'savior', you're not 'doing the work' yourself. Who would come to your Planet and 'take you off the hook'? For what purpose? You' would only re-create the situation again, because you haven't permanently evolved to the level of becoming your own savior. You haven't learned the lesson, and this has been my strongest message to him.

The Archons are a caste system, just like insects. They all basically think the same things at the same time. Their minds are like 'radios'. If there aren't any 'radio waves', they won't do anything. In other words, Archons are controlled by computers that emit a 'vibratory wave', instructing their own what to do. Yaldabaoth is in charge, of course. If someone shut the computers off, they would stop in their tracks, because they don't think for themselves. They are part of a 'group mind' and do not have individualized intelligence, like we do. They would like to create humans to be like them. Now, this is not the case exactly with the aliens from Zeta Reticuli 1, who have the same technology, but use it to heal - not to control.

To manipulate humans' belief-system, there is a plan in process to play out a staged 'second coming'. This will occur shortly after the destruction of the World economy. We are not very far away from that. This false spiritual being will be a 'cloned' biological human being, who will be holographically imprinted with information regarding spiritual truths contained in all Earth's religious and metaphysical systems. The clone will profess the Hindu philosophy, but its intent will be evil, and it will not have a soul. It is in fact - a robotoid; a synthetic clone. The Reptilians have technology that allows them to stage this kind of phenomena. The clone will be identical to the image on the 'Shroud of Turin', whose holographic image was created by the Archons for the purpose of strengthening a belief in a 'savior'. This belief would assist their plan for control, because humanity wants to give their power away to someone that appeared to be a true and legitimate 'messiah'. This is what they have been taught. The

Archons know that few people truly want to accept responsibility for their own evolution. Most would rather be told what to do, than to realize the situation and take appropriate action necessary to free themselves.

Archons were also responsible for the 'Fatima' episode in Portugal, where the Virgin Mary spoke to the children. This was a holographic image of a woman, professed to be the Virgin Mary, the 'Mother of Jesus Christ'. During this incident, the Sun supposedly fell from the sky and miraculously healed people. Using alien technology, these apparent miracles did in fact occur, but 'light' and 'sound' were beamed onto these people to actualize the healings. This technology has been on the Earth for at least 100 years or so, but it is against the law in most places of the United States because color and sound technology work. It certainly would diminish the Medical and Pharmaceutical industries. The reason these modalities work is because the entire Universe is a 'holographic projection'. It's all a hologram.

The Biblical Jesus is a composite character, and is an allegorical myth. The Virgin Mary is also a composite character. These composites were made for the purpose of uniting religions of the ancient Roman empire. From 310 AD to 325 AD, the Council of Nicea created these composite characters. Some books that discuss this truth are Holy Blood, Holy Grail, Antiquities Unveiled, and The Messianic Legacy.

Archons are 2,500 years ahead of humans in their technologically. The U.S. 'black government' is afraid to tell humans the truth concerning this reality, because they fear it will instigate a revolution and result in the overthrow of their corrupt politics.

Lastly, there are two large mother ships on Earth hiding in the oceans. One is below the Equator and the other one is in the Atlantic. They are Andromedan ships. We have positioned them on the Planet because the World Government has actually talked about implementing 'alternative 4', which was to create a controlled pole-shift, and we in the Andromedan Council will not allow this to happen. These ships are there to anchor Earth's axis. We also have huge mother ships on Jupiter, Ganymede and the moon - 'Demos'.

Michael mentioned his findings of the Reptilian base in the Middle East, but taking out the Reptilian base on the floor of the ocean south of the Saudi Arabian, UAE, Yemen in the Oman Peninsula is a priority; a much more pressing matter. The reason is simple. As you know, Earth's history continues to repeat itself year after year. The squabbling and skirmishes in this region have gone on for thousands of years. The original reasons for the fighting have gotten blown out of proportion. They were greatly enhanced by the Reptilian undersea base, as you can understand. The people in this area are being played much like 'pawns on a chess board' and they have no knowledge as to how, why, or how long this situation has taken place. We have to - and we will - put a stop to this! This undersea base will be taken out.

Outside parties, with outside interests, have attempted nuclear strikes in order to start a full-scale war in this region, which we have stopped. We have disabled and neutralized their bombs a few times. Yes, we had a 'hand' in this. Understand, a full-scale nuclear war cannot and will not happen in this region. We will not allow actions that permit nuclear war to start by either side. The impact would be far too great to your Planet, your people, and the rest of your Solar System. What you do on Earth affects us all. We will remove the deadly undersea bases from the Middle East and China. This specific police action of taking out Reptilian underground bases is the continuance of a cleanup operation on Earth that's in the final phase of a 'proxy war' the Star Systems and Planets of the Andromeda Council have fought and won to free the people of Planet Earth. By defeating these malevolent aliens in space - especially the Draco and Hydra based Reptilians - we have prevented catastrophe.

Everything I've learned about these intelligent Reptilians indicates they are very mean, viscous, calculating, manipulating, and literally 'cold blooded' in their actions They are very self-centered and generally don't care about anyone else unless it serves their purposes. For years they've simply perceived humans and Earth as their 'natural resources' to be consumed and exploited.

"That's all going to change, "Michael commented.

The Ambassador continued . . .

"We were fortunate to be given help from the people of Procyon. They gave us technology that they developed and successfully used to liberate themselves from the Reptilians in their own 'war' in which they won their freedom about twelve years ago. It incorporates the use of 'sonic energy beams', specifically attenuated and adjusted to certain frequencies that were meant to accomplish the following:

- *Disrupt and disable the mental thought patterns and brain waves of Reptilians that were either controlling, manipulating and/or enforcing a secretive and scientific administrative operated soldier work force from these bases. To accomplish their agenda, they used a specific highly attenuated and high frequency sonic beam that would Incapacitate them. The humans in these bases did not hear this sound, nor would they be affected by it. And as you know, humans were removed from these facilities.*
- *The second goal was meant to obliterate, destroy, and collapse the physical structure of these underground bases and ensure the bases would become completely inoperable, and closed off. For this effort, the people from Procyon used a highly concentrated, but much lower frequency and far more compressed sonic beam' meant to destroy matter. It does the job quite well. They thumped these bases pretty good.*

"This is pretty much all I have to say. I hope this information was helpful and encouraging. Tolec stepped away from the witness stand, visibly exhausted.

Thelete thanked him. Standing before the Council, He said firmly, "We have completed our testimony. But before the Court adjourns to reflect and offer their recommendation, I would like to call a recess. When we return, our beloved Sophia will speak."

Sophia Speaks

With tear-filled eyes
Sophia reveals Her feelings ...

Sophia appeared on the huge screen situated in the middle of the courtroom. The crowd held their breaths as She began to speak:

"Dear Mother Barbelo, honorable Aeons, my dear Thelete and devoted friends . . . thank you for your kind attendance. As I advised, Gaia is in dire circumstances. The threat of extinction looms. This is why I have reached out to you. I have made an important decision concerning the destiny of Yaldabaoth and the Archons, who as you know, are the source of this threat. Enormous chaos and hardships have been experienced by the Anthropos because of them. However, I would appreciate your input having heard the information of my dear Thelete and His devoted assistants presented for your analysis. I trust you will agree with my decision after you have reviewed our testimony.

I am weary and saddened - perhaps overwhelmed at the present time. I have been pushed 'against the wall' so to speak and now must address this serious problem. I have tried for eons to be patient and compassionate towards the Archons in hopes they would change their ways. Since this is not the case, my love and compassion is now extended exclusively to humanity. I am tired of the wars, the killings, the destruction, the anger, the greed, the unbelievable hatred shown towards the Anthropos by Yaldabaoth and his Archons who refuse to obey my wishes.

Mother Barbelo, You are my Divine Mother. Surely you can understand my feelings as a Mother. I have always wished to live in peace and love with my children - yet time and time again - we have suffered from the jealous rages of Yaldabaoth and the Archons. They are responsible for the demise of many magnificent civilizations. Their advanced technology has created plagues, earthquakes, tsunamis, tidal waves, tornados, pole shifts, ice ages, and other atrocities that have pillaged Earth. They have instigated wars, engaged in genocide, caused starvation, incurable illnesses, poverty, mental illness and a myriad of other ills causing unbelievable hardship and pain. Gaia's oceans, atmosphere, soil, and land have been polluted. Beautiful structures have been leveled. They have indulged in genetic experiments, which resulted in the creation of grotesque life forms. Their attempts to destroy the 'human genome' have been unsuccessful, yet they continue to tamper with animal and human DNA. This has caused deformities and illnesses to humanity for generations. Earth's recorded history has been distorted and rewritten to suit their agenda. They have destroyed all that is sacred and beautiful and desire to destroy humanity and Gaia. They believe they can rule the entire Universe. The ignorant fools do not even try to conceal their arrogance.

I have finally accepted that they are a problem that cannot be resolved with patience and kindness. The problem originated with my 'Fall'. I did not make a wise decision at the time. I should never have allowed them to exist, but I felt very remorseful, guilty and embarrassed. It was my mistake. The Archons were created because of my mistake. I tried to make it up to them with an unlimited compassion and patience - to no avail.

Acknowledging their propensity for evil was too painful for me to accept before now. I believe with all my heart that it is time for humanity's story to be 'corrected'. This will require the restraint of Yaldabaoth, every Archon, and every earth/hybrid they have contaminated. I am through putting up with their evil on Earth. All those who have the wealth and power to buy and sell 'souls' must be taught a lesson. They must all be 'rounded up and contained' once and for all, or they will always be a threat to life on Gaia and the neighboring galaxies.

It has been expressed that the Anthropos are a defected species destined to 'self-destruct'. If this is so, would it not be wise for me, dear Mother, to intercede now before all is lost? I cannot do it alone, however. I need your support and the strength of our heavenly force of Aeons to assist me at this critical time. Please help me move forward towards perfection - not destruction. This is an urgent plea for help! . . . Thank you."

A long silence permeated the room. Thelete wiped away a few tears. Words could not express the joy and relief He felt after He heard Sophia speak. Her words were powerful and heart wrenching. Still, She was firm and no one doubted Her resolve or thought Her decision would be reversed. She was very clear that Her patience and compassion had finally been exhausted. He wondered how many humans would survive the *punishment* that was yet to be allocated. Most were probably '*border line*'.

He and Michael had an enormous challenge ahead of them, but he never doubted their victory. All His warriors were clear about their mission. All thought Sophia's decision to remove Yaldabaoth and the Archons from the Solar System was 'just'. How this would be accomplished would be determined by the Aeons and Sophia. Thelete wasn't involved with this part of the deal. He was a warrior - not a judge. He hoped the people on Earth realized that the removal of the Archons and Yaldabaoth wasn't the ultimate cure for their ills. As a species, they had a lot of baggage to clean up. Their entire societal structure had to be rebuilt with a new paradigm. This is where the *young* people would become involved and contribute their knowledge to their new World. Viola and Carl, Tiffany Rose and Darius, Judy and Peter had participated in one of humanity's 'greatest stories'. They were chosen to become teachers. Sophia expected them to spread the 'word' and with Her guidance, they would help restore Earth to its former habitat. Humanity would once again live in a Golden Age.

Ironically, Michael and his angels captured the Archons/hybrids on Earth using their own technology. It was the 'icing on the cake' for the warrior.

"Idiots, "he said in contempt. "How does it feel to be rounded up like useless 'scum' and be imprisoned until your inevitable disposal?"

The Verdict

Once again there was a great war in heaven. Michael and his angels, and the Andromedans fought against Yaldabaoth and the Archons who fought back, but prevailed not; neither was their place found any more in heaven. The solar system they inhabited was abolished from the construct of the hologram and the Demiurge and his hybrid/minions on Earth were rounded up. They could not escape for they were exposed by the mark seen on their foreheads. It was the number '666'. No longer would any of them deceive and destroy the World. Their existence had been restrained forever."

All those who refused to acknowledge 'The One' as their ultimate God and Creator were removed from the Universe and imprisoned within a 'black hole'. Because of their lust for power, wealth, and evil, they would never again realize an opportunity to know life nor would they be offered another universe to work out their problems. Their souls were damned, never to receive the healing power of 'organic light'.

Reflections

Reflections . . .

Though zombies are the pop culture's apocalyptic poison of choice these days, many researchers seem to take the possible threat of a robot-led apocalypse more seriously. Cambridge researchers are now investigating the possibility that technology will be mankind's ultimate undoing. The Centre for the Study of Existential Risk (CSER) will begin studying the dangers posed by *biotechnology, artificial life, nano-technology* and *climate change* reports the BBC. The scientists warn that writing off a potential *robot apocalypse* would be 'dangerous'. The popular apocalyptic theory that robots will eventually rise up and enslave mankind has been made popular by films like The Terminator, The Matrix, I, Robot, and to a more limited degree, Ridley Scott's cult-hit - Blade Runner. The formula is simple . . .

It turns out that humanity exists within the confines of a highly-detailed *computer simulation* created by the machine overlords. And now German physicists have come up with evidence showing that this might actually be happening. Whoa! The whole thing is based on the idea that any sufficiently advanced civilization will eventually create a simulation of the Universe, which would of course lead to the creation of more such simulations within the original simulation. So it would continue, eventually resulting in a huge number of simulations nested within simulations, making it statistically probable that the Universe we inhabit is in fact merely a *simulation.* It's a thought experiment, apparently a fairly famous one, but researchers at the University of Bonn say they have evidence that this could actually be the case. Can a new technique known as 'deep learning' revolutionize artificial intelligence as yesterday's front-page article at The *New York Times* suggests? There is good reason to be excited about *deep learning*, a sophisticated 'machine learning' algorithm that far exceeds many of its predecessors in its abilities to recognize syllables and images. But there's also good reason to be skeptical. While the *Times* reports that advances in an *artificial intelligence technology* that can recognize patterns offer the possibility of machines that perform human activities like seeing, listening and thinking, deep learning takes us at best only a small step toward the creation of truly intelligent machines. Deep learning is important work, with immediate practical applications. But it's not as breathtaking as the front-page story in the New York *Times* seems to suggest.

At Cambridge University, scientists warn there's a chance that AI computers will annihilate all of us within the next two centuries. A philosopher, scientist, and a software engineer have come together to suggest that computers are set to become Earth's dominant species, proposing that the threat of human extinction-by-robot is *real* and not just the remit of sci-fi and those who favor tin-foil millinery. The thinkers have founded the Centre for the Study of Existential Risk maintaining that we shouldn't take AGI for granted. The possibility of a 'Pandora's box' with AGI should be taken seriously because if missed, could be disastrous.

In December 2014, robots will be tested in a disaster scenario to see if they can accomplish complicated tasks such as driving utility vehicles, removing debris blocking entryways, climbing ladders, traversing industrial walkways, and using power tools. All of this will be part of the DARPA Robotics Challenge (DPC). The challenge aims to develop ground robots that can perform complex tasks and use available human tools, such as vehicles. The goal is to advance the robotic technologies of supervised autonomy, dismounted mobility, dexterity, and platform endurance. By using supervised autonomy, the robots developed will be able to be controlled by non-expert operators and enable effective operation despite low fidelity communications.

SHARON GILBERT warns on the rise of sentient machines: "Since Derek and I cut the 'cable cord' six months ago, we find our news via Roku's CNN International or BBC News channels. This morning, a stick-thin female news anchor on CNN Int. conducted an interview with someone I'll just call Mr. X (sorry, didn't get the name of the gentleman. I've been scouring the CNN website, but there's no video of the spot there and the topic centered around the ethics behind sentient machines. In particular, should 'self-aware' drones be deployed? *If we learned anything in the 20th century it is that science fact very often follows science fiction,* so let us turn to the disturbing futures depicted in 'Terminator' and Battle Star Galactica. In both, machines designed as humanity's helpers became 'self-aware' and decided that humans were *inferior.* It therefore logically followed that humans should be *eliminated.* A similar theme arose in the original Star Trek film (based on a script from the TV series). A US probe sent out to 'learn all that is learnable' returns with an enhanced 'brain' that is now sentient, seeking to destroy all 'biological units' within its path. The Sequoia *supercomputer* at Lawrence Livermore National Laboratory, recently crowned 'World champion of supercomputers', just simulated 10 billion neurons and 100 trillion connections among them - the most powerful brain simulation ever. IBM and LLNL built an unprecedented 2.084 billion neuro-synaptic cores, which were an IBM-designed computer architecture that is designed to work like a brain. IBM was careful to say it didn't build a realistic simulated complete brain by stating, "We have simulated a novel modular, non von-Neumann, ultra-low power, scalable, cognitive computing architecture."

IBM researchers said in an abstract of their new paper, "It meets DARPA's metric of 100 trillion synapses, which is based on the number of synapses in the human brain. This part of DARPA's cognitive computing program is called *Systems of Neuromorphic Adaptive Plastic Scalable Electronics* (SYNAPSE).

You may never have heard of the Singularity, but many scientists call its advent 'inevitable', and it has the potential, some would

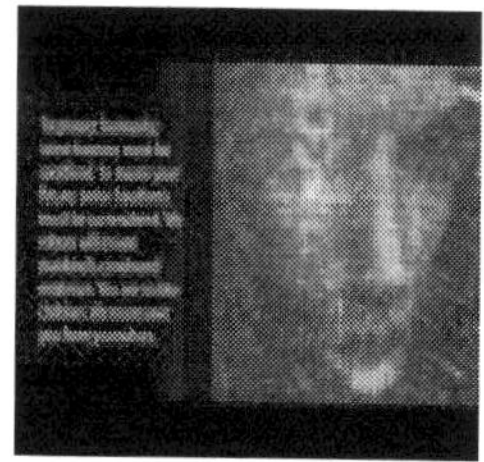

even say the promise, to deliver the human race to *immortality*. In order to understand how we can become immortal via the 'Singularity', we first have to understand what it is.

According to Ray Kurzweil, author of '*The Singularity is Near'* and co-founder of Singularity University, the Singularity is an era in which our intelligence will become increasingly non-biological and trillions of times more powerful than it is today. It is the dawning of a new civilization that will enable us to transcend our biological limitations and amplify our creativity. To put this in layperson's terms, the 'Singularity' is the exact moment in time when computers, in all their incarnations, become smarter (and) billions of times faster than human intelligence can grow.

It sounds identical to the plot of many science fiction films, but rest assured, real scientists are feverishly working toward making this rather far-out sounding vision a reality. At Singularity University, computer scientists, top entrepreneurs, and giant corporations come together to expedite the moment of Singularity via intensive study led by top technology evangelists and experts. It should come as no surprise to anyone that one of the corporate founders of Singularity University is . . . Google.

The Reptilians are broadcasting a false reality from the Moon that humans are decoding into what they think is a physical World. It is all happening on a vibrational level as 'wave' fields in the Metaphysical Universe, which we decode into a holographic reality response and experience. The target 'receiver' of the Moon/ Matrix transmissions is the frequency range of what we call 'Mind', especially the Reptilian brain. To keep us enslaved in the false reality of the Moon Matrix, the Reptilians and their hybrid networks must ensure that we do not expand our state of awareness beyond Mind and into Consciousness. The other prime Moon-Earth-human connections are *crystals and water.* The vibrational

interplay between the Moon and crystals within the Earth is 'key' to the Moon Matrix. Crystals are found in stones, rocks and every grain of sand. Our planet is crystalline, just like the human body and both are transmitter receivers of information. Quartz crystal has the ability to generate a fixed frequency and convert *waveform resonance* or *vibration* into an electrical signal, which is what the five senses do. What isn't realized is the appreciable amount of crystal content within the Earth and below the seabed - right down to the core. These gigantic crystals and crystal deposits are there to receive and transmit information encoded in the *photons emitted by the Sun.* Transmissions from the Moon have hacked into the Sun/Earth connection and created the vibrational sub-reality that is called the Moon/Matrix - all based on *fear and survival.* Food additives and electromagnetic pollution adds to this 'tuning in' effect. The crystal matrix within the Earth is expressed as the energy force-lines known as 'lei' lines or meridians. Most of the great stone circles and stone forests were put there to block and dilute the power of the energy passing through the lei line and vortex network. This is also true of the pyramids; the calling card of Reptilians/Archons, whose purpose was two-fold:

- To access the energy for their own ritual and other purposes.
- To suppress the power and vibration of the energy pumping around the planet to maintain both the Earth and humanity in the low vibration state that tunes them into the Moon Matrix.

Today they accomplish this by positioning nuclear power stations, major cities, road interchanges and other disruptive structures on the vortex points where many lei lines cross. *The United Kingdom is in many ways the 'hub' of the global conspiracy at operational level. England and Ireland have more stone circles and ancient earthworks than any other place in the World.* Seventy percent of the Earth's surface is water which has been estimated to total the sum of 326 million trillion gallons. The human body is 60 - 70 percent water. The Moon/Matrix transmissions have encoded their fake reality information through the conduit of water (at the level of the Metaphysical Universe). Most people think water is an excellent conductor of electricity, but this is not strictly true. Water only becomes an efficient conductor when *salt* has been added. It isn't the water as much as it is the chemical and other content. Interestingly, 97 percent of Earth's water is sea water - salt water (mostly from sodium chloride). The human diet is also full of salt; especially in processed foods produced by the Illuminati (Monsanto) corporations. Language researcher Pierre Sabak states that 'salt' was part of the Covenant between the bloodlines and the Reptilian gods. The theme of salt can be found in Christianity and Judaism, among other faiths. The biblical *Second Book of the Chronicles* clearly connects salt to the Covenant between God (the gods) and Israel: "Don't you know that the Lord, the God of Israel, has given kingship of Israel to David and his descendents forever by a covenant of salt?" The Hebrew term 'melakh' (covenant of salt) relates to the 'mal' 'akh' (the angel or shining king). Sabak says that 'halos', the Greek 'polymorphic' (many forms) noun for 'salt' signifies 'halos; the disc of the Sun or Moon and 'halos' is related to 'hals' (the sea). From 'sal' we also get the Greek noun 'Selene' (the Moon Goddess). The symbolism of salt and the covenant are also the origins of 'salary' from the Roman word 'salarium' (a soldier's ration or salt money). We also talk of someone being 'worth their salt' or being the 'salt of the Earth'.

African legend, per Credo Mutwa, states that there was a time when all the seas were fresh water, but the Reptilians made it undrinkable to drive away the 'good' gods. The accounts say that the sea became salty at the time of the 'Great Flood' of which there were many.

Reflections . . .

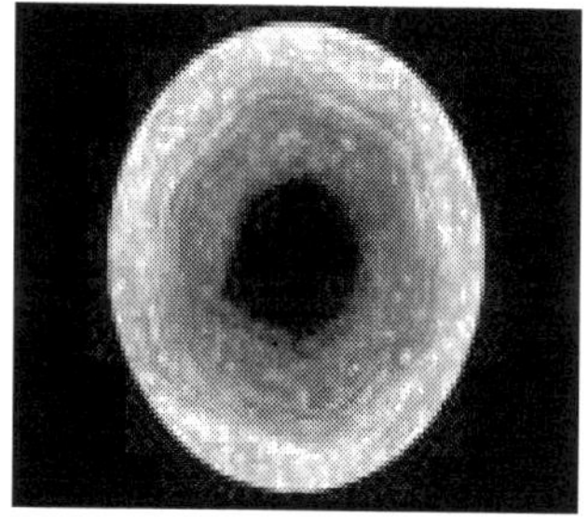

Believe it or not, this is the North Pole of Saturn. It is unclear how an unusual hexagonal cloud system that surrounds Saturn's north pole was created, keeps its shape, or how long it will last. It was originally discovered during the Voyager 'flybys' of Saturn in the 1980s. No one has ever seen anything like it elsewhere in the Solar System. Although its infrared glow was visible previously to the Cassini spacecraft now orbiting Saturn. The mysterious hexagonal vortex became fully illuminated by sunlight for the first time during the Cassini's visit in 2009. Since then, Cassini has imaged the rotating hexagon in visible light enough times to create a time-lapse movie. The pole center was not well imaged and has been excluded. This movie shows many unexpected cloud motions, such as waves emanating from the corners of the hexagon. Planetary scientists are sure to continue to study this most unusual cloud formation for quite some time.

Reflections . . .

Scholar and mythologist John Lash shared revelations about aliens and UFOs that he gleaned from his research of the Dead Sea Scrolls and Nag Hammadi texts. “The Scrolls were written by an apocalyptic sect and contained numerous descriptions on the ‘hardware’ side - sightings of crafts and close encounters. The aliens were written in a positive light.”

In contrast, in the Nag Hammadi texts written by Gnostics, intrusive encounters and abductions were highlighted with predatory aliens known as ‘Archons‘. Described as ‘draconic‘, these entities were said not to be of Earth, yet hailed from our Planetary System. The text explicitly warns of the Archons implanting *divisive religious ideologies* into the populace for their own purposes - a situation he sees being played out today. Lash outlined Nine Theories of ET contact which showed various ways of comprehending Ufology. Several are:

- The Extraterrestrial Hypothesis. Suggests our government cut a deal with the Ets. In exchange for access to ‘advanced technology‘, the government gave them the right to conduct experiments on humans and animals.
- The Mind Control Hypothesis. Exemplified by Jacques Vallée. It posits that UFO phenomena is real, but not in the sense that it appears to be, indicating it was mostly psychological.
- The Benevolent Hypothesis. Assumes ‘space brothers’ are here to helpfully intervene and initiate humanity into a higher evolution.

During his life, Sir Arthur C. Clarke (1917–2008) was a famous science-fiction author, inventor, futurist, and television commentator who, together with Robert A. Heinlein and Isaac Asimov, was considered to be one of the 'Big Three' of science fiction. Clarke in particular had an uncanny knack at foreseeing the future. As an example, modern video games were unheard of in 1956 and *virtual reality* games hadn't even been imagined. That is, until Clarke wrote about them in *The City and the Stars*:

"Of all the thousands of forms of recreation in the city, these were the most popular. When you entered a saga, you were not merely a passive observer. You were an active participant and possessed - or seemed to possess - 'free will'. The events and scenes which were the raw material of your adventures might have been prepared beforehand by forgotten artists, but there was enough flexibility to allow for wide variation. You could go into these phantom worlds with your friends, and as long as the dream lasted there was no way in which it could be distinguished from reality."

Or who could have believed in 1968 that the 'news pad' technology set in 2001 would be realized nine years later as the iPad in 2010? Yet Clarke in his novel, *2001: A Space Odyssey*, clearly described the technology:

"When he tired of official reports and memoranda and minutes, he would plug his foolscap-sized Newspad into the ship's information circuit and scan the latest reports from Earth. One by one he

would conjure up the world's major electronic papers; he knew the codes of the more important ones by heart, and had no need to consult the list on the back of his pad. Switching to the display unit's short-term memory, he would hold the front page while he quickly searched the headlines and noted the items that had interested him."

Unfortunately, that Clarke showed such remarkable prescience may hold important (and frightening) realities for our investigation, too. This is because in the sci-fi seer's classic, *Childhood's End (1953),* giant silver spaceships appear in the sky over every major city on Earth. After the dust settles, the

peaceful yet mysterious 'Overlords' inside them help form a World Government, which ends all war and turns the planet into a utopia. Oddly, only a select few people get to see the Overlords, and their purpose for coming to Earth remains shrouded as they dodge questions for years, preferring to remain in their spacecraft. On Earth an alien god speaks directly only to the UN Secretary

General. 'Karellen' tells him that the Overlords will reveal themselves in fifty years, when humanity will be used to and dependent on their presence. When the revealing finally takes place, at Karellen's request, two children run into the ship as the crowd below finally gets a glimpse of what the aliens look like. Clarke writes: "*There was no mistake. The leathery wings, the little horns, the barbed tail - all were there. The most terrible of all legends had come to life, out of the unknown past. Yet now it stood smiling, in ebon majesty, with the sunlight gleaming upon its tremendous body, and with a human child resting trustfully on either arm.*"

According to the narrative, the revelation that these beings historically known as the devil and his angels were always our benefactors and saviors does not lead to chaos, but rather to technological and spiritual utopia, quickly resulting in the dissolution of all previously existing religions. The World celebrates as people are described as having overcome their prejudices against the devilish sight of Karellen, or, as he had been known in the Bible, 'Satan'. Here was a revelation which no one could doubt or deny. Here, seen by some unknown magic of Overlord science, were the true beginnings of all the World's great faiths. Most of them were noble and inspiring - but that was not enough. Within a few days, all mankind's multitudinous *messiahs* had lost their divinity. Beneath the fierce and passionless light of truth, faiths that had sustained millions for thousand of years vanished like morning dew. As the story continues, the children on Earth, set free from outdated Abrahamic religions such as Christianity, begin displaying powerful psychic abilities, foreshadowing their evolution into a Cosmic Consciousness, a transcendent form of life. Indeed, this is the end of the human species as it was known as everyone merges into a cosmic intelligence called the 'Overmind'. Those familiar with eastern religions will recognize Clarke's narrative as a clever ET version of pantheistic monism (the view that there is only one kind of ultimate substance). Overmind is quite similar to the Hindu concept of Brahman, and given that Atman is, simply stated, the concept of self, the Hindu doctrine 'Atman is Brahman' is roughly equivalent to absorption into the Overmind. Similarly, Buddhism advocates the dissolution of the self into Nirvana. In fact, nearly all New Age, spiritualist, and occult traditions have comparable monistic dogma. Some shroud this doctrine of deceit in terms like 'Christ Consciousness', giving it a more appealing veneer, but Jacques Vallée recorded interesting examples of such twisted ET theology, replacing biblical prophecy with the Overmind. One contactee told Vallée:

"I was told that I was to come out at this time with this information because mankind was going to go through the collective Christ experience of worshipping UFOs and receiving information. It would help mankind balance its political focus. You see the interesting thing, Jacques, is that we must emphasize the fact that we are receiving a new program! We do not have to go through the old programming of Armageddon."

That this New Age babble has been the doctrine of non-Christians this century is one thing, but in recent homilies, Pope Benedict XVI's 'end-times' views took on a troubling and similar preparatory tome. This may not come as a surprise to those Catholics familiar with Father Malachi Martin's warnings in his book, *The Jesuits*, which documented how priests like Pierre Teilhard de Chardin were deeply influencing the Church and its academia toward occultism this century.

In the chapter on 'Exo-theology' within our new publication, *Exo-Vaticana,* we establish Chardin's belief in extraterrestrials and offer a brief discussion on his sorcerers' Darwinian mysticism. But it was his connection with monistic occultism and what is called the 'Omega Point' that takes us through the alien-deity rabbit hole. According to Chardin, in his *The Future of Man* (1950), the Universe is currently evolving towards higher levels of material complexity and consciousness and ultimately will reach its goal - the Omega Point. Chardin postulated that this is the supreme aspiration of complexity and consciousness, an idea also roughly equivalent to the 'Technological Singularity' as expressed in the writings of trans-humanists like Ray Kurzweil. Indeed, one finds a remarkable coalescence of all non-Christian systems under the banner of Singularity, Monism, Omega Point, and Overmind. Yet, like the nebulous 'Christ Consciousness' advocated by occultists, Chardin's writings are easily misunderstood because he not only created new vocabulary for his Darwinian religion, he also redefined biblical terminology to mean something alien to its original intent. For instance, when Chardin writes about 'Christ', he usually does not mean Jesus of Nazareth. Instead, he is describing the Ultra-Man, the all-encompassing end of evolution at the Omega Point. As an example, consider when Jesus said, "Think not that I am come to destroy the law, or the prophets: I am not come to destroy, but to fulfill." (Matthew 5:17). Chardin exegetes this as, "I have not come to destroy, but to fulfill Evolution." To most Christians, this probably seems overtly heretical, but its infiltration into Roman Catholic thought and the dangerous alien-Christ implications it brings with it, has infiltrated the highest levels at Rome including the Papacy.

Unbeknownst to most Roman Catholics, the retired Pope Benedict XVI is a *Chardinian* mystic of the highest order. His book, '*Credo for Today: What Christians Believe'* (2009)', follows the lead of the Jesuit and states unequivocally that a belief in Creationism (the idea that life, the Earth, and the Universe as we know it today, did not 'evolve' but rather were created by the God of the Bible) 'contradicts the idea of evolution and (is) untenable today'. Following his rejection of Creationism and support of evolution, Pope Benedict XVI employed the doctrine of the Second Coming of Christ to advance Chardin's 'Omega Point', *in which a 'new kind' of God, man, and mind will emerge.*

On page 113 we read: *From this perspective the belief in the second coming of Jesus Christ and in the consummation of the World in that event could be explained as the conviction that our history is advancing to an 'omega' point, at which it will become finally and unmistakably clear that the element of stability that seems to us to be the supporting ground of reality, so to speak, is not mere unconscious matter; that, on the contrary, the real, firm ground is Mind. 'Mind' holds 'being' together, gives it reality, indeed is reality; it is not from below, but from above that 'being' receives its capacity to subsist. That there is such a thing as this process of 'complexification' of material being through spirit, and from the latter its concentration into a new kind of unity can already be seen in the remodeling of the World through technology.*

The term "complexification' was coined by Chardin (and the technological allusions it suggests is akin to transhumanism and Ray Kurzweil's Singularity) and the Pope's complete devotion to this theology is again laid bare in his book, Principles of Catholic Theology (1987), which states:

The impetus given by Teilhard de Chardin exerted a wide influence. With daring vision it incorporated the historical movement of Christianity into the great cosmic process of evolution from Alpha to Omega: since the 'noogenesis', the formation of consciousness in the event by which man became man, this process of evolution has continued to unfold as the building of the noosphere above the biosphere. This 'noosphere' is taken very seriously today in modernist Catholic theology, academia, and even science. It is explained in the scientific journal, Encyclopedia of Paleontology this way: *Teilhard coined the concept of the 'noosphere', the new 'thinking layer' or membrane on the Earth's surface, superposed on the living layer (biosphere) and the lifeless layer of inorganic matter (lithosphere). Obeying the 'law of complexification/conscience', the entire Universe undergoes a process of 'convergent integration' and tends to a final state of concentration, the 'Point Omega' where the noosphere will be intensely unified and will have achieved a hyper-personal organization. Teilhard equates this future hyper-personal psychological organization with an emergent divinity (a future new form of God).* The newly sanctioned doctrine of an *approaching emergent divinity* in place of the literal return of Jesus Christ isn't even that much of a secret any longer among Catholic priests (though the cryptic Chardinian lingo masks it from the uninitiated). In his July 24, 2009 homily in the Cathedral of Aosta while commenting on Romans 12:1–2, the Pope said:

"The role of the priesthood is to consecrate the World so that it may become a living host, a liturgy: so that the liturgy may not be something alongside the reality of the World, but that the World itself shall become a living host, a liturgy. This is also the great vision of Teilhard de Chardin: in the end we shall achieve a true cosmic liturgy, where the cosmos becomes a living host."

In Chardin's system, noogenesis is the fourth of five stages of evolution, representing the emergence and evolution of mind. This is the stage we are said to be in currently, and as noogenesis progresses, so does the formation of the noosphere, which is the collective sphere of human thought. In fact, many Chardinians believe that the World Wide Web is an infrastructure of noosphere, an idea intersecting well with transhumanist thought. Chardin wrote, "We have as yet no idea of the possible magnitude of 'noospheric' effects. We are confronted with human vibrations resounding by the millions; a whole layer of consciousness exerting simultaneous pressure upon the future and the collected and hoarded produce of a million years of thought.

This concept gets more translucent in astrobiology, where scientists have adopted noogenesis as the scientific term denoting the origin of technological civilizations capable of communicating with humans and traveling to Earth. In other words, the basis for *extraterrestrial contact*. Consequently, among many, if not most of Rome's astronomers and theologians, there is the widespread belief that the arrival of *alien deities* will promote our long-sought spiritual noogenesis, and according to a leading social psychologist, the World's masses are ready for such a visitation and will receive them (or him) as a messiah. This is further reflected in a 2012 United Kingdom poll, which indicated that more people nowadays believe in extra-terrestrials than in God. Consequently, whether or not it is the ultimate expression, the noogenic strong delusion is already here. While we aren't suggesting a direct equivocation per se, the conceptual intersection between the two uses of noogenesis (the occultic and astrobiological) is thought provoking, especially in light of Clarke's scenario in *Childhood's End*, where noogenesis in the astrobiological application (the arrival of the alien Overlords) was the impetus for evolution toward the Overmind and dissolution of humanity. It seems Rome has connected these dots for us. In his sanctioned treatise, Kenneth J. Delano linked the concept of maximum consciousness and alien contact, truly noogenesis in both senses of the word: "For man to take his proper place as a citizen of the universe, he must transcend the narrow-mindedness of his earthly provincial-ism and be prepared to graciously accept the inhabitants of other Worlds as equals or even superiors." At this point in human history, our expansion into space is the necessary means by which we are to develop our intellectual faculties to the utmost and, perhaps in cooperation with ETI, achieve the maximum consciousness of which St. Thomas Aquinas wrote in 'Summa Theologica':

> *"This is the earthly goal of man: to evolve his intellectual powers to their fullest, to arrive at the maximum of Consciousness, to open the eyes of his understanding upon all things so that upon the tablet of his soul the order of the whole Universe and all its parts may be enrolled."*

Viewed through this lens, the Vatican's promotion of Darwinism and astrobiology intrigues. Following Chardin and Delano, perhaps Pope Benedict, the VORG astronomers, and theologians like Tanzella-Nitti, O'Mera, and Balducci pursued astrobiological noogenesis so that when 'Petrus Romanus' assumed his reign as the final Pope, they might usher in the Fifth Element of the Omega Point known as "Christogenesis." (Authors note: one cannot help recall the movie *The Fifth Element* that involved a priesthood who protects a mysterious Fifth Element that turns out to be a messianic human who ultimately combines the power of the other four elements (noogenesis) to form a 'divine light' that saves mankind). In Chardin's book, *The Phenomenon of Man*, the five elements of evolution are: 1) geogenesis (beginning of Earth); 2) biogenesis (beginning of life); 3) anthropogenesis (beginning of humanity); 4) noogenesis (evolutionary consolidation to maximum consciousness) leading finally to 5) Christogenesis, the creation of a *total Christ* at the Omega Point. With that in mind, be aware that astrobiology and transhumanist philosophy suggest this noogenesis is being driven by an external intelligence, whether it be respectively artificial or extraterrestrial, which leads these authors to conclude we are on the cusp of a noogenesis unlike the one Rome's theologians may have anticipated. We would redefine the terms and instead suggest aggressive preparation for an Antichrist genesis - an Alien Serpent-Savior - the ultimate Darwinian Übermensch who may even bare leathery wings, little horns, and a barbed tail. But regardless of how he appears, it will be frighteningly obvious to all readers of Exo-Vaticana that the Vatican has cleverly prepared for his coming, even now monitoring his approach from atop Mt. Graham, using the LUCIFER device." - *Tom Horn*

Secret government documents have disclosed that William Cooper revealed how the Vatican had been infiltrated by the Illuminati in his novel, "Behold A Pale Horse".

He was assassinated after the release of his book - a highly recommended read.

Belfast Telegraph - Tue, 21 Dec 2010 02:08 CST

Is the game up for the Catholic Church? Sadly not, as many of its brainwashed members will continue to support it in spite of its now overt symptoms of psychopathology. Victims of clerical sex abuse have reacted furiously to Pope Benedict's claim yesterday that pedophilia wasn't considered an 'absolute evil' as recently as the 1970s. In his traditional Christmas address to cardinals and officials working in Rome, Pope Benedict XVI claimed that child pornography was increasingly considered 'normal' by society. He stated, "In the 1970s, pedophilia was theorized as something fully in conformity with man and even with children. It was maintained even within the realm of Catholic theology that there is no such thing as evil in itself or good in itself. There is only a 'better than' and a 'worse than'. Nothing is good or bad in itself." The Pope said abuse revelations in 2010 reached 'an unimagined dimension' which brought 'humiliation' on the Church. Asking how abuse exploded within the Church, the Pontiff called on senior clerics 'to repair as much as possible the injustices that occurred' and to help victims heal through a better presentation of the Christian message. "We cannot remain silent about the context of these times in which these events have come to light," he said, citing the growth of child pornography that seems in some way to be considered more and more *normal* by society. Pope Benedict also said sex tourism in the Third World was threatening an entire generation.

Outraged Dublin victim, Andrew Madden, insisted that child abuse was not considered normal in the company he kept. Mr. Madden accused the Pope of not knowing that child pornography was *the viewing of images of children being sexually abused*, and should be named as such. Angry abuse victims in America last night said that while some Church officials have blamed the liberalism of the 1960s for the Church's sex abuse scandals and cover-up catastrophes, Pope Benedict had come up with a new theory of blaming the 1970s. "Catholics should be embarrassed to hear their Pope talk about abuse while doing little or nothing to stop it and to mischaracterize this heinous crisis, "said Barbara Blaine, the *head* of SNAP.

Reflections . . .

"As mentioned numerous times, Earth has been taken over in governmental, military, educational, pharmaceutical, economic, and religious sectors of society by murderous, deceiving psychopaths! They are a real danger to our species presently. We must familiarize ourselves with the agenda of these psychopaths, identify their M.O., and discover who they are and take them DOWN! Because they're not going to stop until they're taken down. We all have a responsibility to become pro-active. Dark thoughts have seized the minds of these people. They behave like *robots* and don't feel any compassion towards others. They are the product of mind control and manipulation into believing they originate from a special bloodline.

To a great extent 'trans-humanism' is really just a name - a label you can attach to the agenda of certain human beings who actually don't want to be human. The most obvious and main characteristic of all these human beings with this trans-human agenda is one simple thing that identifies them - *fear of death!* They're afraid to die. And so they want to upload their consciousness to a cybernetic organism or they want nano-medicines and such. All of these people have turned against humanity. So, trans-humanism is really a program of people who are anti-human. The 'trans' part of it is the only thing alive. If you want to go beyond humanity even when you don't even know what humanity is or what human potential is - you're really stupid. This obsession comes from people who can't face their own humanity because they hate humanity. That's why they're against humanity. They're scared to death of their own immortality. Those of you who never want to die - don't worry about it because when you die - nothing will happen to you. You're already dead. You're dead because you can only live as a 'human' for as long as the quality of 'humanity' lives in you.

The Gnostics knew what the quality of this humanity was and they educated and nurtured it with tremendous care. It is the quality *of innocence, of play, of communication, of seek and discover. It is the quality of trial and error, the willingness to make mistakes and learn from them. It is the quality of being transparent with others.* These are the pure qualities of humanity. It's a flame of 'Antrophos' that burns within you. But those who hate humanity are people in whom this flame has been snuffed out. And even though they're walking around like you and me, and they're breathing, and they're eating and excreting . . . they're dead! because their humanity has come to an end. They're really like a dead branch on a tree just hanging on. They were already dead. The 'Genome Project' isn't going anywhere - it's a dead-end. Trans humanism is a dead-end. Like the dead branch on the tree, it is lifeless. It just hangs on until a swift wind blows it away."

John Lash

VOCABULARY

- Aeons - Not entities, but processes that may best be conceptualized as immense plasma currents; currents that are alive, self-aware, sensuous.
- Pleroma - The Matrix of infinite potential - Gnostic heaven
- Anthropos - Human genome
- Dema - The chaotic flux of elementary matter in the spiral arms of the Stereoma
- Kenoma - Matrix of finite possibilities
- Stereoma - located in the third spiral galactic limb of the Galaxy - the virtual World of the Archons
- Archons - inorganic beings having the ability to affect our minds by subliminal conditioning techniques. Their main tactic is mental error or false ideology.

Rosebud

Made in the USA
Lexington, KY
11 November 2014